Dec., 1984     750
meth.

# The Lyrics
# of Noël Coward

# BOOKS BY NOËL COWARD

# Noël Coward

# The Lyrics

METHUEN · LONDON

*The Lyrics of Noël Coward*
first published in Great Britain
by William Heinemann Ltd in 1965
Republished in simultaneous hardback
and paperback editions in 1983
by Methuen London Ltd,
11 New Fetter Lane, London EC4P 4EE
Copyright in all the lyrics and the introduction
is by the Estate of the late Noël Coward

ISBN 0 413 54310 2 (hardback)
ISBN 0 413 53810 9 (paperback)

Printed in Great Britain
by Richard Clay (The Chaucer Press) Ltd,
Bungay, Suffolk

TO JAMES POPE-HENNESSY

# *Contents*

# *Introduction*

I can only assume that the compulsion to make rhymes was born in me. It cannot have been hereditary for neither my mother nor my father nor any of my forebears on either side of the family displayed, as far as I know, the faintest aptitude for writing poetry or verse. I believe that a certain Miss Veitch, a far-back ancestress of my mother's, who lived in Dawick House, Moffat, near the Scottish border, wrote a number of spirited novels at the beginning of the nineteenth century. I have been unable to trace these but even had I succeeded in finding them, I doubt whether they would have been written in rippling verse. In fact, I am beginning to doubt if they were ever written at all.

There is no time I can remember when I was not fascinated by words 'going together': Lewis Carroll, Edward Lear, Beatrix Potter, all fed my childish passion, in addition to all the usual nursery rhymes that the flesh is heir to, beginning, to the best of the belief, with 'Pat-A-Cake, Pat-A-Cake, Baker's Man'. I can still distinctly recall being exasperated when any of these whimsical effusions were slipshod in rhyming or scansion. One particularly was liable to send me into a fury. This was 'Little Tommy Tucker'.

> 'Little Tommy Tucker
> Sings For His Supper
> What Shall He Have
> But Brown Bread And Butter?'

That 'Tuck' and that 'Sup' and that 'But' rasped my sensibilities to such a degree that a deep scar must have formed in my subconscious, for many many years later the untidy little verse sprang, unbidden by me, from the lips of one of my favourite characters, Madame Arcati, in *Blithe Spirit*. She recites it irritably in the séance scene in order to catch the attention of her 'child control' on 'the Other Side'. 'I despise that,' she says, 'because it doesn't rhyme at all, but Daphne loves it.'

Some years later when I was rushing headlong towards puberty I wrote a series of short couplets under the general heading, 'Vegetable Verse'. These, I am relieved to say, have disappeared as completely as the novels of the late Miss Veitch. I remember at the time of writing them I read them to my mother who was immensely struck by their brilliance. Apart from her and a few contemporary cronies nobody set eyes on them. Even my own memory, which is retentive to an extraordinary degree, has refused to hold on to them. I can recall only two tantalizing fragments:

> 'In A Voice Of Soft Staccato
> We Will Speak Of The Tomato'

and

> 'The Sinful AspaRAGus
> To Iniquity Will Drag Us'.

The rest is silence. The emphasis on the third syllable of 'asparagus' in order to make it rhyme with 'drag us' indicates a certain precocious ingenuity, but aside from this brief flicker of promise, I fear they were undistinguished.

Later in my teens, inspired and at the same time slightly irritated by the feverish industry of my childhood friend, Esmé Wynne, who wrote a vast number of sensuous love poems between the ages of thirteen and seventeen, heavily influenced by the Eastern nostalgia of Laurence Hope and the highly-coloured imagery of Oscar Wilde, I decided after a few competitive failures to strike out on a line of my own. I had the edge on her because, being a natural musician, I found it easier to write to tunes jangling in my head than to devote myself to mastering iambics, trochees, anapaests, or dactyls. If a tune came first I would set words to it. If the words came first I would set them to music at the piano. This latter process almost invariably necessitated changing the verse to fit the tune. If you happen to be born with a built-in sense of rhythm, any verse you write is apt to fall into a set pattern and remain within its set pattern until it is completed. This is perfectly satisfactory from the point of view of reading or reciting, but when you attempt to set your pattern to a tune, either the tune gives in and allows itself to be inhibited by the rigidity of your original scansion or it rebels, refuses to be dominated and displays some ideas of its own, usually in the form of unequal lines and unexpected accents. This is why I very seldom write a lyric first and set it to music later. I think that the best lyrics I have written are those which have developed more or less at the same time as the music. All of this of course inevitably makes the reading of lyrics more complicated than the reading of straight verse which was never initially intended to have a musical setting. Unless the reader happens to know the tune to which the lyric has been set, his eye is liable to be bewildered by what appears to be a complete departure from the written rhythm to which his ear has subconsciously become accustomed. In fact, what I am trying to explain to the reader of this formidable volume is that in many instances, the words and rhythms he reads, divorced from the melody line that holds them together, may appear to be suddenly erratic, inept or even nonsensical.

In *The Noël Coward Song Book* which was published a few years ago and contained some fifty of my better-known songs, I divided the contents up into decades with a brief introductory preface to each. In this book I propose to follow the same procedure. When the idea was first discussed it was suggested that the lyrics should be printed in alphabetical order. This idea I hastily discarded when the complete retyped manuscript was delivered to me. It was a little too humiliating to discover late on in the book a crude fatuous little ballad sandwiched between two of my more modern and accomplished efforts just because its first line happened to start with a W. Also, as a great number of my lyrics happened to have been written specifically for musical comedies or operettes, these looked curiously forlorn separated from the original context and in many instances made no sense at all.

The original idea behind the publishing of this book was to put on record, presumably for the gratification of posterity, every lyric, good, bad or indifferent, that I have ever written in my life. On mature consideration I decided that although in theory it would be flattering to feel that every rhymed couplet, every cliché-ridden four-line verse, should faithfully be recorded if only as a tribute to my industry, in practice such a procedure would be a waste of print, paper and time. I know of no professional writer who would not recoil in horror from the suggestion that everything he had ever written since his childhood should be published. There are indeed a great number of prose exercises of my own written between the ages of eleven and seventeen which are locked away in trunks and strong-boxes and which I am determined will never see the light of day in my lifetime. After I am dead is quite another matter. If at that time some yet unborn biographer should feel that he might acquire a more psychologically accurate knowledge of my character by reading them, he is welcome to if he can find them. By then I shall be past caring. In the meantime, however, those early immature whimsies will be left to gather the dust they so richly deserve for so long as there is breath in my body.

The same thing applies to the lyrics I intend to eliminate from this volume. It is not that I am ashamed of having written them, even the worst ones; it is merely impractical to overweight an already weighty book with a lot of repetitions and inferior work merely for the dubious reason that I happened to have written it. I have left, however, enough of my naïf, youthful, catchpenny, 'made-to-order' material to provide a basis of comparison with the more mature rhyming of my later years. I hope and trust that the gentle reader will be able to detect the difference.

*The Twenties*

## NOTE ON 'THE TWENTIES'

Actually a few of the lyrics appearing under this heading were written before 1920, but there are not enough of them to merit a section of their own, also 'The Tens' as a designation looks somehow foolish. Whereas everyone refers to 'The Twenties', 'The Thirties', 'The Forties', etc., nobody either talks or writes about 'The Tens', perhaps because 'The Tens', with the 1914–18 War in the middle of it, was such a desolate decade in our history that people instinctively wish to relegate it to oblivion. For me it was a period rich with promise. I became a professional actor in 1911. I was fourteen when the war started and eighteen when it finished and, apart from the fact that I was yanked briefly into the army towards the end of it, I was too young and ambitious and filled with my own concerns for it to have much significance for me. In later years when I had matured enough to be able to view it historically and set it in perspective, its horrors and muddles and tragedies became very profoundly significant. Indeed my retrospective rage against its waste of life and utter futility inspired me in the late 'Twenties' to write a bitter, sentimentally-ironic war play called *Post Mortem*. The idea of the play was good and if I had taken a little more trouble with it from the point of view of construction and devoted more time to character delineation and less to emotional fervour, it might have been a great deal better. Even as it was there were two or three genuinely moving scenes in it. However, while the war was actually going on and I was growing up with it, it meant little more to me than a gloomy, almost anti-climactic background against which I was fated to play out my adolescence. In course of this 'playing out' process I managed to write two novels, both embarrassing, and eight or nine plays, only one of which, *The Rat Trap* (1917) later achieved production. I also wrote some of the early lyrics that appear in this book and I earnestly advise any reader who has not a clinical passion for analysing my life's work to skip lightly through them and get on to those which, during 'The Twenties', were written specifically for musical shows: *London Calling* (1923), *On With The Dance* (1925), both English and American editions of *This Year Of Grace* (1928), and *Bitter Sweet* (1929).

The late Oscar Hammerstein wrote wisely and accurately in the preface to his own published book of selected lyrics, that the perfect lyric for a musical should be inspired directly by the story and the characters contained in it. In fact, ideally, a song in a musical should carry on whenever the dialogue leaves off. Apart from one or two rare exceptions I concur with him entirely. Revue writing is of course different because there is no definite story line on which to hang the numbers. But any young potential lyric writer should learn early that if he wishes to write a successful 'book show' he must eschew irrelevance and stick to the script.

3

# London Calling

## TAMARISK TOWN

*from* LONDON CALLING

Verse 1   On an island far across the sea,
A maid sat dreaming,
While above the Tamarisks,
The moon was softly gleaming,
And as the perfumed Southern breeze caressed her,
She dreamed of how her lover's arms had pressed her.
And she was sighing, sighing.

Refrain 1   Come to Tamarisk Town,
When the birds in Spring are mating,
I'm tired of waiting
I love you so.
The honey-wind is blowing o'er the bay,
It calls to mind the day you went away.
From the look in your eyes
I can tell your heart is yearning
To be returning to me
In Tamarisk Town again.

Verse 2   Softly o'er the skies the silver dawn came creeping,
Weary were her eyes and sad her heart, with weeping.
Then suddenly she saw a sail appearing,
And then a graceful schooner swiftly nearing.
With joy bells ringing,
She's gaily singing, singing.

Refrain 2   Come to Tamarisk Town,
When the birds in Spring are mating,
I'm tired of waiting
I love you so.
The honey-wind is blowing o'er the bay,
It calls to mind the day you went away.
From the look in your eyes
I can tell your heart is yearning
To be returning to me
In Tamarisk Town again.

## OTHER GIRLS

*from* LONDON CALLING

Verse 1    I've always longed to see
Myself at twenty-three
In some dramatic situation,
A slightly cruel man,
With some fair courtesan,
Serenely driving in the Bois,
Though when you're young it's nice
To dream of gilded vice
With all its lurid fascination,
I've learnt to see beyond
The flaunting *femme-du-monde*
And hitch my wagon to a star.

Refrain 1    She hasn't rings and sables and things,
Like other girls I know,
She hasn't stockings,
Openwork clockings,
Other girls would show,
Her eyes would never cause a stir,
She's such a simple character,
I don't know why,
But I'd say goodbye
To other girls for her.

Verse 2    When young men leave their schools,
They make a lot of rules,
They feel their destiny is calling,
They want to burn their boats
And sow the wildest oats
And lead a life of scarlet sin,
I had such smart ideas
But now around my ears
My youthful dreams are gently falling,
My plans have all gone wrong,
Since this girl came along
I've never wanted to begin.

Refrain 2    She hasn't guiles and feminine wiles,
Like other girls I've seen,
She never races
Or goes to places
Other girls have been,

  She has such sweet simplicity,
  So full of domesticity,
  I don't know why,
  But I'd say goodbye
  To other girls for her.

## WHEN MY SHIP COMES HOME

*from* LONDON CALLING

Verse 1  Sometimes when I'm weary
     And the world seems grey
     And the firelight flickers blue,
     Somewhere in the future,
     Maybe far away,
     There are dreams that may come true.
     Cinderella's story is so lovely, to pretend,
     Some day soon my story too
     May have a happy end.

Refrain 1 When my ship comes home,
     When my ship comes home,
     Silks and velvets and cloth of gold,
     Caskets bursting with wealth untold,
     When my ship comes home.
     Through the world I'll roam,
     Open skies above me,
     Someone dear to love me,
     When my ship comes home.

Verse 2  Life is nothing but a game of make-believe
     Until true love comes your way,
     Such a dreary pattern
     Through the years you weave.
     If you can't afford to pay
     Fate is sometimes cruel,
     And a new dawn soon may break,
     Every single jewel
     I'll be wearing for your sake.

Refrain 2 When my ship comes home,
When my ship comes home,
No more waiting through empty years,
Pearls and diamonds in place of tears,
When my ship comes home.
Through the world I'll roam,
Open skies above me,
Someone dear to love me,
When my ship comes home.

## CARRIE

### *from* LONDON CALLING

Verse 1 Carrie as a baby was a darling little pet,
And everybody loved her from the Vicar to the Vet.
Her manners when at school were most ingenuous and quaint,
She had the reputation of a little plaster saint.

Refrain 1 Carrie was a careful girl,
Such a very careful girl,
Nobody imagined from the day that she was weaned,
That underneath her sweetness was the temper of a fiend,
Carrie was a careful girl,
Quite a little cultured pearl,
The teachers all adored her and the pupils did the same,
At every sort of girlish sport she quickly made a name
And nobody suspected that she played a double game,
Carrie was a careful girl.

Refrain 2 Carrie was a careful girl,
Such a very careful girl,
She stole out on the landing while the others were at prayers,
And rubbed a lot of grease upon the dormitory stairs,
Carrie was a careful girl,
In her little cot she'd curl,
The teacher fell down half a flight and landed on her head,
And naturally to Carrie not a single word was said
'Cos they found a pat of butter in her little sister's bed,
Carrie was a careful girl.

Verse 2 Carrie had a father with a rather mottled past,
And evils of heredity are bound to show at last,
But Carrie always realized the danger from the start,
So she stole dear father's diary and learnt it off by heart.

Refrain 3  Carrie was a careful girl,
           Such a very careful girl,
           When papa departed to the angels meek and mild,
           He left a lot of souvenirs and maxims to his child,
           Carrie was a careful girl,
           And when in the social whirl,
           Though she wasn't tempted by the usual forms of vice,
           She said she thought that games of chance were really awfully nice
           But still she never played a game without her father's dice,
           Carrie was a careful girl.

Refrain 4  Carrie was a careful girl,
           Such a very careful girl,
           So far and no further she was quite prepared to go,
           But still she took precautions 'cos of course you never know,
           Carrie was a careful girl,
           Once she met a noble Earl,
           He thought that Carrie lived alone and so she let him think,
           She asked him to her flat one night to have a little drink
           But she had her Auntie Jessie underneath the kitchen sink,
           Carrie was a careful girl.


## THERE'S LIFE IN THE OLD GIRL YET

*from* LONDON CALLING

Verse 1   I'm a naughty little lady,
          Full of winsome girlish tricks;
          Though I'm rather past my heyday,
          I began with Seymour Hicks:
          With the chorus boys behind me
          I'm a sight you can't forget,
          Though the years have rather lined me
          I am still a firm soubrette.

Chorus    Tell us why, tell us which, tell us what, tell us how;
          Tell us when, tell us soon, tell us now.

Refrain 1 They call me Kitty,
          Because I'm pretty,
          And because I have a dainty curl;
          Men pursue me and woo me, and ask me to dine
          But I'm always in bed by a quarter past nine:
          I'm awfully sporty

And I'll be forty
On October the twenty-third:
Though there may be one or two notes that I can't quite get,
There's life in the old girl yet.

Verse 2    I'm as playful as a kitten,
Love has seldom passed me by;
I have more than once been bitten,
Though I'm hardly ever shy,
Though if Winter came, my style would
Be a little undermined;
Still the Spring of second childhood
Can't be very far behind.

Chorus    Pretty soon, pretty near, pretty quaint, pretty queer;
Pretty poll, pretty pet, pretty dear.

Refrain 2    They call me Flossie,
Because I'm mossy,
And because I always go the pace;
I show traces of laces, and silk underneath,
I'm as old as my tongue but much older than my teeth:
My Goodness Gracious
I'm so vivacious,
Always ready for a kiss or two:
Though at one time people always called me 'Gladstone's Pet',
Still, there's life in the old girl yet.

## RUSSIAN BLUES

### *from* LONDON CALLING

Verse    I'm just a Russian Refugee,
There's nothing left in all the world for me,
But within my brain
I seem to hear those lovely melodies again
That made my Motherland what she used to be,
I'm weary and my heart is sore
For, even though I do return once more,
Skies are overcast
And I'll have nothing but my memories of the past
To make me weep for days that have gone before.

Refrain  All day long I've got those Russian Blues,
The blues I'll never lose
Until I die.
For while I'm sleeping,
The lovely melodies come creeping,
Just to remind me of days gone by.
Fairy tales
That I learnt at my mother's knee,
And the echo of nightingales
In a magical tree.
Then I find I'm waking with a sigh,
That's the reason why
I've got those Russian Blues.

Patter  Bowled over, bowled over,
Morning noon and night
I'm simply longing for the sight
Of dear old Petrograd and Moscow gay
And the jolly little tinkle of a bell upon a sleigh!
The Northern lights gleaming,
Samovars steaming,
Maybe I'll return some day.
It may be hysteria
But even if it means Siberia
Start your locomotive, rock your little boat,
I shall feel so happy when I know that I'm afloat,
I've been too long away.


# PRENEZ GARDE, LISETTE

*from* LONDON CALLING

Verse 1  Lisette was witty and naughty and pretty,
She started flirting when she was ten,
And she intended
When schooldays were ended
To grow up a soignée Parisienne.
Young men would sigh
As she passed by,
And all her anxious relatives
Would rush at her and cry:

Refrain 1  Prenez Garde, Lisette,
           You are rather young as yet,
           Though of soldiers and of sailors you
           May be extremely fond,
           We don't wish you to turn into
           A flaming demi-monde,
           Prenez Garde, Lisette,
           You seem to be a born coquette,
           But when the Poilus come marching right up to your door,
           They'll love you and leave you but wiser than before,
           Allons enfants de la Patrie,
           Mais Prenez Garde, Lisette.

Verse 2    Lisette was charming, alluring, disarming,
           Desiring, acquiring experience.
           Military honour
           Was showered upon her,
           Her love for her country was so intense,
           Soldiers adored,
           Raved and implored,
           But when she only laughed at them they cried with one accord:

Refrain 2  Prenez Garde, Lisette,
           You have caught us in your net,
           Though where ignorance is bliss they say 'tis folly to be wise,
           We never knew
           An ingénue
           With quite your kind of eyes,
           Prenez Garde, Lisette,
           But she had made her plans you bet,
           And when the Generals came marching right up to her door,
           They'd love her and leave her but richer than before,
           Allons enfants de la Patrie,
           Mais Prenez Garde, Lisette.


## SENTIMENT

*from* LONDON CALLING *and* CHARLOT'S REVUE, New York 1924

Verse 1    People have said sentiment's dead
           But it's a lie!
           Listen to what I say—
           It has remained firmly ingrained
           Never will die
           Look at the world today.

Refrain 1   Sentiment, it's simply sentiment
           That makes the world go round at all,
           It keeps the undiscerning
           Home fires burning
           Though the skies may fall,
           Many a loving couple have their motives misconstrued,
           For there's a fundamental code with which we're all imbued,
           If they're alone together after half past ten it's rude,
           Sentiment that's all!

Refrain 2   Sentiment, it's simply sentiment
           That makes the world go round at all,
           The British as a race
           Just hate to face
           The faintest moral squall,
           Foreigners' immorality may make us look askance,
           Though we are not above it if we get the slightest chance.
           What is it makes an Englishman enjoy himself in France?
           Sentiment, that's all!

Verse 2     People may laugh, people may chaff,
           Brush it away!
           Thinking the time is ripe,
           Nevertheless you must confess
           Here it will stay,
           We are so true to type.

Refrain 3   Sentiment, it's simply sentiment
           That makes the world go round at all,
           Though people deprecate it,
           Say they hate it,
           All the same they fall,
           What is it makes a magistrate when some divorce is filed,
           Lecture the woman sternly on the wrongs of running wild?
           Then give the husband custody of someone else's child?
           Sentiment that's all!

Refrain 4   Sentiment, it's simply sentiment
           That makes the world go round at all,
           You'll find the Public Taste
           Is fiercely chaste
           No matter what befall,
           When some poor girl falls victim to the local ne'er-do-well,
           When it's too late to wonder as to 'should a woman tell',
           What is it makes her marry him though hating him like hell?
           Sentiment that's all!

# PARISIAN PIERROT

*from* LONDON CALLING

Verse 1 Fantasy in olden days
In varying and different ways
Was very much in vogue,
Columbine and Pantaloon,
A wistful Pierrot 'neath the moon,
And Harlequin a rogue.
Nowadays Parisians of leisure
Wake the echo of an old refrain,
Each some ragged effigy will treasure
For his pleasure,
Till the shadows of their story live again.

Verse 2 Mournfulness has always been
The keynote of a Pierrot scene,
When passion plays a part,
Pierrot in a tragic pose
Will kiss a faded silver rose
With sadness in his heart.
Some day soon he'll leave his tears behind him,
Comedy comes laughing down the street,
Columbine will fly to him
Admiring and desiring,
Laying love and adoration at his feet.

Refrain Parisian Pierrot,
Society's hero,
The Lord of a day,
The Rue de la Paix
Is under your sway,
The world may flatter
But what does that matter,
They'll never shatter
Your gloom profound,
Parisian Pierrot,
Your spirit's at zero,
Divinely forlorn,
With exquisite scorn
From sunset to dawn,
The limbo is calling,
Your star will be falling,
As soon as the clock goes round.

# WHAT LOVE MEANS TO GIRLS LIKE ME

*from* LONDON CALLING

Verse 1    A little word, four letters only,
And yet it means a lot you must admit.
It seems absurd,
But when I'm lonely
I lose my sense of values just a bit.
If men are really willing,
I must say I find it thrilling
Just to listen to the charming things they say.
Though I'm not exactly fickle,
I enjoy a slap and tickle
In a quiet unassuming sort of way.

Refrain 1    It isn't that I'm naughty or capricious,
It isn't that I single out my prey,
I'm sure that I've a mind
Too essentially refined
To flaunt my girlish charms in any way.
I sometimes think that Eve was very thoughtless
To wrench the fruit of knowledge from the tree,
More abstemious she'd have been,
Could she only have foreseen
What love means to girls like me.

Verse 2    If love is blind and people say so,
I'm certain that that statement's incorrect.
I shouldn't mind,
If he would stay so,
It's when he starts to see things I object.
To say that Cupid hates me,
And deliberately baits me,
Would really not exaggerate the case.
You could wheel away in barrows
All the bleeding blunted arrows
That from time to time he's fired in my face.

Refrain 2    It isn't that I'm thoroughly degraded,
It isn't that I go from bad to worse,
It isn't that I pine
For Roses, Love and Wine,
I'm a victim of a temperamental curse.
I often try to suffocate my passion,
Though all the time I yearn to set it free,

Cleopatra at her best
Would have shuddered if she'd guessed
What love means to girls like me.

Refrain 3 It isn't that I'm consciously alluring,
It isn't that I'm altogether bad.
A girl may have her dreams
Without going to extremes,
Though I shouldn't like to mention some I've had.
It isn't that I take all and give nothing,
I'm sure I'm generous-hearted as can be,
But poor Mary, Queen of Scots,
Would have tied herself in knots
For what love means to girls like me.

## WHEN WE WERE GIRLS TOGETHER

*from* LONDON CALLING 3rd Edition

Verse 1 Once we were maidens of bashful fifteen,
    Ah fal la la
    Whack folly olly O,
Though we were not what we ought to have been,
    Hey lack-a-day
    Nin nonny nonny no,
I used to bloom like a flowering shrub,
I was the toast of the Ham and Bone Club,
People would cycle for miles and miles
To bask in the light of our radiant smiles.

Refrain 1 When we were girls together,
Ready to do and dare,
Roguish and winsome and naughty and gay,
Bold at our lessons and
Rascals at play,
Don't give a jot for weather,
Spiced with devil-may-care,
Dreams of romance we would never dismiss,
Life was a frolic of virginal bliss
Wanting the magic of somebody's kiss,
That was our maiden's prayer.

Verse 2    Oh how the gallants of Battersea Rise,
                   Ah fal la la
                   Whack folly olly O,
            Followed us round with lascivious eyes,
                   Hey lack-a-day
                   Nin nonny nonny no,
            Medical students besieged me in mobs,
            I was a riot at Arding and Hobbs,
            Roués would tempt us to amorous sin,
            Their patience gave out
            But we never gave in.

Refrain 2  When we were girls together,
                   Brushing our golden hair
            Over the fire when daytime was done,
            Whispering fragments of naughtiest fun,
            Fresh as the wind-blown heather,
            Laying our secrets bare,
            Biblical stories we'd always believe,
            All kinds of knowledge we tried to achieve,
            And oh for the apple the Serpent gave Eve,
            That was our maiden's prayer.

Verse 3    One Sunday evening we met a young man,
                   Ah fal la la
                   Whack folly olly O,
            Though it was rash we fell in with his plan,
                   Hey lack-a-day
                   Hi nonny nonny no,
            I had misgivings I'm bound to confess,
            I kept myself to myself more or less,
            Maybe we did go a little too far
            But we didn't get tired as he'd such a nice car.

Refrain 3  When we were girls together,
                   Oh, what an elfin pair,
            As we grew older
            We're bound to admit
            Our maidenly fancies
            Developed a bit,
            Often our thoughts we'd tether,
            Though we were well aware
            We'd done naughty things that we oughtn't to do,
            We wanted no longer to bill and to coo
            But marriage with someone
            We didn't care who,
            That was our maiden's prayer.

## SPANISH GRANDEE

*from* LONDON CALLING 3rd Edition

Verse    Spain with its mountains and streams
Is a country of dreams
Where romance always seems
To be found
There in the coolness of night
When the stars are alight
And the moonlight is bright
On the ground,
Spain sunshine and rain
Deep in my brain
Calling ever,
Spain must I remain
See you again
Never, never.

Refrain    Somewhere there's a Spanish Grandee
Waiting for a lover like me
And while he whispers my name
My heart he'll claim
Under a flaming tangerine moon.
Swept off my feet
By kisses sweet
I hope I'll meet
Him terribly soon.
Some day we'll assuredly be
Lovers by the warm southern sea
With passion flowers swaying
And mandolins playing,
My thoughts ever straying
To my Spanish Grandee.

# On with the Dance

## COSMOPOLITAN LADY

*from* ON WITH THE DANCE

Verse    When I was quite a little mite of seven,
I secretly decided on my course;
Though maybe I'm not heading straight for heaven,
I have never put the cart before the horse.

Chorus    She wouldn't do that of course!

Verse    It's seldom that my 'joie de vivre' forsakes me,
I frequently succeed where others fail,
And when the day of judgment overtakes me,
I shall make a very firm appeal for bail!

Chorus    She seems successfully to dominate
And utterly control her fate,
We'll try to follow firmly on her trail!

Refrain    I'm a cosmopolitan lady,
With a cosmopolitan soul,
Every dashing blonde
Of the demi-monde
Starts to quake when I take a stroll
As my past's incredibly shady,
And my future grows more doubtful every day.
Though determined to be pleasant,
I shall utilize the present
In a cosmopolitan way.

Verse    The world to me will always be a gamble,
I don't care if I win or if I lose;
The straight and narrow path is such a scramble,
And is such an unattractive life to choose.

Chorus    We'd like to be in your shoes!

Verse    I much prefer a flutter at the tables,
I treat my whole existence as a game,
And if I end in sackcloth or in sables,
I shall not have lived for nothing, all the same!

Chorus  We're really quite impatient to begin
        A life of unassuming sin,
        And try to reach your pinnacle of fame!

Refrain  I'm a cosmopolitan lady,
         With a cosmopolitan heart,
         And I've lived so long
         Between right and wrong,
         That I can't tell the two apart,
         Though my past's incredibly shady,
         And my future grows more doubtful every day;
         Though my methods may be breezy,
         I find virtue very easy,
         In the cosmopolitan way.

## I'M SO IN LOVE

*from* ON WITH THE DANCE

HE:  Ever since I met you,
     I've been absolutely crazy, dear;
     Just why I can't explain,
     Even though your character
     Is languid, loose and lazy, dear,
     My love will still remain,
     Look down and say my pleading and my prayers are not in vain.

### *Refrain 1*

I'm so in love with you,
Sort of a cross between a habit and a vice,
You thrill me through and through
Though you behave exactly like a block of ice.
Beneath the spell of your endearing young charms,
I'd break the Ten Commandments,
And jazz the Psalms,
I'm so in love with you,
And if I have to keep proposing till I'm blue,
I'll override your dignity,
I'll grab you tight and shake you,
Until I make you say that you're in love with me.

SHE: Ever since we met that night,
You take delight in shattering
My perfect peace of mind;
All my winsome girlish dreams
You make a point of scattering
Like leaves upon the wind.
You have such perfect charm and fearful selfishness combined.


*Refrain 2*

I'm so in love with you,
Sort of passion Mister Plato wouldn't pass;
I don't know what to do,
When I'm away from you I feel as bold as brass,
But when I gaze into your wonderful eyes
I find them undermining
My enterprise.
I'm so in love with you,
If you could only understand my point of view,
Just think how happy we could be,
I'd never once divorce you,
Unless of course you started in divorcing me!


## POOR LITTLE RICH GIRL

*from* ON WITH THE DANCE

Verse    You're only
A baby,
You're lonely,
And maybe
Some day soon you'll know
The tears
You are tasting
Are years
You are wasting,
Life's a bitter foe,
With fate it's no use competing,
Youth is so terribly fleeting;
By dancing
Much faster,
You're chancing
Disaster,
Time alone will show.

Refrain Poor little rich girl,
        You're a bewitched girl,
        Better beware!
        Laughing at danger,
        Virtue a stranger,
        Better take care!
        The life you lead sets all your nerves a jangle,
        Your love affairs are in a hopeless tangle,
        Though you're a child, dear,
        Your life's a wild typhoon,
        In lives of leisure
        The craze for pleasure
        Steadily grows.
        Cocktails and laughter,
        But what comes after?
        Nobody knows.
        You're weaving love into a mad jazz pattern,
        Ruled by Pantaloon.
        Poor little rich girl, don't drop a stitch too soon.

Verse 2 The role you are acting,
        The toll is exacting,
        Soon you'll have to pay.
        The music of living,
        You lose in the giving,
        False things soon decay.
        These words from me may surprise you,
        I've got no right to advise you,
        I've known life too well, dear,
        Your own life must tell, dear,
        Please don't turn away.


## FIRST LOVE

*from* ON WITH THE DANCE

HE:  If you could only realize
     And knew how I idealize
     The very slightest thing
     You say or do.

SHE: I've guessed and felt a little bit
     Depressed because I know that it
     Leads to complications,
     Think of your relations'
     Point of view.

*Chorus*

HE: First love,
Completely unrehearsed love,
Has all the spontaneity of youth.

SHE: Well, to tell the truth,
I am quite unversed, love,
In treating suitably
These adolescent scenes;
You're indisputably
The victim of your teens.
New love must always seem the true love,
Experience will teach you as you go,
Till you really know
Just the way to woo, love.

HE: I wish you'd show me how my passion should be nursed,

SHE: Your papa must raise my wages first, love.

HE: I've burned to kiss your darling hand,
And yearned to make you understand
That you're the only one
In life for me!

SHE: I fear I can't reciprocate,
But, dear, I do appreciate
Having made you suffer,
Darling little duffer,
You'll soon see.

*Chorus*

SHE: First love
Is generally the worst love.

HE: I'm trying to restrain it all the time.
I've a feeling I'm
Really going to burst, love.

SHE: I fully realize
Your true romantic soul,
But you must utilize
A little self-control.

HE: Calf love
Is never half and half love,
To me you're just the fairest of your sex.
How I love you.

SHE: Excuse me if I laugh, love.

HE:   Let's plunge in passion till we're totally immersed.

SHE: I shall have to ask my husband first, love.


## COULDN'T WE KEEP ON DANCING?

*from* ON WITH THE DANCE

Refrain 1    If we try, you and I,
             Couldn't we keep on dancing?
             Man and wife, what a life!
             Wouldn't it be entrancing?
             Never mind if we find
             People a bore,
             Never blue,
             Follow through
             Every encore.
             Couldn't we, couldn't we,
             Couldn't we keep on dancing?

Verse 1      With our fingers interlacing,
             We'll go rapturously pacing,
             Hand in hand, dear,
             Fairyland, dear.
             Couldn't be more grand, dear,
             I should welcome growing older
             With your head upon my shoulder.
             Lights are gleaming
             While we're scheming,
             What a lovely dream!

Verse 2      Absent-minded syncopation
             So improves the circulation,
             Law-abiding
             Love is hiding
             As we're gently gliding;
             In my dreams I've contemplated
             Being rhythmically mated.
             Never leave me,
             That would grieve me,
             Let us make believe!

Refrain 2  If we try, you and I,
              Couldn't we keep on dancing?
              Man and wife, what a life!
              Wouldn't it be entrancing?
              Never mind if we find
              People a bore,
              Never blue,
              Follow through
              Every encore.
              Couldn't we, couldn't we,
              Couldn't we keep on dancing?

Interlude  Drifting through the world to some sweet tune,
              What a fascinating honeymoon!
              Happiness acquiring,
              Never tiring,
              Don't let's wake too soon.

Refrain 3  If we try, you and I,
              Couldn't we keep on dancing?
              Man and wife, what a life!
              Wouldn't it be entrancing?
              Never mind if we find
              People a bore,
              Never blue,
              Follow through
              Every encore.
              Couldn't we, couldn't we,
              Couldn't we keep on dancing?

## RASPBERRY TIME IN RUNCORN

*from* ON WITH THE DANCE
FÊTE GALANTE

CHORUS:  When it's raspberry time in Runcorn,
            In Runcorn, in Runcorn,
            The air is like a draught of wine,
            The undertaker cleans his sign,
            The Hull express goes off the line,
            When it's raspberry time in Runcorn.

SOLO:  The happy-hearted Rural Dean—

CHORUS:  In Runcorn, in Runcorn—

SOLO:  Plays cricket on the village green—

CHORUS: In Runcorn, in Runcorn—

SOLO:    And as before the vestry door
         With cricket bat he poises,
         From far and near you always hear
         The most peculiar noises.

CHORUS: For it's raspberry time, raspberry time, raspberry
        time in Runcorn.


## SPINSTERS' SONG

*from* ON WITH THE DANCE
FÊTE GALANTE

We're little Parish workers,
With indefinite desires,
Determined to improve the shining hour
Though years of firm repression
May have quenched our inward fires,
Undoubtedly we've turned a trifle sour.
We're busy little beavers,
And we decorate the Church.
Our moral standard's very, very high.
The flower of English manhood
May have left us in the lurch
But we know we'll go to Heaven when we die.


## THE VICARAGE DANCE

*from* ON WITH THE DANCE
FÊTE GALANTE

I'm just seventeen and a rogue of a girl;
My heart is a-throbbing with carnival's whirl.
Lovers in plenty I'll have before dawn,
As I dance in my semi of mercerized lawn!

Refrain  Come with me, come to the vicarage dance.
         Quick to the ball we must hasten.
         Those who have gout are allowed to sit out
         Under the lavatory basin.

Several old deans behind Japanese screens
Give naughty Cupid a chance,
Though I get cramp
I'm no end of a scamp
Down at the vicarage dance.


## CHOIR BOYS' SONG

*from* ON WITH THE DANCE
FÊTE GALANTE

We're six dirty little choir boys
With really frightful minds,
We scream and shout and rush about
And pinch our friends' behinds.
Nobody could admire boys
With dirty hands and knees,
But the countryside rejoices
At our sweet soprano voices,
So we do what we damn well please.


# EVEN CLERGYMEN ARE NAUGHTY NOW AND THEN

*from* ON WITH THE DANCE
FÊTE GALANTE

*Verse 1*

People have a wrong idea of Members of the Cloth;
It's really an enjoyable profession.
And though we don't indulge in much frivolity and froth
We really haven't cause for much depression.
Our lives are full of jollity and gaiety and fun,
With christenings and funerals and such,
There's not a week goes by
In which someone doesn't die,
So we really mustn't grumble very much.

*Refrain 1*

When we wake up in the morning and the birds are trilling
There is something thrilling
In the air;

CURATE: I can feel my pulses starting
        As I struggle with my parting,
        And my thoughts go gaily darting
        Here and there.

        When we visit village invalids on New Year's Day
        We're really just as gay
        As other men;

VICAR:  Mrs Jones whom I was chaffing
        Had a fit and died from laughing.

BOTH:   Even clergymen are naughty
        Now and then.


*Verse 2*

VICAR:  The villagers will never disregard a festive cause
        To join in any jumble sale or raffle,
        And every Christmas evening I appear as Santa Claus,
        A good disguise which never fails to baffle.
        A whist drive in the Parish Room
        Could only be described
        As a positively brilliant affair.
        And when old Mrs Meyer
        Gives a picnic for the choir
        It's really almost more than we can bear.


*Refrain 2*

BOTH:   When we wake up in the morning and the weather's bad
        We're really always glad
        To be alive.

VICAR:  With a faithful repetition
        Of our family tradition
        Every year a new addition
        Will arrive.

BOTH:   Though we fill the cup of duty to the very brim
        Ideas may sometimes swim
        Into our ken.

CURATE: When our thoughts are most volcanic
        We remember in our panic
        Even clergymen are naughty
        Now and then.

## CHURCH PARADE

*from* ON WITH THE DANCE
FÊTE GALANTE

Verse    On every Sunday morning
See the righteous leave their houses,
With perching hats adorning,
Feather boas and dressy blouses,
Their souls devoid of base emotions,
They're on their way to their devotions.

Refrain 1   Church parade, church parade,
See the different types displayed.
Tall ones, short ones, thin and stout,
Everyone looking quite aggressively devout.
Church parade, church parade,
Truculent and undismayed,
There's Mrs Bowls in grey sateen,
Her hat's the queerest shape I can remember having seen,
It makes me quite suspicious as to what it might have been
On Church parade.

Refrain 2   Church parade, church parade,
See the different types portrayed.
Christian women, large and small,
With nothing in their faces to distinguish them at all.
Church parade, church parade,
Truculent and undismayed,
Those young ladies don't read Freud,
Their virginal mentalities are otherwise employed;
Maybe that's the reason that they look so unenjoyed
On Church Parade.

## COME A LITTLE CLOSER

*from* ON WITH THE DANCE

HE:   Sometimes you whisper
After a kiss,
How much I mean to you.

SHE: You're so persistent,
Just think of this.
What is a girl to do?
When you are pleading
Close by my side,
Gaily unheeding
Time and tide.
If you have meant the nice things you say,
I might relent
And look your way.

### Refrain

Come a little closer, closer dear to me;
If you answer, 'No, Sir,' how annoyed I'll be.
Why do you crush me and try to rush me,
Each single word I say?
Come a little closer, please don't turn away.
Sometimes you're sweet and adorably small,
'Then you're so grand I can't reach you at all.
Come a little closer, closer dear to me.

HE: Think of the rapture
When we're at last
Lost in our love intense.

SHE: Try to recapture
Out of the past
One little shred of sense.
You're so tenacious
With your desire;
If you were gracious
You'd soon tire.

HE: That isn't fair, dear,
Doubting me so,
I couldn't bear
To let you go.

### Coda

I'll never falter, take me on trust!
If at the altar you would just
Come a little closer, closer dear to me.

# This Year of Grace

## WAITING IN A QUEUE

*from* THIS YEAR OF GRACE

Verse    In a rut
In a rut
In a rut
We go along,
Nothing but
Nothing but
Nothing but
The same old song,
To those who view us lightly
We must seem slightly
Absurd,
We never break the ritual,
One habitual
Herd.

Refrain    Waiting in a queue
Waiting in a queue
Everybody's always waiting in a queue,
Fat and thin
They all begin
To take their stand—it's grand—queueing it.
Everywhere you go
Everywhere you go
Everybody's always standing in a row,
Short and tall
And one and all
The same as sheep—just keep—doing it.
No one says why
No one says how
No one says what is this for,
No one says no
No one says go
No one says this is a bore,
If you want to do
Anything that's new,
If you're feeling happy, furious or blue,
Wet or fine
You get in line
For everybody's waiting in a queue.

## MARY MAKE-BELIEVE

*from* THIS YEAR OF GRACE

Verse   I have been reading in this book of mine
      About a foolish maiden's prayer
  And every gesture, word and look of mine
      Seems to be mirrored there.
  She had such terribly pedantic dreams
      That her romantic schemes
      Went all awry,
      Her thoughts were such
      She claimed too much
  And true love passed her by.

Refrain  Mary make-believe
  Dreamed the whole day through,
      Foolish fancies,
      Love romances,
  How could they come true?
  Mary make-believe
  Sighed a little up her sleeve,
      Nobody claimed her,
      They only named her
  Mary make-believe.

*Counter Melody sung by Chorus*

  She's just a girl who's always blowing mental bubbles
      Till she's quite out of breath—quite out of breath,
  She seems to have the knack of magnifying troubles
      Till they crush her to death—crush her to death.
      She's just a duffer
      Of the ineffective kind,
      She's bound to suffer
      From her introspective mind,
  Her indecisions
  Quite prevent her visions
  Coming true.
      Imagination
      Is a form of flagellation,
      If a sensitive child
      Let's it run wild
  It dims the firmament
  Till all the world is permanently blue.
  She's simply bound
  To make a bloomer

Until she's found
Her sense of humour,
If love should touch her ever
    She'll never, never see it through.

## I'M MAD ABOUT YOU

*from* THIS YEAR OF GRACE

### *Verse*

HE:    Dear, your personality
Is bad for my morality,
It's more than I can bear.

SHE:    Though I surmise it isn't wise
To set my cap at you,
I've lost all control and on the whole
I can't live through a single minute,
Dear, without your image in it.

HE:    When you are inclined to be
Encouraging and kind to me
I simply walk on air,
Maybe I'll wake up soon and break my heart
To find that you—aren't there.

### *Refrain*

HE:    I'd like to tell you that I'm mad about—
    Mad about you—mad about you.

SHE:    But there is one thing that I'm sad about—
    Sad about—sad about too.

HE:    When you met me you swore
    You were essentially nice
But I wasn't so sure
    When we had kissed once or twice.

SHE:    For all I know you're just a gadabout—
    Gadabout—gadabout who
Is always eager to exchange old love for new.

BOTH:    I've a feeling—you've been concealing
    A thousand or two
Mad about, mad about, mad about you!

# LORELEI

*from* THIS YEAR OF GRACE

Verse 1  When the day
Fades away,
Twilight dies,
Sirens rise
Combing their hair with cool green fingers,
Crooning out their song,
Let him beware who loves and lingers
Over-long.

Refrain 1 Lorelei, Lorelei,
Call to sailors drifting by,
Cooo, cooo, come hither,
While they're sailing
A voice is wailing
A beckoning tune.
No use praying,
They'll all be paying
A reckoning soon.
Under the moon.

Lorelei, Lorelei,
Silver voices fade and die
Smiling with glee
Into the sea,
They slither
Down in the depths profound,
Where passionate joys are drowned,
There lie the lovers wooed by the Lorelei.

Verse 2  All that is past
And now at last
Everything's altered and changed about,
Progress goes on,
Glamour has gone
From where the schooners once ranged about.
Speed and power,
Hour by hour,
Liners tower high,
Onward churning,
Never turning
For a yearning cry,
Coal dust and grime,

No one has time
For any simple romance at all,
Beckon and coo
Till you are blue,
Mermaids have got no damned chance at all.

Refrain 2    Lorelei, Lorelei,
Sit around and weep and cry,
Days are so long,
Everything's wrong
Completely.
All the sirens
In these environs
Are sorry they spoke,
Coaling steamers
Are belching streamers
Of horrible smoke
Making them choke.

Lorelei, Lorelei,
Sadly sigh
And wonder why
Every new ship
Gives them the slip
So neatly.
What could be more obscene
Than vamping a submarine?
Pity the languid left-alone Lorelei.


## A ROOM WITH A VIEW

*from* THIS YEAR OF GRACE

### Verse 1

HE:     I've been cherishing
Through the perishing
Winter nights and days
A funny little phrase
That means
Such a lot to me
That you've got to be
With me heart and soul
For on you the whole
Thing leans.

SHE:   Won't you kindly tell me what you're driving at,
       What conclusion you're arriving at?

HE:    Please don't turn away
       Or my dream will stay
       Hidden out of sight
       Among a lot of might-
       Have-beens!

### Refrain 1

HE:    A room with a view—and you,
       With no one to worry us,
       No one to hurry us—through
       This dream we've found,
       We'll gaze at the sky—and try
       To guess what it's all about,
       Then we will figure out—why
       The world is round.

SHE:   We'll be as happy and contented
       As birds upon a tree,
       High above the mountains and the sea.

BOTH:  We'll bill and we'll coo-oo-oo
       And sorrow will never come,
       Oh, will it ever come—true,
       Our room with a view.

### Verse 2

SHE:   I'm so practical
       I'd make tactical
       Errors as your wife,
       I'd try to set your life
       To rights.
       I'm upset a bit
       For I get a bit
       Dizzy now and then
       Following your mental flights.

HE:    Come with me and leave behind the noisy crowds,
       Sunlight shines for us above the clouds.

SHE:   My eyes glistened too
       While I listened to
       All the things you said,
       I'm glad I've got a head
       For heights.

*Refrain 2*

SHE:   A room with a view—and you,
And no one to give advice,
That sounds a paradise—few
Could fail to choose,
With fingers entwined we'll find
Relief from the preachers who
Always beseech us to—mind
Our P's and Q's.

HE:   We'll watch the whole world pass before us
While we are sitting still
Leaning on our own window-sill.

BOTH:   We'll bill and we'll coo-oo-oo,
And maybe a stork will bring
This, that and t'other thing—to
Our room with a view.


# IT DOESN'T MATTER HOW OLD YOU ARE

*from* THIS YEAR OF GRACE

Verse 1   Life is just a gamble
And without preamble
I should like to state my case.
I'm no Messalina,
I've a slightly cleaner
Outlook on the human race.
Don't imagine that I'm hewn from
Marble or stone,
I'm not utterly immune from
Pangs of my own.
Though I'm over forty
I can still be naughty
In an unassuming way.
Beauty doesn't always win the day
I say.

Refrain 1   It doesn't matter how old you are
If the joys of life are sweet.
It doesn't matter how cold you are
If you've still got central heat.

I've seen raddled wrecks
With false pearls hung round their necks
Get away with lots of sex appeal
And though I may have been through the mill
I'm a creature of passion still,
It doesn't matter how old you are,
It's just how young you feel.

Verse 2 Though I'm not a gay girl
I'm a 'come-what-may' girl,
Nothing in my life is planned.
Men with love get blinded
But I'm so broad-minded
I just smile and understand,
Men don't always want to marry,
They're not to blame,
I'm quite certain that Dubarry
Felt just the same.
Too much love is nauseous,
One can't be too cautious,
Cupid's such a wily foe,
Though I never let myself quite go,
I know.

Refrain 2 It doesn't matter how old you are
If your heart can still beat fast,
It doesn't matter how bold you are
When the dangerous age is past,
Though my face is lined
And my outlook too refined
I shall never let my mind congeal,
Pompadour found her love a curse
But I'll go further and fare much worse,
It doesn't matter how old you are,
It's just how young you feel.

Refrain 3 It doesn't matter how old you are
If you've still the strength to care,
However naughty you're told you are
It's entirely your affair.
Though I come a smack
And go rolling off the track
It will never be from lack of zeal.
You may laugh when you look at me
But watch the papers and wait and see!
It doesn't matter how old you are,
It's just how young you feel.

# TEACH ME TO DANCE LIKE GRANDMA

### *from* THIS YEAR OF GRACE

Verse   I'm getting tired of jazz tunes
Monotonous,
They've gotten us
Crazy now.
Though they're amusing as tunes
Music has gone somehow.
I hear the moaning
Groaning
Of a saxophone band,
It simply shakes me,
Makes me
Want to play a
Lone hand.
Please understand
I want an age that has tunes
Simple and slow,
I'm feeling so
Lazy now.

Refrain  Teach me to dance like Grandma used to dance,
I refuse to dance—Blues.
Black Bottoms, Charlestons, what wind blew them in,
Monkeys do them in zoos.
Back in the past the dancing signified
Just a dignified glow.
They didn't have to be so strong
Though they revolved the whole night long.
Teach me to dance like Grandma used to dance
Sixty summers ago!

# LITTLE WOMEN

### *from* THIS YEAR OF GRACE

### *Verse 1*

ALL:     We're little girls of certain ages
Fresh from London town,
Like an instalment plan of Drage's
We want so much down.

We have discovered years ago
That flesh is often clay,
We're not a new sin,
We're on the loose in
Quite the nicest way.
We have renounced domestic cares
For ever and for aye,
We're not so vicious,
Merely ambitious,
If there must be love
Let it be free love.


*Refrain*

We're little women,
Alluring little women,
Cute but cold fish
Just like goldfish
Looking for a bowl to swim in.
We lead ornamental
But uncreative lives,
We may be little women
But we're not good wives.


VIOLET:   I am just an ingénue
And shall be till I'm eighty-two,
At any rude remark my spirit winces,
I've a keen religious sense
But in girlish self-defence
I always have to put my faith in princes.


ALL:   Do not trust them, gentle maiden,
They will kick you in the pants.


RUTH:   I'm not a type that is frequently seen,
I wear my hair in a narrow bang,
I have remained at the age of eighteen
Since I left home in a charabanc,
Though men all pursue me
When they woo me
They construe me as innocent,
But when I hear things suggestively phrased
I'm not unduly amazed.


ALL:   It takes far more than that to wake
Sweet wonder in her eyes.

JANE:    I waste no time on things
           That other girls are arch about,
           I much prefer to march about
           Alone.
           I am a baby vamp,
           I'd take a postage stamp,
           I just believe in grabbing
           Anything that's offered me.
           If Mother Hubbard proffered me
           A bone
           I should not be upset,
           Have the darned thing re-set.

ALL:     Much further than the Swanee River
           She keep her old folks at home.

IVY:     I am a girl whose soul with domesticity
              abounds,
           I know a man of six foot three who's worth
              a million pounds,
           Though he is like a brother
           I haven't told my mother
           He's given me a lovely house and grounds!

ALL:     Be it ever so humbug
           There's no place like home.

### Second Refrain

ALL:     We're little women,
           Alluring little women,
           Cute but cold fish
           Just like goldfish
           Looking for a bowl to swim in.
           Though we're very clinging
           Our independence thrives,
           We may be little women
           But we're not good wives.

## THE LIDO

*from* THIS YEAR OF GRÁCE

ALL: A narrow strip of sand
Where Byron used to ride about,
While stately ships would glide about
The sea on either hand.
But now the times have changed,
For civilized society
With infinite variety
Has had it rearranged.
No more the moon
On the still Lagoon
Can please the young enchanted,
They must have this
And they must have that
And they take it all for granted.
They hitch their star
To a cocktail bar
Which is all they really wanted,
That narrow strip of sand
Now reeks with asininity
With in the near vicinity
A syncopated band
That plays the blues—all the day long—
And all the old Venetians say
They'd like a nice torpedo
To blow the Lido away.

WIVES: Beneath the blue skies
Of sunny Italy
We lie on the sand
But please understand
We're terribly grand.
We firmly married
The old nobility,
But we can spend happy days here,
Take off our stays here,
Tarnish our laurels,
Loosen our morals.
Oh! you'll never know
The great relief it is
To let our feelings go,
We're comme-il-faut
You see and so
It doesn't matter what vulgarity
We show!

HUSBANDS: Ladies of abundant means
And less abundant minds,
Although we're not romantic
We crossed the cold Atlantic
To choose a few commercial queens
Of different sorts and kinds.
Returning with a cargo
Of girlhood from Chicago,
Though we regret it more from day to day
We think it only fair to you to say:
It wasn't for your beauty that we married you,
It wasn't for your culture or your wit,
It wasn't for the quality that Mrs Glyn describes
As 'It', just it.
It wasn't your position in society
That led us on to making such a fuss.

Forgive us being frank,
But your balance in the bank
Made you just the only wives for us.

ALL:          This narrow strip of sand
Makes something seem to burst in us,
Brings out the very worst in us,
But kindly understand
We've got the blues all the day long
And every year we always say
We'd like a nice torpedo
To blow the Lido away!


# ENGLISH LIDO

*from* THIS YEAR OF GRACE

### Opening Chorus

ALL:          Hurray, hurray, hurray!
The holidays!
The jolly days
When laughter, fun and folly days
Appear
Hurray, hurray, hurray!
The laity
With gaiety
And charming spontaneity
Must cheer.

MR. HARRIS:  I've left my bowler hat and rubber collar far behind.

MRS. HARRIS:  I wish to God you'd left that awful Panama behind,
It looks gaga behind.

ALL:          But never mind
Because the holidays are here,
Our tastes are very far from Oriental,
We have a very fixed idea of fun,
The thought of anything experimental
Or Continental
We shun.
We take to innovations very badly,
We'd rather be uncomfortable than not,
In fighting any new suggestion madly
We'd gladly
Be shot!
We much prefer to take our pleasures sadly
Because we're thoroughly contented with our lot.


## MOTHER'S COMPLAINT

*from* THIS YEAR OF GRACE

We're all of us mothers,
We're all of us wives,
The whole depressing crowd of us,
With our kind assistance
The Motherland thrives.
We hope the nation's proud of us.
For one dreary fortnight
In each dreary year
We bring our obstreperous families here.
We paddle and bathe while it hails and it rains,
In spite of anaemia and varicose veins,
Hey nonny, ho nonny, no no no!

Our lodgings are frowsy,
Expensive and damp,
The food is indigestible.
We sit on the beach
Till we're tortured with cramp
And life is quite detestable.

The children go out with a bucket and spade
And injure themselves on the asphalt parade,
There's sand in the porridge and sand in the bed,
And if this is pleasure, we'd rather be dead,
Hey nonny, ho nonny, no no no!


# BRITANNIA RULES THE WAVES

*from* THIS YEAR OF GRACE

CHORUS:  Hail, Neptune's daughter,
           The pride of Finsbury Park,
           Behold a modest clerk
           Is goddess of the water.
           Hail, pioneer girl,
           Though rain and wind have come
           You've swum and swum and swum,
           You really are a dear girl.

DAISY:  Kind friends, I thank you one and all
           For your delightful greetings.
           I merely heard my country's call
           At patriotic meetings.

CHORUS:  Just think of that,
           Just think of that,
           She got her inspiration at
           A patriotic meeting.
           Oh, tell us more,
           Oh, tell us more,
           Oh, tell us what you do it for,
           It must be overheating.

DAISY:  Kind friends, I thank you all again
           And since you ask me to
           I will explain.

*Verse*

DAISY:  Like other chaste stenographers
           I simply hate photographers,
           I also hate publicity.

CHORUS:  She lives for sheer simplicity.

DAISY:   For any woman more or less ·
A photo in the daily press
Is horribly embarrassing.

CHORUS:  It must be dreadfully harassing.

DAISY:   The British male
May often fail,
Our faith in sport is shaken,
So English girls awaken
And save the nation's bacon.

### Refrain 1

Up girls and at 'em
And play the game to win,
The men must all give in
Before the feminine.
Bowl 'em and bat 'em
And put them on the run,
Defeat them every one,
Old Caspar's work is done.
We'll do our bit till our muscles crack,
We'll put a frill on the Union Jack,
If Russia has planned
To conquer us and
America misbehaves,
Up girls and at 'em,
Britannia rules the waves!

### Refrain 2

DAISY:   Up girls and at 'em,
Go out and win your spurs
For England much prefers
Applauding amateurs.
Man is an atom
So break your silly necks
In order to annex
Supremacy of sex.
Valiantly over the world we'll roam,
Husbands must wait till the cows come home.
The men of today
Who get in our way
Are digging their early graves.
Up girls and at 'em,
Britannia rules the waves!

*Refrain 3*

DAISY:      Up girls and at 'em
AND         And play the game to win,
CHORUS:     The men must all give in
            Before the feminine.
            Bowl 'em and bat 'em
            And put them on the run,
            Defeat them every one,
            Old Caspar's work is done.
            We'll do our bit
            Till our muscles crack,
            We'll put a frill
            On the Union Jack.

DAISY:      Here's to the maid
            Who isn't afraid,
            Who shingles and shoots and shaves.

CHORUS:     Up girls and at 'em,
            Britannia rules the waves!


## DANCE LITTLE LADY

*from* THIS YEAR OF GRACE

Verse       Though you're only seventeen
            Far too much of life you've seen,
            Syncopated child.
            Maybe if you only knew
            Where your path was leading to
            You'd become less wild.
            But I know it's vain
            Trying to explain
            While there's this insane
            Music in your brain.

Refrain     Dance, dance, dance little lady,
            Youth is fleeting—to the rhythm beating
            In your mind.
            Dance, dance, dance little lady,
            So obsessed with second best,
            No rest you'll ever find,
            Time and tide and trouble
            Never, never wait.

Let the cauldron bubble
Justify your fate.
Dance, dance, dance little lady,
Leave tomorrow behind.

Patter    When the saxophone
Gives a wicked moan,
Charleston hey hey,
Rhythms fall and rise,
Start dancing to the tune,
The band's crooning—
For soon
The night will be gone,
Start swaying like a reed
Without heeding
The speed
That hurries you on.
Nigger melodies
Syncopate your nerves
Till your body curves
Drooping—stooping,
Laughter some day dies
And when the lights are starting to gutter
Dawn through the shutter
Shows you're living in a world of lies.

## CHAUVE-SOURIS

*from* THIS YEAR OF GRACE

QUINTETTE:    Ish con broshka
Whoops dad illoshka
Whoops dad illoshka
Inkle drob vaard.

Ish con broshka
Whoops dad illoshka
Whoops dad illoshka
Inkle drob vaard.

Wheeshka eeglee
Wheeshka bombolom
Wheeshka weedlewee
Chock chock wish laa.

Wheeshka eeglee
Wheeshka bombolom
Wheeshka weedlewee
Inkle drob vaard.


## TRY TO LEARN TO LOVE

*from* THIS YEAR OF GRACE

### *Verse 1*

HE:  In kindergartens
In country or town
Our education begins,
Like little Spartans
We're taught to crush down
The inclination to sin.
When we change to gentle adolescence
Things get rather strained,
There's a strange, peculiar effervescence
No one has explained.

### *Refrain 1*

First you learn to spell
A little bit,
Then, if you excel
A little bit,
Other things as well
A little bit
Come your way;
Though the process may be slow to you
Knowledge of the world will flow to you,
Steadily you grow a little bit,
Day by day;
Though you're too gentle, sentimental,
In fact, quite a dreary bore,
Though you're aesthetic, apathetic
To all men but Bernard Shaw,
Use the velvet glove
A little bit,
Emulate the dove
A little bit,
Try to learn to love a little bit more.

*Verse 2*

SHE: The art of wooing,
I'm firmly resolved,
For men is terribly crude.
To be pursuing
Is not so involved
As having to be pursued.
Doubts and fears
Make women work much faster
Though they're frail and weak,
Taking years
Successfully to master
Feminine technique.

*Refrain 2*

First you droop your eyes
A little bit,
Then if you are wise
A little bit
Register surprise
A little bit,
If he's bold,
Stamp your foot with some celerity,
Murmur with intense sincerity
That his immature temerity
Leaves you cold.
But when you get him
You must let him
Have the joy he's yearning for
And whisper sweetly,
Indiscreetly,
He's the boy that you adore.
Use the moon above
A little bit,
Emulate the dove
A little bit,
Try to learn to love—a little bit more.

## CABALLERO

*from* THIS YEAR OF GRACE

Verse 1  Night falls, love calls tender and sweet, just there in the street below,
Teach me, reach me,
Wooing with song an echo of long ago.
Though all my dreams are in your serenade,
I'm afraid dreams must fade.

Refrain  Caballero,
You've simply swept me off my feet,
I love to listen to you sweetly
Serenading in the street
Outside.
Caballero,
I haven't got a heart of stone,
I'm waiting here for you alone,
You're sure to win me, if you only
Tried;
The southern night is soft and tender,
I'm simply burning to surrender,
Caballero.
The creamy passion flowers swoon,
Beneath a honey-coloured moon,
I'm only praying to be soon
Your bride.

Verse 2  Star shine, carmine life for the asking, passion unmasking soon,
Hold me, fold me,
Blossoms are fragrant, wooed by your vagrant tune;
I hear the echo of romance gone by;
That is why now I sigh.

## FINALE LONDON PRODUCTION

*from* THIS YEAR OF GRACE

STAGE HANDS:  We're eight stage hands,
Weary and winsome,
Embassy Club be blowed.
We've got wives and a nice drop of gin
Somewhere in the Old Kent Road.
Goodnight! Goodnight!

CHORUS GIRLS: One, two, three, four,
Five, six, seven, eight
All going home to bed.
Nobody's asked us to supper,
We wish we were dead.
Though we know quite
Well if we are late
Mother will leave the light.
We're feeling depressed
'Cos no one wants us;
So it would be best
For us to say goodnight.

SHOW GIRLS: You'll never know girls
Nicer than show girls,
For our behaviour
Reeks of Belgravia,
We're so restrained that
Men have complained that
We've nothing left to show,
Goodnight, goodnight, goodnight.

SMALL PARTS: Though we hardly speak parts
We support the weak parts
In our unpretentious way.
Now that you have seen us
Kindly choose between us,
We shall all be stars some day.
Goodnight and in the next revue that Cochran produces
We'll see our talents have more definite uses.

PRINCIPALS: Now you know our
Personalities,
What is it all about?
We're most surprised to discover
You haven't walked out.
We've exhausted
Our vitalities,
Sorry we've been so bright,
Just hurry and go
And put your coats on,
We've come to the moment
When we say goodnight,
Goodnight, goodnight, goodnight.

ALL:        We are the cause
Of all the traffic jam in Piccadilly,
Motoring laws
We disregard because they are so silly,
Toot-toot—toot-toot,
Toot-toot—toot-toot—toot-toot.
We're driving home in our
Driving home in our
High-powered cars,
You'd better hurry and take cover
For our knowledge of driving is slight,
Toot-toot—toot-toot,
Toot-toot—toot-toot—toot-toot
So good goody good goodnight.

You'ver seen the revue right through.
We hope you're applauding too
For it's according to
You—the money speaks.
We hope you can rouse
Keith Prowse
To something sensational,
Their approbation'll
House us here for weeks.
We thought it best to have a try-out,
We're not allowed to shirk,
Please don't let us fly out
Of work.
The best we can do
It's true
May not make you yearn again
Soon to return again to
This dreary revue.


## LOVE, LIFE AND LAUGHTER

*from* CHARLOT'S 1924 REVUE,

also THIS YEAR OF GRACE, New York 1928

LA FLAMME:  Hark to the music enthralling, appalling,
It dies away, and then—

RUPERT:    Women like you, so inviting, exciting,
Play fast and loose with men.
Fate has smiled on our meeting.
Feel my pulse madly beating.

LA FLAMME: Call for more drinks,
This is what the world thinks
Is La Vie Parisienne.

BOTH:     Love, life and laughter,
To the devil with what comes after.

RUPERT:   Hearts are on fire
With the flame of desire.

LA FLAMME: Lovers surrender
Regardless of gender.
Away care and sorrow,
Never worry about tomorrow.

BOTH:     We will rule passion's kingdom for a day.
For that's just the Bohemian way.

RUPERT:   Teach me the bliss of profanity's kiss
As we sway beneath the moon.

LA FLAMME: Lovers may sip
Passion's wine from my lip
To a gay romantic tune.

RUPERT:   Cupid's dart has impaled me,
All my breeding has failed me,
I want to smite you and beat you and bite you
And swoon and swoon and swoon.

BOTH:     Love, life and laughter,
To the devil with what comes after.

RUPERT:   Here is my heart, you can tear it apart,
Nothing suffices but decadent vices.

BOTH:     And mirth, folly, madness,
Never giving a thought to sadness.

LA FLAMME: If you told me to die I should obey.

BOTH:     For that's just the Bohemian way.

## WORLD WEARY

*from* THIS YEAR OF GRACE
(used in American production)

Verse 1    When I'm feeling dreary and blue,
I'm only too
Glad to be left alone,
Dreaming of a place in the sun.
When day is done,
Far from a telephone;
Bustle and the weary crowd
Make me want to cry out loud,
Give me something peaceful and grand
Where all the land
Slumbers in monotone.

Refrain 1    I'm world weary, world weary,
Living in a great big town,
I find it so dreary, so dreary,
Everything looks grey or brown,
I want an ocean blue,
Great big trees,
A bird's eye view
Of the Pyrenees,
I want to watch the moon rise up
And see the great red sun go down,
Watching clouds go by
Through a Winter sky
Fascinates me
But if I do it in the street,
Every cop I meet
Simply hates me,
Because I'm world weary, world weary,
I could kiss the railroad tracks,
I want to get right back to nature and relax.

Verse 2    Get up in the morning at eight,
Relentless Fate,
Drives me to work at nine;
Toiling like a bee in a hive
From four to five
Whether it's wet or fine,
Hardly ever see the sky,
Buildings seem to grow so high.
Maybe in the future I will
Perhaps fulfil
This little dream of mine.

Refrain 2  I'm world weary, world weary,
           Living in a great big town,
           I find it so dreary, so dreary,
           Everything looks grey or brown,
           I want a horse and plough,
           Chickens too,
           Just one cow
           With a wistful moo,
           A country where the verb to work
           Becomes a most improper noun;
           I can hardly wait
           Till I see the great
           Open spaces,
           My loving friends will not be there,
           I'm so sick of their
           God-damned faces,
           Because I'm world weary, world weary,
           Tired of all these jumping jacks,
           I want to get right back to nature and relax.

## LILAC TIME

*from* THIS YEAR OF GRACE
(used in American production)

HE:    Oh tell me, little maiden, pray
       Why should you choose to hide away
       On such a lovely summer's day?

SHE:   (*aside*) He does not know that I am the
       Princess, disguised as a beggar maid. Ah
       me! (*To him*):

       Kind sir, I know not who you are
       But if you should presume too far
       I shall seek refuge with Mamma.

HE:    (*aside*) She does not know that I am the
       Crown Prince, disguised as a gardener. Ah
       me!

SHE:   Spring is the time for folly—Ah ah—ah ah—

HE:    Fly away melancholy—Ah ah—ah ah—

SHE:   Spring is the time

HE:    Spring is the time

SHE:   Spring is the time

HE:    Spring is the time

SHE:   For folly,

HE:    So melancholy fly away—
       For it is Spring and life is gay and jolly.

### Refrain 1

BOTH:  Lilac time, lilac time,
       Blossoms are o'er the lea.

HE:    Birds are chirruping love's sweet song,

SHE:   Church bells ring-a-ding-ding-ding-dong!

HE:    Steal a kiss
       Just like this.

SHE:   You are too bold and free.

BOTH:  That is why it's lilac time
       Under the chestnut tree.

### Verse 2

SHE:   I am engrossed as you can see
       In reading some philosophy.

HE:    Literature this year must be
       So very much in vogue,
       Why should you bury that dainty nose
       In so much dry and dusty prose?

SHE:   You're making love to me, I suppose.

HE:    You charming little rogue.

SHE:   A charming little rogue.

BOTH:  A charming, charming, charming little rogue.

*Refrain 2*

BOTH:   Lilac time, lilac time,
        Blossoms are o'er the lea.

HE:     Birds are mating near and far

SHE:    Tra-la-lalala—la, la, la.

HE:     Steal a kiss
        Just like this.

SHE:    You are too bold and free.

BOTH:   That is why it's lilac time
        Under the chestnut tree,
        Ah ah—ah ah—
        Ah ah—ah ah—ah ah ah ah ah ah,
        Heigho nin nonny no,
        Heigho wack jolly-o,
        Heigho nin nonny no,
        Heigho lackaday do,
        That is why it's lilac time,
        That is why it's lilac time,
        Ha ha ha ha ha ha ha ha ha ha ha ha ha ha ha ha!


# I CAN'T THINK

*from* THIS YEAR OF GRACE
(used in American production)

Verse 1   It was early in September
          That we met each other first,
          And my entrance, I remember,
          Was distinctly unrehearsed.
          I had been to buy some butter
          And some raspberries and some eggs,
          When I slipped up in the gutter
          And clasped him round the legs.

Refrain 1  I can't think why he looked at me so queerly,
           I can't think why he scowled and walked away,
           I feel, as I apologized sincerely,
           He might have—well, perhaps I shouldn't say.
           I can't think how he managed to resist me,
           Perhaps the wish was father to the thought,
           I can't think why he didn't even kiss me,
           But I *do* think he did nothing of the sort.

Verse 2    It was later in October
        When we met—heigho!—once more,
        I believe that I was sober,
        But I couldn't be quiet sure.
        It was early in the morning
        And the air was pure and sweet,
        When I staggered without warning
        And fell prostrate at his feet.

Refrain 2   I can't think why my balance so betrayed me,
        I can't think why he hiccoughed and then frowned,
        I feel as he had not the strength to raise me,
        He might at least have joined me on the ground.
        I can't think why his manners so depressed me,
        Perhaps he was too social and refined,
        If you think he attempted to molest me,
        I *do* think he did nothing of the kind.


## THE SUN, THE MOON AND YOU
### (Burlesque of American Musical)

*from* THIS YEAR OF GRACE
(Finale, American production)

Verse 1    Little Girlie,
        Late or early,
        I just dream of you.
        Since that happy Tuesday when we met,
        If you only knew,
        One and one are two,
        That's a thing you never should forget.

Refrain    I want the sun, the moon and you,
        They simply thrill me through and through,
        The little stars that shine above
        Just fill me full of thoughts of love,
        My heart is throbbing,
        For you're robbing
        Me of all my pride,
        So listen, baby,
        Don't say maybe,
        You will be my bride.
        Sweetheart, I could never be blue
        With just the sun, the moon and you.

## PLAYING THE GAME

*from* THIS YEAR OF GRACE
(Part of Finale American production)

Playing the game
You have to biff the ball
And bang the ball,
In playing the game
You have to whiff the ball
And whang the ball,
And rah rah—rah rah—rah rah—rah rah—rah rah—
We're so collegiate—so collegiate—
You are to blame
For all the speed of it,
Your need of it
Is really a terrible shame,
Rah rah—rah rah—rah rah—rah rah—rah rah—
Everybody plays the game.

# *Bitter Sweet*

## THE CALL OF LIFE

*from* BITTER SWEET

LADY S.: Your romance could not live the length of a day,
You hesitate and analyse,
Betray your love with compromise,
Till glamour fades away;
And all too soon you realize
That there is nothing left to say.

CHORUS: Hey, hey—hey, hey,
How does she get that way?
She'd be more light-hearted
If she started—to Charleston;
She's never danced it,
She's never chanced it;
Perhaps her muscles are disinclined,
Perhaps she hasn't the strength of mind.

LADY S.: Love that's true can mean naught to you but a name,
A thing that isn't part of you;
Can never touch the heart of you;
It's nothing but a game,
A fire without a flame.

MEN: We find it difficult to grasp your meaning.

LADY S.: Maybe the past is intervening.

CHORUS: We very much regret that times have changed so,
Life is more speedily arranged so.

LADY S.: In your world of swiftly turning wheels
Life must be extremely grey.

CHORUS: We've no time to waste on Love Ideals,
That which to our senses most appeals
Is all we can obey.

61

LADY S.: No—no. Not so:
There must be something further on,
A vision you can count upon,
To help you to acquire
A memory when Youth is gone
Of what was once your heart's desire.

There is a call that echoes sweetly
When it is Spring and Love is in the air;
Whate'er befall, respond to it completely,
Though it may bring you sadness and despair;
Fling far behind you
The chains that bind you,
That love may find you
In joy or strife;
Though Fate may cheat you,
And defeat you,
Your Youth must answer to the Call of Life.

## IF YOU COULD ONLY COME WITH ME

*from* BITTER SWEET

Though there may be beauty in this land of yours,
Skies are very often dull and grey;
If I could but take that little hand of yours,
Just to lead you secretly away.
We would watch the Danube as it gently flows,
Like a silver ribbon winding free;
Even as I speak of it my longing grows,
Once again my own dear land to see.
If you could only come with me,
If you could only come with me.

## I'LL SEE YOU AGAIN

*from* BITTER SWEET

CARL: Now Miss Sarah, if you please,
Sing a scale for me.

SARAH: Ah—Ah—Ah—

CARL: Take a breath and then reprise
In a different key.

SARAH: Ah—Ah—Ah———

CARL: All my life I shall remember knowing you,
All the pleasure I have found in showing you
The different ways
That one may phrase
The changing light, and changing shade;
Happiness that must die,
Melodies that must fly,
Memories that must fade,
Dusty and forgotten by and by.

SARAH: Learning scales will never seem so sweet again
Till our Destiny shall let us meet again.

CARL: The will of Fate
May come too late.

SARAH: When I'm recalling these hours we've had
Why will the foolish tears
Tremble across the years,
Why shall I feel so sad,
Treasuring the memory of these days
Always?

CARL: I'll see you again,
Whenever Spring breaks through again;
Time may lie heavy between,
But what has been
Is past forgetting.

SARAH: This sweet memory,
Across the years will come to me;
Though my world may go awry,
In my heart will ever lie
Just just the echo of a sigh,
Goodbye.


## WHAT IS LOVE?

*from* BITTER SWEET

SARAH: Play something gay for me,
Play for me, play for me;
Set me free,
I'm in a trance tonight,

Can't you see
How I want to dance tonight?
Madly my heart is beating,
Some insane melody possessing me,
In my brain thrilling and obsessing me;
How can I leave it to call in vain?
Is it joy or pain?
Live your life, for time is fleeting,
Some insistent voice repeating;
Hear me—hear me,
How can I leave it to call in vain?
Is it joy or pain?

*Refrain*

Tell me—tell me—tell me, what is love?
Is it some consuming flame;
Part of the moon, part of the sun,
Part of a dream barely begun?
When is the moment of breaking—waking?
Skies change, nothing is the same,
Some strange magic is to blame;
Voices that seem to echo round me and above,
Tell me, what is love, love, love?

Play something gay for me,
Play for me—play for me;
Tell me why
Spring has so enchanted me;
Why this shy
Passion has been granted me;
Am I awake or dreaming?
Far and near
Every lover follows you,
Swift and clear,
Flying as the swallows do;
Leave me no longer to call in vain,
Are you joy or pain?
Leave me not by love forsaken,
If I sleep, then let me waken;
Hear me—hear me,
Leave me no longer to call in vain
Are you joy or pain?

# THE LAST DANCE

*from* BITTER SWEET

MEN: They've all gone now—have no fear—

GIRLS: Sarah's mother may be near,
If she should hear

ALL: She might be rather cross with us,
Elderly people make too much fuss.

MEN: Always insist on a chaperone,
Never leave love alone.

GIRLS: We feel frightened, if you please
Don't flirt or tease.

MEN: Gentle and sweet in your purity,
We give our hearts as security.

GIRLS: We shall be scolded a lot for this.

MEN: You won't miss just one kiss.
(*They all kiss*)

GIRLS: Think of the consequences, please, you haven't realized
What an appalling thing for us to be so compromised,
So dreadfully, dreadfully, dreadfully compromised.

MEN: Everything's ending,
The moon is descending,
Behind the tall trees in the park.

GIRLS: Silence falls,
Slumber calls.

MEN: We men together
Were wondering whether
We might have a bit of a lark.

GIRLS: No jokes in the dark, please,
What sort of a lark, please?

ALL: Just a slight dance,
One more dream-of-delight dance,
Just a sort of good-night dance
Would be glorious fun.

MEN:    Won't you let us, please let us, just stay for a while,
        Won't you, please won't you, be gay for a while?
        All we desire is to play for a while
        Now the party's done.

GIRLS:  Just a fast waltz,
        Till the world seems a vast waltz,
        Very often the last waltz
        Is the birth of romance.

ALL:    It's a June night,
        There's a thrill in the moonlight;
        Let's give way to the tender surrender
        Of one last dance.


## EENY MEENY MINY MO
### (Finale Act I)

*from* BITTER SWEET

GLORIA:     Eeny meeny miny mo

HARRIET:    Catch a nigger by his toe

VICTORIA:   If he hollers let him go

ALL:        O.U.T. spells out and so

GLORIA:     Out goes she. (*She points to Effie*)

EFFIE:      Out goes me. (*Skipping about*) This is the loveliest, loveliest
            part of the party.

GLORIA:     Eeny meeny miny mo

HARRIET:    Catch a nigger by his toe

VICTORIA:   If he hollers let him go

ALL:        O.U.T. spells out and so

GLORIA:     Out goes she. (*She points to Harriet*)

HARRIET:    Out goes me. (*She and Effie take hands and twirl around*)

| | |
|---|---|
| HARRIET<br>EFFIE } : | Now we're free to know who'll be he! |
| GLORIA: | Eeny meeny miny mo |
| VICTORIA: | Catch a nigger by his toe |
| SARAH: | If he hollers let him go |
| ALL: | O.U.T. spells out and so |
| VICTORIA: | Out goes she. (*She points to Gloria*) |
| GLORIA: | Out goes me. (*She joins Effie and Harriet*) |
| HARRIET<br>EFFIE } :<br>GLORIA | This is the loveliest, loveliest part of the party. |
| VICTORIA: | Eeny meeny miny mo |
| SARAH: | Catch a nigger by his toe |
| JANE: | If he hollers let him go |
| JANE: | Out goes she. (*Points to Victoria*) |
| VICTORIA: | Out goes me. (*She joins Effie, Harriet and Gloria*) |
| ALL: | This is the loveliest, loveliest part of the party. |
| EFFIE }:<br>HARRIET | Only three of them left now, we're excited to see |
| GLORIA }:<br>VICTORIA | Who is going to be blind man, who's it going to be. |
| SARAH: | I have a strange presentiment it's me. |
| JANE: | Eeny meeny miny mo<br>Out goes she. (*She points to Honor, who joins the others*) |
| SARAH: | Eeny meeny miny mo<br>Out goes she. (*She points to Jane*)<br>I'm HE—it's me,<br>It's me—I'm HE. |

GIRLS:       Just get a handkerchief and bind it around her eyes.

SARAH:       Not too tight, not too tight. (*They blindfold her*)

GIRLS:       She mustn't see a thing no matter how much she tries.

SARAH:       That's all right—that's all right.

GIRLS:       She will cheat if she can,
             That corner's raised a bit,
             Turn her round till she's dazed a bit,
             Are you ready now.
             One, two, three!

SARAH:       Since the party began,
             Something's been taunting me,
             Some presentiment haunting me,
             What can it be?

GIRLS:       Start now—start now,
             She can see the ground,
             She can see the ground.

SARAH:       Somehow, somehow,
             Some forgotten sound,
             Some forgotten sound,
             Echoes deep in my heart,
             Strangely enthralling me,
             Someone secretly calling me,
             Like a melody far away.

GIRLS:       Oh, for Heaven's sake start,
             Here go along with you,
             We can see nothing wrong with you,
             We want to play.

SARAH:       Should happiness forsake me,
             And disillusion break me,
             Come what may,
             Lead the way,
             Take me, take me.
             Although I may discover
             Love crucifies the lover,
             Whate'er Fate has in store,
             My heart is yours evermore.

CARL:        Oh, Lady, you are far above me,
             And yet you whisper that you love me,
             Can this be true or is it just some foolish dream?

SARAH:       (*speaking*) You know it's true, look in my eyes—can't you
             see?

CARL:        (*speaking softly*) Oh, my dear, dear love.
             (*singing*) Now though your fears are sleeping,
             Look well before the leaping.
             Love of me
             May be repaid
             By weeping.
             Life can be bitter learning,
             When there is no returning,
             Whate'er Fate has in store,
             My heart is yours for evermore,
             I love you—I love you—I love you.

GLORIA:      You cannot realize the things you say.
             You quite forget yourself, please go away.

HARRIET:     Now leave all this to me, my dear,
             It's really too absurd.

EFFIE:       It's quite the most romantic thing that I have ever heard!


## FOOTMEN QUARTETTE

### *from* BITTER SWEET

             Now the party's really ended,
             And our betters have ascended,
             All with throbbing heads,
             To their welcome beds,
             Pity us, who have to be up,
             Sadly clearing the debris up,
             Getting for our pains
             Most of the remains.

             Though the Major-Domo is a trifle tight,
             Though the mistress hiccoughed when she said good night,
             We in our secluded garret,
             Mean to finish up the claret
             Cup all right.

When we've doused the final candles,
We'll discuss the latest scandals
We have overheard,
Pleasure long deferred.
When the Duke of So-and So stares
At his wife, we know below stairs,
While she smirks and struts,
That he hates her guts.
Though we all disguise our feelings pretty well,
What we mean by 'Very good' is 'Go to hell'.
Though they're all so grand and pompous,
Most of them are now non compos,
Serve them right,
Good night.


# LIFE IN THE MORNING

*from* BITTER SWEET

WAITERS:      Life in the morning isn't too bright,
              When you've had to hurry round and carry plates all night;
              And the evening isn't too gay,
              When you know you've got to rise and be at work all day.
              This café merely caters
              For a horde of drunken satyrs,
              Why, oh why, we're waiters
              Nobody can say.

CLEANERS:     Oh dear, it's clear to see that cleaners lead a worse life,
              Every day we curse life;
              More and more
              The muscles on our brawny arms like iron bands are
              Scrubbing till our hands are
              Sore;
              We scour and polish till our fingers ache.

WAITERS:      (*humming*) Hum—hum————!

CLEANERS:     Each hour we feel as though our backs would break,

WAITERS:      Hum—hum————!

CLEANERS:     We weep and keep our growing families as well,
              Why we're here at all nobody can tell.

WAITERS: Life in the morning isn't too bright,
When you've had to hurry round and carry plates all night.

CLEANERS: Oh dear, it's clear to see that cleaners lead a worse life.

WAITERS: And the evening isn't too gay
When you know you've got to rise and be at work all day.

CLEANERS: You see the reason why each day we want to curse life.

WAITERS: For this café merely caters

CLEANERS: Weary

WAITERS: For a horde of drunken satyrs;

CLEANERS: Dreary

WAITERS: Why, oh why, we're waiters nobody can say.

CLEANERS: Every day.

WAITERS: Ah—Ah—Ah——

CLEANERS: Ah—Ah—Ah——


## LADIES OF THE TOWN

*from* BITTER SWEET

Though we're often accused of excessively plastic, drastic sins,
When we're asked to decide on the wrong or the right life,
Night life wins,
We know that destiny will never bring
A wedding ring about.
Our moral sense may really not be quite the thing
To fling about,
Sing about;
We'll achieve independence before it's too late, and
Wait and see.
What care, what care we?

Refrain  Ladies of the town, ladies of the town,
         Though we've not a confessional air,
         We have quite a professional flair,
         Strolling up and down, strolling up and down,
         We employ quite an amiable system
         Of achieving renown,
         Though the church and state abuses us,
         For as long as it amuses us,
         We'll remain, no matter how they frown,
         Haughty, naughty ladies of the town.

         We can often behave in a very disarming, charming way,
         Which can frequently add to the money we lay by,
         Day by day.
         If we are told of something on the Stock Exchange
         We pry a bit,
         And if it's safe we get some kindly banker
         To supply a bit, buy a bit,
         And if later our helpers may wish to forget us,
         Set us free,
         What care, what care we?

Refrain  Ladies of the town, ladies of the town,
         Though we're socially under a cloud,
         Please forgive us for laughing aloud,
         Strolling up and down, strolling up and down,
         Disapproval may sometimes submerge us,
         But we none of us drown,
         We have known in great variety
         Members of the best society,
         And should we decide to settle down,
         We'll be wealthy ladies of the town.


## IF LOVE WERE ALL

*from* BITTER SWEET

         Life is a very rough and tumble,
         For a humble
         Diseuse,
         One can betray one's troubles never,
         Whatever
         Occurs,
         Night after night,

Have to look bright,
Whether you're well or ill
People must laugh their fill.
You mustn't sleep
Till dawn comes creeping.
Though I never really grumble
Life's a jumble.
Indeed————
And in my efforts to succeed
I've had to formulate a creed————

Refrain  I believe in doing what I can,
In crying when I must,
In laughing when I choose.
Heigho, if love were all
I should be lonely,
I believe the more you love a man,
The more you give your trust,
The more you're bound to lose.
Although when shadows fall
I think if only————
Somebody splendid really needed me,
Someone affectionate and dear,
Cares would be ended if I knew that he
Wanted to have me near.
But I believe that since my life began
The most I've had is just
A talent to amuse.
Heigho, if love were all!

Though life buffets me obscenely,
It serenely
Goes on.
Although I question its conclusion,
Illusion
Is gone.
Frequently I
Put a bit by
Safe for a rainy day.
Nobody here can say
To what, indeed,
The years are leading.
Fate may often treat me meanly,
But I keenly
Pursue
A little mirage in the blue.
Determination helps me through.

# PEACE ENFOLD YOU
## (Evermore and a Day)

*from* BITTER SWEET

### Verse

CARL: Why are you weeping, dear?
What shadow haunted you in sleeping, dear?
Though portents and fears your courage may be plundering.
Your faith in my love should leave no time for wondering.
Even your dreams are in my keeping, dear.

SARI: Ah, no! my sweet,
Fate knows our happiness is too complete.
Though now in our love's security we live awhile
A little of heart's content the gods may give awhile,
Time's on the wing, my love, and time is fleet.

### Refrain

CARL: Peace enfold you;
Here in my arms I will hold you,
Fears receding further and further away.

SARI: Peace enfold me;
Here in your arms you will hold me,
Fears receding further and further away.

CARL: Though the world may divide us,
And ill-fortune betide us,
Yet our love is a token
That cannot be broken
Or stolen away.
There's a passionate glory
In the heart of our story;
We have something to guide us
Evermore and a day.

CARL⎱:
SARI⎰ Though the world may divide us,
And ill-fortune betide us,
Yet our love is a token
That cannot be broken
Or stolen away.
There's a passionate glory
In the heart of our story;
We have something to guide us,

We have something to guide us,
Evermore and a day,
Evermore and a day.

SARI: Peace enfold me,
Here in your arms you will hold me.

CARL: Peace enfold you,
Here in my arms I will hold you.

BOTH: Fears receding further and further away.
Fears receding further and further away.


# DEAR LITTLE CAFÉ

### *from* BITTER SWEET

CARL: We share a mutual ambition
Which naught can disarrange,

SARI: Based on the hopeful supposition
That soon our luck will change.

CARL: Though we very often wonder whether
Poverty will win the day,

SARI: Just as long as we remain together
Troubles seem to fade away.

BOTH: However hard the bed one lies on
The same old dreams begin,
We're always scanning the horizon
For when our ship comes in.

### *Refrain*

CARL: We'll have a sweet little café
In a neat little square,

SARI: We'll find our fortune
And our happiness there.

CARL: We shall thrive on the vain and resplendent

SARI: And contrive to remain independent.

CARL: We'll have a meek reputation
       And a chic clientèle,

SARI: Kings will fall under our spell.

BOTH: We'll be so zealous
       That the world will be jealous
       Of our sweet little café in a square.

SARI: Can you imagine our sensations
       When we've security?

CARL: And all our dreary deprivations
       Are just a memory.

SARI: Though we're very often driven frantic,
       Peace is very hard to find.

CARL: All these dreadful days will seem romantic
       When we've left them far behind.

BOTH: Fate needn't be quite such a dragon,
       He knows how tired we are.
       We'll hitch our hopeful little wagon
       Onto a lucky star.

*Refrain*

CARL: We'll have a sweet little café
       In a neat little square,

SARI: We'll find our fortune
       And our happiness there.

CARL: We shall thrive on the vain and resplendent

SARI: And contrive to remain independent.

CARL: We'll have a meek reputation
       And a chic clientèle,

SARI: Kings will fall under our spell.

BOTH: We'll be so zealous
       That the world will be jealous
       Of our sweet little café in a square.

## OFFICERS' CHORUS

*from* BITTER SWEET

OFFICERS: We wish to order wine, please,
Expressly from the Rhine, please,
The year we really don't much care.

LADIES: Oh dear,
Now that you're here
Think of the wear and tear.

OFFICERS: We hope without insistence
To overcome resistance
In all you little ladies fair.

LADIES: Oh well,
How can we tell
Whether you'd really dare?

OFFICERS: We sincerely hope it's really not a thankless task
Amusing us,
Won't you please agree?

LADIES: Ah me!

OFFICERS: You could quickly break our hearts by everything we ask

Refusing us;
Cruel that would be,
Ladies, can't you see!

We're officers and gentlemen,
Reliable and true,
Considerate and chivalrous
In everything we do.

Though we're gay and drunk a trifle,
All our laughter we should stifle,
Were we summoned by a bugle call.
We're amorous and passionate,
But dignified and stern,
Which if you play us false you'll quickly learn.
Do not let our presence grieve you,
When we've loved you we shall leave you,
For we're officers and gentlemen, that's all!

# TOKAY

*from* BITTER SWEET

OFFICERS:   Tokay!

CAPTAIN A.:  When we're thoroughly wined and dined,
            And the barracks are left behind,
            We come down to the town to find
            Some relief from the daily grind.
            Love is kind,
            Love is blind.

OFFICERS:   Tokay!

CAPTAIN A.:  When the thoughts of a man incline
            To the grapes of a sunlit vine,
            On the banks of the golden Rhine,
            Slowly ripening pure and fine,
            Sweet divine,
            Lovers' wine.
            Lift your voices till the rafters ring,
            Fill your glasses to the brim and sing:

            *Refrain*
            Tokay!
            The golden sunshine of a summer day,
            Tokay!
            Will bear the burden of your cares away,
            Here's to the love in you,
            The hate in you,
            Desire in you.

OFFICERS:   Wine of the sun that will waft you along,
            Lifting you high on the wings of a song.

CAPTAIN A.:  Dreams in you,
            The flame in you,
            The fire in you,
            Tokay—Tokay.

OFFICERS:   So while forgetfulness we borrow,
            Never minding what tomorrow has to say,

CAPTAIN A.: Tokay!

ALL:        The only call we all obey,
            Tokay—Tokay—Tokay!

## BONNE NUIT, MERCI!

*from* BITTER SWEET

MANON: Lorsque j'étais petite fille
En marchant parmi les prés
J'entendis la voix d'ma tante
Qui murmura à côté,
'N'oublie pas la politesse
Lorsque viendra un amant
Car tout le bonheur réside là dedans.'

*Refrain*

C'est pourquoi dans mes affaires,
Soit de cœur ou soit d'esprit,
C'est pourquoi je tâche de plaire
Toute la foule de mes amis,
Soit qu'ils m'offrent pied-à-terre
Ou me montrent une bonne affaire
J'leur réponds, 'Vas-y. Bonne nuit,
Merçi!'

Lorsque je suis v'nue à Paris
J'étais bien sage de nature,
Mais que faire dans la vie
Étant trop jeune pour rester pure!
Quand ma politesse m'obligea
Lorsqu' je suivais par hasard
Une aventure dans les bôites des boulevards.

*Refrain*

Et j'ai rencontré en ville
Un monsieur bien comme-il-faut,
Il m'a dit, ,Ma petite fille,
Veux-tu faire un p'tit do-do?'
Lorsqu' j'arrive chez lui toute de suite
Il m'dit, 'Deshabilles-toi vite!'
J'me suis dit, 'Vas'y. Bonne nuit,
Merçi!'

## KISS ME

*from* BITTER SWEET

MANON: 'Tis time that we were parted,
You and I,
However broken-hearted,
'Tis goodbye!
Although our love has ended
And darkness has descended,
I call to you with one last cry:

Kiss me
Before you go away!
Miss me
Through every night and day,
Though clouds are grey above you,
You'll hear me say I love you!
Kiss me
Before you go away!

Parmi les chansons tristes
De l'amour,
Joies et chagrins existent
Tour à tour,
Et presqu'avec contrainte
On risque la douce étreinte
Qui nous sépare enfin toujours.

*Refrain*

Je t'aime,
Tes baisers m'ont grisés,
Même
A l'heure de t'en aller,
La volupté troublante
Brise mes lèvres brulantes,
Je t'aime,
A l'heure de t'en aller.

## TARARA BOOM-DE-AY

*from* BITTER SWEET

ALL:        Tarara  boom-de-ay,
             Tarara boom-de-ay,
             We are the most effectual,
             Intellectual
             Movement of the day.
             Our moral standards sway
             Like Mrs Tanqueray,
             And we are theoretically
             Most aesthetically
             Eager to display
             The fact that we're aggressively
             And excessively
             Anxious to destroy
             All the snobbery
             And hob-nobbery
             Of the hoi-polloi.
             Tarara boom-de-ay,
             It's mental washing day,
             And come what may
             We'll scrub until the nation's morals shrink away.
             Tarara boom-de-ay.

EXQUISITES:  Though we are languid in appearance
             We're in the vanguard,
             We feel we can guard
             The cause of Art.
             We shall ignore all interference,
             For our complaisance
             With this renaissance
             Is frightfully smart.
             Please do not think us unrelenting,
             Our charming frolic
             With the symbolic
             Is meek and mild.
             We merely spend our time preventing
             Some earnest stripling
             From liking Kipling
             Instead of Wilde.

             Now that we find the dreary nineteenth century is closing,
             We mean to start the twentieth in ecstasies of posing.

ALL:           Tarara boom-de-ay,
               It's mental washing day,
               And come what may
               We'll scrub until the tiresome bourgeois shrink away.
               Tarara boom-de-ay.


## ALAS THE TIME IS PAST

*from* BITTER SWEET

SEXTETTE:  Alas the time is past when we
           Could frolic with impunity.
           Secure in our virginity,
           We sometimes look aghast
           Adown the lanes of memory,
           Alas the time is past.
           Ah, then the world was at our feet,
           When we were sweet and twenty,
           We never guessed that what we'd got,
           Though not a lot—was plenty.
           We gaily sought some Abélard
           To cherish, guard and own us,
           But all we know of storm and strife
           Our married life—has shown us.
           Alas, the time is past when we
           Could frolic with impunity.
           Secure in our virginity,
           We sometimes look aghast
           Adown the lanes of memory.
           Alas, the time is past.
           Alack-a-day me—alack-a-day-me!
           Ah, then the world was at our feet,
           Alas the time is past.


## GREEN CARNATION

*from* BITTER SWEET

QUARTETTE:  Blasé boys are we,
            Exquisitely free
            From the dreary and quite absurd
            Moral views of the common herd.

We like porphyry bowls,
Chandeliers and stoles,
We're most spirited,
Carefully filleted 'souls'.


*Refrain*

Pretty boys, witty boys, too, too, too
Lazy to fight stagnation,
Haughty boys, naughty boys, all we do
Is to pursue sensation.
The portals of society
Are always opened wide,
The world our eccentricity condones,
A note of quaint variety
We're certain to provide,
We dress in very decorative tones.
Faded boys, jaded boys, womankind's
Gift to a bulldog nation,
In order to distinguish us from less enlightened minds,
We all wear a green carnation.


We believe in Art,
Though we're poles apart
From the fools who are thrilled by Greuze.
We like Beardsley and Green Chartreuse.
Women say we're too
Bored to bill and coo,
We smile wearily,
It's so drearily true!


*Refrain*

Pretty boys, witty boys, you may sneer
At our disintegration,
Haughty boys, naughty boys, dear, dear, dear!
Swooning with affectation.
Our figures sleek and willowy,
Our lips incarnadine,
May worry the majority a bit.
But matrons rich and billowy
Invite us out to dine,
And revel in our phosphorescent wit,
Faded boys, jaded boys, come what may,
Art is our inspiration,
And as we are the reason for the 'Nineties' being gay,
We all wear a green carnation.

*Refrain*

Pretty boys, witty boys, yearning for
Permanent adulation,
Haughty boys, naughty boys, every pore
Bursting with self-inflation.
We feel we're rather Grecian,
As our manners indicate,
Our sense of moral values isn't strong.
For ultimate completion
We shall really have to wait
Until the Day of Judgment comes along.
Faded boys, jaded boys, each one craves
Some sort of soul salvation,
But when we rise reluctantly but gracefully from our graves,
We'll all wear a green carnation.


## 'ZIGEUNER'

*from* BITTER SWEET

Verse 1　Once upon a time,
　　　　　Many years ago,
　　　　　Lived a fair Princess,
　　　　　Hating to confess
　　　　　Loneliness was torturing her so.
　　　　　Then a gipsy came,
　　　　　Called to her by name,
　　　　　Woo'd her with a song,
　　　　　Sensuous and strong,
　　　　　All the summer long;
　　　　　Her passion seemed to tremble like a living flame.

Refrain　Play to me beneath the summer moon,
　　　　　Zigeuner!—Zigeuner!—Zigeuner!
　　　　　All I ask of life is just to listen
　　　　　To the songs that you sing,
　　　　　My spirit like a bird on the wing
　　　　　Your melodies adoring—soaring,
　　　　　Call to me with some barbaric tune,
　　　　　Zigeuner!—Zigeuner!—Zigeuner!
　　　　　Now you hold me in your power,
　　　　　Play to me for just an hour,
　　　　　Zigeuner!

Verse 2  Bid my weeping cease,
         Melody that brings
         Merciful release,
         Promises of peace,
         Through the gentle throbbing of the strings.
         Music of the plain,
         Music of the wild,
         Come to me again,
         Hear me not in vain,
         Soothe a heart in pain,
         And let me to my happiness be reconciled.


## I'LL SEE YOU AGAIN

*from* BITTER SWEET

Reprise  I'll see you again,
         I live each moment through again.
         Time has lain heavy between,
         But what has been
         Can leave me never;
         Your dear memory
         Throughout my life has guided me.
         Though my world has gone awry,
         Though the years my tears may dry
         I shall love you till I die,
         Goodbye!

              *     *     *     *     *

         Though my world has gone awry,
         Though the end is drawing nigh,
         I shall love you till I die,
         Goodbye!

# *Miscellaneous*

## FORBIDDEN FRUIT
### (1917)

Verse 1    Ordinary man invariably sighs
Vainly for what cannot be,
If he's in an orchard he will cast his eyes
Up into the highest tree,
There may be a lot of windfalls
Lying all around,
But you'll never see a man enjoy the fruit that's on the ground.

Refrain 1    Every peach out of reach is attractive
'Cos it's just a little bit too high,
And you'll find that every man
Will try to pluck it if he can
As he passes by.
For the brute loves the fruit that's forbidden
And I'll bet you half a crown
He'll appreciate the flavour of it much much more
If he has to climb a bit to shake it down.

Verse 2    If a man's engaged and feels that he is loved,
Blasé he will quickly be,
Often on one side his ladylove is shoved
While he goes upon the spree.
Then perhaps she'll marry,
And you can bet your life
He'll want her very badly when she's someone else's wife.

Refrain 2    Every peach out of reach is attractive
'Cos it's just a little bit too high,
Though it isn't very sane
To make the things you can't attain,
Still you always try.
If you find that you're blind with devotion
For delightful Mrs Brown,
You'll appreciate eloping with her much much more
If her husband comes along and knocks you down.

Verse 3    Women haven't altered since the days of Eve,
Anxiously through life they prowl,
Always trying to better what their friends achieve,
Either by fair means or foul.
A girl may be quite careful
Of the sort of life she picks,
But to be a real success she's got to know a lot of tricks.

Refrain 3  Every peach out of reach is attractive
'Cos it's just a little bit too high,
Even well-brought-up young girls
Will look at other women's pearls
With a yearning eye.
If they fight day and night persevering
And a small string they collect,
They'll appreciate the colour of them much much more
If they've sacrificed a little self-respect.

# WE MUST ALL BE VERY KIND TO AUNTIE JESSIE

Verse 1    I remember clearly when a tiny little child
My Auntie came to stay with us.
Maybe as a family we were a trifle wild,
Our spirits ran away with us.
Every single day
When we were at play
Mother used to creep into the nursery and say:

Refrain 1  We must all be very kind to Auntie Jessie,
For she's never been a Mother or a Wife,
You mustn't throw your toys at her
Or make a vulgar noise at her,
She hasn't led a very happy life.
You must never lock her playfully in the bathroom
Or play tunes on her enamelled Spanish comb.
Though unpleasant to behold
She's a heart of purest gold
And Charity you know begins at home.

Verse 2    Relatives who come to stay are generally inclined
To fray the children's nerves a bit,
Something in a maiden aunt just stupefies the mind,
From Virtue's path one swerves a bit,

Though our childish joys
May have made a noise
Mother used to murmur though I *know*,
Boys will be Boys.

Refrain 2 We must all be very kind to Auntie Jessie,
And do everything we can to keep her bright.
If when you're in the Underground
You hear her make a funny sound
It's very rude to laugh at her outright.
You must never fill her nightdress case with beetles
Or beat up her Horlick's Malted Milk to foam,
Though her kiss is worse than death
It's unkind to hold your breath
For Charity you know begins at home.

Refrain 3 We must all be very kind to Auntie Jessie,
And encourage her to see the sunny side,
It isn't kind to rush at her
And hurl the blacking brush at her,
It's things like this that trample on her pride,
Don't molest her with a pail of *Icy* water,
If when wandering at night she chanced to roam,
Though the attic stairs are steep
Death comes peacefully in sleep
And Charity *we hope* begins at home.

## SHE WAS A GOOD GIRL THEN

Verse 1   I remember Mary at a very early age,
She was sweet, sweet, sweet as pie,
She was like a fairy who has fallen on Life's stage
And forgotten how to fly.
She was full of charming and alluring little ways,
Her modesty would leave you quite aghast.
Innocence to her was like a cosy little cage,
But alas! those days are past.

Refrain 1  Take it from me she was a good girl then,
She was as fragrant as the blooming cyclamen.
If a schoolboy
Brought her a bunch of flowers
She'd weep with joy for hours,
She was never misled
And was always in bed

By ten;
Take it from me
That child could do no wrong
Though lots of horrible temptations came along.
One occasion
When her watch was stolen by her sister Nell,
Mary promptly offered her the chain as well.
Take it from me she was a good girl then.

Verse 2 Mary growing older was extremely comme-il-faut
And her ignorance was bliss.
No one ever told her all the things a girl should know,
And the reason why was this.
She was unsophisticated, dancing to and fro
She didn't know the value of her charms,
Dwelling in such innocence it only goes to show
That she seldom suffered qualms.

Refrain 2 Take it from me she was a good girl then,
Above her bed was hung 'The Monarch of the Glen',
In the morning
She never pulled the blind up
Till she had made her mind up,
And she finished her prayers with a very devout 'Ah-men',
Take it from me she never went too far.
One day a young man took her driving in his car
And I must say
Though he drove her straight to a barbed wire fence
She had never fallen in the stricter sense.
Take it from me she was a good girl then.

Refrain 3 Take it from me she was a good girl then,
She really hadn't much experience of men.
She would always blush with surprise if teased much,
Give piercing cries if squeezed much,
And she looked on the world as a sort of lions' den,
Take it from me she was as pure as snow,
She seemed to know by instinct just how far to go.
In the morning
When she took her cousin Jack his early tea
Neither of them had their lunch till half past three.
Take it from me she was a good girl then.

Refrain 4 Take it from me she was a good girl then,
Peculiar thoughts had never crept into her ken.
She was never really depressed or humpy,
Maybe her nerves were jumpy,

But she left it at that—
And took lots of Sanat-ogen.
Take it from me she was a bit run down,
The doctor looked at her with quite a worried frown,
Then he told her
Tactfully and firmly that she needed care,
So she went to Canada and had it there.
Take it from me she was a good girl then.


## JESSIE HOOPER

Verse 1    Have ye heard of Jessie Hooper?
On the banks of Loch MacRae.
Stepping lightly from her truckle,
To salute the coming day.
All the sheep and cows adored her,
She was sonsie, braw and gay,
As she rocked with girlish laughter
On the banks of Loch MacRae.

Refrain 1   Where are ye now, Jessie, where are ye now?
Never a sheep will say, nary a cow,
For Jessie she hangs to the willow tree bough.
Where are ye now, Jessie? Where are ye now?

Verse 2    Do not weep for Jessie Hooper,
She whose eyes with death are closed
For even though she is a corpse,
She isn't decomposed.
You could hear the haggis wailing
Over bonny loch and brae
When the soul of Jessie Hooper
So completely passed away.

Refrain 2   Where are ye now, Jessie, where are ye now?
Swinging about on the willow tree bough.
Was it the laird who brought ye so low?
Where are ye now, Jessie? Where are ye now?

## HE NEVER DID THAT TO ME

Verse 1    I have been a Movie fan
Since the cinemas first began;
My young brother's a cameraman,
And when I start
Meeting heroes of romance,
I shall firmly take my chance.
Though I find the hero charming,
I prefer the more alarming
Man who plays the villain's part.
The things he does to nice young girls
Aren't easy to forget;
He never minces matters,
When he traps them in his net.

Refrain 1    He never did that to me;
He never did that to me;
Though I must admit
He wasn't a bit
Like what I'd supposed he'd be.
The way that he uses
Ingénues is
Really a sight to see;
He binds them across his saddle tight,
Regardless of all their shrieks of fright,
And carries them upside down all night,
He never did that to me.

Refrain 2    He never did that to me;
He never did that to me;
Though I must admit
He wasn't a bit
Like what I'd supposed he'd be.
I once saw him save
A Christian slave,
And gallantly set her free.
She knelt at his feet with downcast head;
'God will reward you, sir', she said.
He gave her a look and shot her dead
He never did that to me.

Verse 2    Though my disappointment's great,
I shall never procrastinate,
I'm determined to watch and wait,
And then you'll see;
He'll revert to type, perhaps,

Have a violent moral lapse,
When the moment's quite propitious,
He'll do something really vicious.
Think how lovely that will be.
His reputation's terrible,
Which comforts me a lot;
If any girl is seen with him,
She's branded on the spot.

Refrain 3   He never did that to me;
He never did that to me;
Though I must admit
He wasn't a bit
Like what I'd supposed he'd be.
He went in his car
But not too far,
Some mutual friends to see;
The car gave a lurch and then a skid,
We didn't turn over—God forbid!
Whatever you may have *thought* he did,
He never did that to me.

Refrain 4   He never did that to me;
He never did that to me;
Though I must admit
He wasn't a bit
Like what I'd supposed he'd be.
I once saw him fish
The Sisters Gish
From out of a stormy sea;
He locked them in his refined Rolls Royce,
And said in a most determined voice,
'It's death or dishonour—take your choice!'
He never did that to me.


## THE DREAM IS OVER

Verse 1   Just because we're lovers,
Don't let's laugh at fate;
Often one discovers
When it is too late
Vows that have been spoken
When the tide is high
Lie around us broken
When the sands are dry.

Refrain I love you so, but the dream is over,
    Days come and go, but the dream is over.
    I've tried to fool myself,
    School myself into believing
    Our love could still go on,
    But it's gone beyond retrieving.
    My hopes were vain like a fool in clover,
    Never again for the dream is over.

Verse 2 Things can't last for ever,
    Lover's hours are fleet,
    Destiny may sever
    Happiness complete,
    Passion's so uncertain,
    Some unfinished rhyme
    May bring down the curtain
    Long before it's time.

# DOWN WITH THE WHOLE DAMN LOT!
## (Co-Optimists)

Verse 1    We're men of democratic thought
      And independent means,
      We're full of plans of every sort
      To give old England beans.
      Conscription made us go and fight
      Our country's cause to win,
      And now that we've got back all right
      We're going to 'do her in'!

Chorus    Down with the idle rich!
      The bloated upper classes.
      They drive to Lord's
      In expensive Fords
      With their jewelled op'ra glasses.
      Down with the London P'lice!
      We'll quickly have them shot.
      We'll spread destruction everywhere,
      Burn things up in a fine old flare.
      What about the lions in Trafalgar Square?
      Down with the whole damn lot!

Repeat Chorus    Down with the Courts of Law!
                 With flaming swords we'll raid 'em,
                 And slay the blokes
                 Who have laughed at jokes
                 Just because the judges made 'em.
                 We'll have the murder trials
                 Arranged by Malcolm Scott,
                 And as each one to death is sent
                 The court will rock with merriment.
                 What about the people who are innocent?
                 Down with the whole damn lot!


Verse 2          We're really men of sterling worth.
                 Democracy's our aim.
                 We're going to Bolshevize the earth,
                 Protected by that name.
                 To outrage any sacred law
                 We'd give our dying breath,
                 And if we started Civil War
                 We'd laugh ourselves to death!


Chorus 2         Down with the working man!
                 We'll starve his wives and sisters,
                 For any sin
                 Can be fitted in
                 With our 'Democratic Vistas'.
                 Down with the London stage!
                 We'll let them have it hot.
                 If Laurillard or Sachs resists
                 We'll kill them both as Royalists.
                 What about the frolicking Co-Optimists?
                 Down with the whole damn lot!


Repeat Chorus 2  Down with the daily Press!
                 We'll wipe it out completely.
                 I'd hate the lives
                 Of my murdered wives
                 To be published indiscreetly.
                 Editors and their staffs
                 Shall languish till they rot.
                 We'll stop the London *Mail* each week.
                 On every side our spite we'll wreak.
                 What about the paragraphs of Pip and Squeak?
                 Down with the whole damn lot!

Verse 3          With Ireland we're offended quite.
We trusted her for years.
She's now infringed our copyright
And stolen our ideas.
We're holding back our hand to strike
And bash her well and good.
We'll show her what the feeling's like
To be 'Misunderstood'.

Chorus 3        Down with the bold Sinn Fein!
We'll rout them willy-nilly.
They flaunt their crimes
In the *Belfast Times*,
Which makes *us* look so silly.
Down with the Ulster men!
They don't know which from what.
If Ireland sunk beneath the sea
How peaceful everyone would be!
You haven't said a word about the R.I.C.?
Down with the whole damn lot!

Repeat Chorus 3  Down with the modern dance!
That craze we'll quickly smother.
It looks all right
If your coat's on tight
And you *really love* each other.
Down with the Shimmie Shake
That makes poor Auntie hot!
We'll see that every dance club fails,
And slap Pavlova till she wails.
What about Salomé and her seven veils?
Down with the whole damn lot!

Extra Chorus   Down with the Garrick Club,
And Kensington Museum!
The Albert Hall
Must abruptly fall,
And the London Coliseum.
Down with the Marble Arch!
It's always been a blot.
England in its blood shall souse,
Mother, father, husband, spouse.
You haven't said a word about the 'Corner House'!
Down with the whole damn lot!

'Reproduced by permission of the copyright
owner Francis, Day & Hunter Ltd.'

## BACK TO NATURE
### (Co-Optimists)

Verse 1
We're here to make confession,
We're forming a triple alliance.
Our years of drab repression
Have burst into open defiance.
We've bid goodbye to faces dear
And mother-in-laws and wives.
We now intend to disappear
And reconstruct our lives.

Refrain
We're over-civilized,
That's the trouble with us.
Our hearts of pickled oak
Are casting off the yoke.
Though we are undersized
We're not giving a cuss,
We're striking off the chains today.
We find that the town
Is keeping us down,
We're yearning to expand
For life in a bank
Is dingy and dank,
It's more than we can stand.
We mean to abscond
Into the beyond
And roll in blood and sand.
We're going back to nature right away!

Verse 2
The climate rules the nation,
The temperature's rapidly falling,
With over-population
The squalor of life is appalling.
We're tired of trying year by year
To imitate plaster saints,
We mean to change our atmosphere
And lose our self-restraints.

Refrain 2
We're too respectable,
That's what's holding us back,
We lie and dream at nights
Of primitive delights.
Think how delectable
Life would be in a shack
With nobody to say us nay.

I'll jump on my horse,
Side saddle of course,
And ride across the green,
I'll gallop and shoot
And plunder and loot
With none to intervene.
As quick as a wink
I'll carelessly drink
A pail of Ovaltine.
We're going back to nature right away!

Verse 3      We must admit the movies
             Have helped to complete our damnation.
             Now what we want to prove is
             Our utter demoralization.
             We don't intend to waste our time
             With celibacy and such,
             We'll lead a life of social crime
             And like it very much.

Refrain 3    We're too adaptable,
             That's what's wrong with us now,
             There must be hidden charms
             In North Canadian farms.
             We've never slapped a bull,
             Never sworn at a cow,
             We can't distinguish straw from hay,
             But nevertheless,
             I'm bound to confess,
             I'm full of do and dare.
             If life is a bore
             I'll hire a squaw,
             With charming savoir faire,
             Where women are bold
             And quite uncontrolled
             All in the open air.
             We're going back to nature right away!

# WHAT'S GOING TO HAPPEN TO THE TOTS?
(English Version)

(WHITEBIRDS, 1927)

I've a message for the women of the Empire,
A message to the women great and small,
A definite appeal to those who still can feel
That a life of shallow pleasure isn't all.
I've a message for the housemaid and the duchess
Whose feet are drawing nearer the abyss,
You may bow your heads in shame
But you can't escape the blame
For the question I am asking you is this.

What's going to happen to the children, when there aren't any more
    grown-ups?
The hand that rocks the cradle will no longer rule the world
When silver threads amongst the gold are permanently curled.
Who's going to hear their prayers at twilight
And tuck the little darlings in their cots?
If comfort, warmth and nourishment cannot be guaranteed
It's very very hard for any child to overfeed,
If Mother's in the bathroom being massaged by a Swede
What's going to happen to the tots?

I've a message for the mothers who are married,
I've a message for the mothers who are not,
I have a message too for the many and the few
Who always strike the iron—when it's hot.
I've a message for the ingénue of forty
Who multiplies her love affairs by ten,
Who, although she looks a fool,
Still she proves the ancient rule
That the chicken should look older than the hen.

What's going to happen to the children, when there aren't any more
    grown-ups?
The stately homes of England will look desolate and cold
When Grandpa's so athletic that's he's painful to behold.
Who's going to telephone the doctor when the baby's little face
    breaks out in spots?
If Auntie's girlish figure is encased in rubber bands
And Father screams with passion when his diaphragm expands
And Mother is injected with the most peculiar glands,
What's going to happen to the tots?

What's going to happen to the children, when there aren't any more
   grown-ups?
It's very hard on nature when she's made a lot of plans
To have them all frustrated by a lot of Peter Pans.
Who has the baby got to turn to
When his underclothes get tangled up in knots?
One contemplates with nervousness, with horror and dismay
The juvenile behaviour of the parents of today.
When Mother's face is lifted till it's almost whisked away
What's going to happen to the tots?

# The Thirties

# NOTE ON 'THE THIRTIES'

My lyric writing during 'The Thirties' started very satisfactorily with 'Mad Dogs And Englishmen'. The idea of it and the rhythm of it got into my head when I was driving, in February 1930, from Hanoi in Tonkin to Saigon. This drive took about a week and while jungles and rivers and mountains and rice fields were unrolling by the window of the car, I wrestled in my mind with the complicated rhythms and rhymes of the song until finally it was complete, without even the aid of pencil or paper. I sang it triumphantly and unaccompanied to my travelling companion, Jeffrey Amherst, on the verandah of a small jungle guest house. Not only Jeffrey but the gekko lizards and the tree frogs gave every vocal indication of enthusiasm.

Between 1930 and 1940, apart from several plays and the first volume of my autobiography, *Present Indicative*, I wrote a number of revues, musical plays, and plays with music: *Private Lives, Cavalcade, Words and Music, Conversation Piece, To-night at Eight-Thirty, Operette*, and *Set To Music* which was a rehash of *Words and Music*, produced in America in 1938. There were several extra numbers written for this including 'Weary Of It All', 'Never Again', 'Marvellous Party', which I had written some years before, and 'The Stately Homes of England'.

# *Cochran's 1931 Revue*

## ANY LITTLE FISH

*from* COCHRAN'S 1931 REVUE

Verse    I've fallen in love with you,
I'm taking it badly,
Freezing, burning,
Tossing, turning,
Never know when to laugh or cry,
Just look what our dumb friends do, they welcome it gladly.
Passion in a dromedary doesn't go so deep,
Camels when they're mating never sob themselves to sleep,
Buffaloes can revel in it, so can any sheep;
Why can't I?

Refrain 1    Any little fish can swim, any little bird can fly,
Any little dog and any little cat
Can do a bit of this and just a bit of that;
Any little horse can neigh, and any little cow can moo,
But I can't do anything at all
But just love you.

Refrain 2    Any little cock can crow, any little fox can run,
Any little crab on any little shore
Can have a little dab and then a little more;
Any little owl can hoot, and any little dove can coo,
But I can't do anything at all but just love you.

Verse    You've pulled me across the brink,
You've chained me and bound me,
No escape now,
Buy the crêpe now,
When is the funeral going to be?
Whenever I stop to think,
See nature all around me,
Then I see how stupidly monogamous I am,
A lion in the circumstances wouldn't give a damn,
For if there was no lioness he'd lie down with a lamb;
Why can't I?

Refrain 3  Any little bug can bite, any little bee can buzz,
Any little snail on any little oak
Can feel a little frail and have a little joke;
Any little frog can jump like any little kangaroo,
But I can't do anything at all but just love you.

Refrain 4  Any little duck can quack, any little worm can crawl,
Any little mole can frolic in the sun
And make a little hole and have a little fun;
Any little snake can hiss in any little local zoo,
But I can't do anything at all but just love you.

## CITY

*from* COCHRAN'S 1931 REVUE

Only one among millions,
Life's a sad routine,
Striving for a goal that hasn't a meaning,
Lonely, living in shadow, part of a machine,
Rising from depair, the buildings are leaning,
Nearer, nearer each day, pressing life away.

Refrain 1  City, why are you casting this spell on me?
City, what if you crumbled and fell on me!
Unbelievably tiring,
Life passes by me;
Noise and speed are conspiring
To crucify me,
Ever making me crawl for my daily bread,
Never letting me rest till my dreams are dead.
Every weary prisoner
Some day must be free;
City, have pity on me!

Interlude  Day in, day out,
Life will be soon over and done.
Where has it led and why?
Day in, day out,
Where is the moon?
Where is the sun?
Where is the open sky?
Ever seeking, and believing
There is hope for us all.

Sirens shrieking, progress weaving
Poor humanity's pall.
Iron, rot, steel, rust,
Speed, noise, death, dust,
Why should we work?
Why should we live?
Why should we even die?

Refrain 2 City, why are you casting this spell on me?
City, what if you crumbled and fell on me?
Unbelievably tiring,
Life passes by me;
Noise and speed are conspiring
To crucify me,
Ever making me crawl for my daily bread,
Never letting me rest till my dreams are dead.
Every weary prisoner
Some day must be free;
City, please have pity on me!

## HALF-CASTE WOMAN

*from* COCHRAN'S 1931 REVUE

Drink a bit, laugh a bit, love a bit more,
I can supply your need,
Think a bit, chaff a bit, what's it all for?
That's my Eurasian creed.
Sailors with sentimental hearts who love and sail away,
When the dawn is grey
Look at me and say—

Refrain Half-caste woman, living a life apart,
Where did your story begin?
Half-caste woman, have you a secret heart
Waiting for someone to win?
Were you born of some queer magic
In your shimmering gown?
Is there something strange and tragic
Deep, deep down?
Half-caste woman, what are your slanting eyes
Waiting and hoping to see?
Scanning the far horizon
Wondering what the end will be.

Down along the river
The sky is aquiver
For dawn is beginning to break;
Hear the sirens wailing,
Some big ship is sailing
And losing my dreams in its wake.
Why should I remember the things that are past,
Moments so swiftly gone;
Why worry, for the Lord knows time goes on.
Go to bed in daylight,
Try to sleep in vain,
Get up in the evening
Work begins again,
Tinker, tailor, soldier, sailor,
Rich man, poor man, beggar man, thief,
Questioning the same refrain.

# BRIGHT YOUNG PEOPLE
## (Trio)

*from* COCHRAN'S 1931 REVUE

Verse     Look at us three,
Representative we
Of a nation renowned for virility.
We've formed a cult of puerility
Just for fun.
You may deplore
The effects of war
Which are causing the world to decay a bit.
We've found our place and will play a bit
In the sun.
Though Waterloo was won upon the playing fields of Eton,
The next war will be photographed, and lost, by Cecil
Beaton.

Refrain 1    Bright young people,
Ready to do and to dare
We casually strive
To keep London alive
From Chelsea to Bloomsbury Square.
We fondly imagine we're cynical elves,
In charity tableaux we pose upon shelves.
It's just an excuse to exhibit ourselves.
What could be duller than that?

Refrain 2    Bright young people,
             Gay to the utmost degree
             We play funny jokes
             On more dignified folks
             And laugh with extravagant glee.
             We give lovely parties that last through the night,
             I dress as a woman and scream with delight,
             We wake up at lunch time and find we're still tight.
             What could be duller than that?

Verse 2     Things that we do
             'Neath the Red, White and Blue,
             Though they can't be called happy or glorious,
             Certainly keep us notorious.
             And it's grand.
             We've made some chums
             In the heart of the slums,
             And we ask to our parties the rougher ones.
             We find the low class and tougher ones, understand,
             We know a darling Bolshevik
             Who's taught us Dosvidanya
             And he can sing 'God Save the King'
             And lovely 'Rule Britannia'.

Refrain 3    Bright young people,
             Don't think our lives are not full.
             I make little hats
             From Victorian mats
             And I work in tin-foil and wool.
             Our critics are often excessively rude,
             To one of my portraits they always allude:
             It's me, worked in beads, upside down, in the nude.
             What could be duller than that?

Refrain 4    Bright young people,
             Making the most of our youth.
             They speak in the Press
             Of our social success,
             But quite the reverse is the truth.
             Psychology experts we often perplex
             And doctors have warned us we'll end up as wrecks.
             They take a degree if they find out our sex.
             What could be duller than that?

# Cavalcade

## THE GIRLS OF THE C.I.V.

*from* CAVALCADE (MIRABELLE)

We're the girls of the C.I.V.
Form fours, get in line, one two three.
For our bravery is such
That the Boers won't like it much
When we chase them across the veldt and teach
    them Double Dutch.
We're the girls of the C.I.V.
And we're out for a lark and a spree,
In our uniforms so stunning,
We shall soon have Kruger running
From the girls of the C.I.V.


## LOVER OF MY DREAMS

*from* CAVALCADE (MIRABELLE)

SHE: A simple country maid am I,
      As innocent as any flower.
      The great big world has passed me by,
      No lover comes my way to greet me shyly in my bower.

HE: Oh, say not so!
     Such modesty enchants me:
     Could I but stay to while away with you a happy hour.

SHE: It must be Spring that fills my heart to overflowing,
      Ah, whither am I going?
      What is the voice that seems to say:
      Be kind to love, don't let him call to you unknowing.

HE: If true love comes to you don't turn your face away.

SHE: Maybe 'tis something in the air:
    For Spring is made for lovers only.

HE: Live for the moment and take care
    Lest love should fly and leave us lonely.
    Ah, if love should leave us lonely.

*Refrain*

SHE: All my life I have been waiting
    Dreaming ages through;
    Until today I suddenly discover
    The form and face of he who is my lover.
    No more tears and hesitating;
    Fate has sent me you.
    Time and tide can never sever
    Those whom love has bound for ever,
    Dear Lover of my Dreams come true.

## ALL THE FUN OF THE FARM

*from* CAVALCADE (MIRABELLE)

*Verse*

ADA: Though sailors are so brave and bold,
    It really must be dreadfully cold
      To sail across the sea.

TOM:     I quite agree,
      I quite agree,
    I'm sick of the ocean wild and free,
    Heigho, heigho, this is the place for me.

ADA: Now I am weary of the town
    And feel inclined to settle down,
      A milk pail on my arm.

TOM:     I feel afraid,
      A London Maid
    Would never know how the eggs are laid.

ADA: I'd find a cow
      And milk till the pail was full.

TOM: I'd shear the sow
And probably milk the bull.

BOTH: You must agree
That it would be
The height of true rusticity
If you and I should settle on a farm.

*Refrain*

BOTH: Oh, the Fun of the Farmyard,
The roosters are crowing,
The cattle are lowing,
The turkeys go gobbly gobbly goo.
This really is an alarm yard.

ADA: Like little Bo-Peep,
I lose my sheep
And cannot find them anywhere.

TOM: I ought to be shot,
For I forgot
To coax the horse to meet the mare.

BOTH: Who left the canary
Locked up in the dairy?

ADA: Cheep, cheep, cheep, cheep,

TOM: Snort, snort, snort, snort.

ADA: Moo, moo, moo, moo,

TOM: Cock a doodle doodle do!

BOTH: Oh, dear, far from being a calm yard,
Quack, quack, quack, quack,
All the fun of the farm.

# TWENTIETH CENTURY BLUES

### *from* CAVALCADE

Verse   Why is it that civilized humanity
        Must make the world so wrong?
        In this hurly-burly of insanity
        Our dreams cannot last long.
        We've reached a deadline—
        The Press headline—every sorrow,
        Blues value
        Is News value
        Tomorrow.

Refrain Blues,
        Twentieth Century Blues,
        Are getting me down.
        Who's
        Escaped those weary
        Twentieth Century Blues.
        Why,
        If there's a God in the sky,
        Why shouldn't he grin?
        High
        Above this dreary
        Twentieth Century din,
        In this strange illusion,
        Chaos and confusion,
        People seem to lose their way.
        What is there to strive for,
        Love or keep alive for? Say—
        Hey, hey, call it a day.
        Blues,
        Nothing to win or to lose.
        It's getting me down.
        Blues,
        I've got those weary Twentieth Century Blues.

# *Words and Music*

## MAGGIE
### (Opening Chorus)

*from* WORDS AND MUSIC

GIRLS:  We shan't be on tonight,
We shan't be on tonight.
Because the overture is near
We're paralysed with fear.
The opening chorus
Is too complicated for us.
In this damned Revue
We've far too much to do,
We sing till our throats are aching,
Dance till our backs are breaking.
During the applause
We rush and change our drawers,
Tearing at ribbons while our hands are shaking,
Always getting dressed
Without a moment's rest,
We're worked to death,
Out of breath,
Nervous of every music cue,
Anxious the whole performance through.

Maggie!

Have you the scissors handy?

Maggie!

We want a port and brandy.

Maggie!

Our brassières don't set right.

Maggie!

We've upset all our wet-white.

114

MAGGIE:  Oh my God, don't hurry me,
         You'll miss your entrance if you worry me,
         Flurry me.


GIRLS:   Maggie!
         These aren't our first-act stockings.
         Maggie!
         Our shoes are tight.
         Maggie! Maggie!
         Our trunks are far too baggy.
         We shan't be on tonight.


MAGGIE:  Now, Freda dear, you must
         Do *something* with your bust.
         You'd best tie a knot, dear,
         You can't show them all you've got, dear.
         Dorothy my duck,
         Your eyelashes ain't stuck,
         You can't look in every scene, dear,
         Just like an Aberdeen, dear.
         Rosie hold this pin
         And keep your stomach in
         And don't do a pratfall in your first routine, dear.
         Nora, there's a smear
         Of eye-black on your ear.
         You must look right
         Every night,
         You know until the show is through
         I have to take the blame for you.


GIRLS:   Maggie!
         We want an orange stick, dear.
         Maggie!
         We're feeling rather sick, dear.
         Maggie!
         Our mirrors need adjusting.
         Maggie!
         Our make-ups look disgusting.


MAGGIE:  Oh, my God, don't hurry me,
         You'll miss your entrance if you worry me,
         Flurry me.

GIRLS:      Maggie!
            Our shoulder straps are slipping.
            Maggie!
            There's nothing right.
            Maggie! Maggie!
            They've made our wigs too shaggy.
            We shan't be on tonight.
            Maggie! Maggie! Maggie! Maggie!
            Maggie! Maggie!
            Maggie! Maggie! Maggie! Maggie!
            We shan't be on tonight.

CALLBOY:    Overture Beginners!

GIRLS:      La lalalalalalala
            Lalalalala la
            La lalalalalalala
            Lalalalala la.

CALLBOY:    Overture Beginners!

MAGGIE:     All right, all right.

GIRLS:      La lalalala la la la
            La lalalala la la la
            La lalalala la la la
            La lalalala la la la la.
            We shan't be on tonight,
            We shan't be on tonight.

MAGGIE:     They must look right
            Every night.
            Worked to death,
            Out of breath,
            I'll stay and tidy up a bit
            And pray the blasted show's a hit!

GIRLS:      Good evening, Ladies and Gentlemen,
            You'll be tickled to death
            To recognize the Chorus
            And as we're opening the show
            It's really comforting now and then
            To discover for once
            That you are here before us.
            It may astonish you to know
            We're Mr Cochran's Young Invincibles,
            He much prefers us to the Principals,

For every scene he cuts out
He says, 'Just send the Sluts out'
And that's the reason why we have to work our guts out.

GIRLS:   Hallo!
We're always on the trigger.
Hallo!
Please note our girlish vigour.
Hallo!
We have to hop and bustle.
Hallo!
We're straining every muscle.
While we break our necks we feel
That so much animation wrecks appeal.
Sex appeal
Never
Can show when there's too much
Endeavour.
It lays us low,
We don't mind now,
We're really quite resigned now.
Hallo! Hallo! Hallo!


# DEBUTANTES

*from* WORDS AND MUSIC

1 Four little Débutantes are we,
   Born of these restless, changing years,
   Conscious of vague, unwilling fears,
   What is our Destiny to be?
   Shall we escape the strange 'Ennui'
   Of civilized futility?
   When we are old and wearied through
   Shall we regret how wise we were?
   Shall we at last have time to spare
   Tears for the dreams we never knew?

2 The Gin is lasting out,
   No matter whose,
   We're merely casting out
   The Blues,
   For Gin, in cruel
   Sober truth,

Supplies the fuel
For flaming youth.
A drink is known
To help a dream along,
A Saxophone
Provides our Theme Song,
Though we dishevel
Our girlish bloom
To the Devil
With Gloom!
The Gin is lasting out,
No matter whose,
We're merely casting out
The Blues,
For Gin, in cruel
Sober truth,
Supplies the fuel
For flaming youth,
We can't refuse,
The Gin is lasting out,
We're merely casting out
The Blues!

Prelude to Finale    Four little Debutantes, so tired.
Yearning to seek our virgin beds,
Longing to rest our aching heads,
Weary of all that we desired,
When in the morning we awake
Shall we be glad to undertake
Further exhausting hours among
Pleasures and joys so carefully planned,
Shall we continue to withstand
The heavy task of being young?


### LET'S LIVE DANGEROUSLY

*from* WORDS AND MUSIC

Verse    Life won't fool us,
Because we're out to lick it,
We've got its ticket
And we'll kick it
In the pants.
Fate will never catch us asleep,

We'll be ready to leap
When there's the slightest chance.
Life won't rule us,
Determined to subdue it
We'll give the raspberry to it,
Do it in the eye.
We believe in following through
All we're ready to do
Or die.

Refrain   Let's live dangerously dangerously dangerously,
Let's grab every opportunity we can,
Let's swill
Each pill
Destiny has in store,
Absorbing life at every pore
We'll scream and yell for more.
Let's live turbulently turbulently turbulently,
Let's add something to the history of man,
Come what may
We'll be spectacular
And say, 'Hey! Hey!
In the vernacular,
And so until we break beneath the strain
In various ways
We're going to be raising Cain.

Refrain 2   Let's live dangerously dangerously dangerously,
Let's all glory in the bludgeonings of chance,
Let's win
Out in
Spite of the angry crowd,
And if the simile's allowed
Be bloody but unbowed.
Let's live boisterously boisterously roisterously,
Let's lead moralists the devil of a dance,
Let's succumb
Completely to temptation,
Probe and plumb
To find a new sensation,
Where we'll end up
Nobody can tell,
So pardon the phrase,
We mean to be raising Hell!

## CHILDREN OF THE RITZ

*from* WORDS AND MUSIC

*Part 1*  Children of the Ritz,
Children of the Ritz,
Sleek and civilized—fretfully surprised,
Though Mr Molyneux has gowned us
The world is tumbling around us,
Without a sou
What can we do?
We'll soon be begging for a crust,
We can't survive
And keep alive
Without the darling Banker's Trust,
In the lovely gay
Years before the Crash
Mr Cartier
Never asked for cash,
Now shops we patronized are serving us with writs,
What's going to happen to the Children of the Ritz?

We owe Elizabeth Arden
Several thousand pounds,
Though we can't pay
We just blow in
If we're passing that way,
While we're going
On our rounds,
We'll perservere
Till our arteries harden,
Then we shan't much care
Whether our chins
Have a crinkle in them,
Whether our skins
Have a wrinkle here and there,
We shan't much mind
For we shall then have left our dreary lives behind.

Children of the Ritz,
Children of the Ritz,
Vaguely debonair,
Only half aware
That all we've counted on is breaking into bits,
What shall we do,
What's going to happen to
The foolish little Children of the Ritz?

*Part 2* Children of the Ritz,
Children of the Ritz,
Mentally congealed
Lilies of the Field
We say just how we want our quails done,
And then we go and have our nails done,
Each single year
We all appear
At Monte Carlo or at Cannes,
We lie in flocks
Along the rocks
Because we have to get a Tan.
Though we never work,
Though we always play,
Though we always shirk
Things we ought to pay,
Whatever crimes the Proletariat commits
It can't be beastly to the Children of the Ritz.

We all economize madly
Now in every way,
Only one car,
An Isotta,
Though it doesn't go far
Still we potter
Through the day,
The times are changing—
We realize sadly
That we're near the brink.
Nothing to wear
We're in tatters
And we honestly swear
That it shatters us to think,
It's really grim
To wonder just how long we're going to sink or swim.

Children of the Ritz,
Children of the Ritz,
Though our day is past—
Gallant to the last—
Without the wherewithal to live upon our wits.
Please say a prayer
For all the frail and fair
And futile little Children of the Ritz.

## MAD DOGS AND ENGLISHMEN

*from* WORDS AND MUSIC

In tropical climes there are certain times of day
When all the citizens retire
To tear their clothes off and perspire.
It's one of those rules that the greatest fools obey,
Because the sun is much too sultry
And one must avoid its ultry-violet ray.

> Papalaka papalaka papalaka boo,
> Papalaka papalaka papalaka boo,
> Digariga digariga digariga doo,
> Digariga digariga digariga doo.

The natives grieve when the white men leave their huts,
Because they're obviously definitely nuts!

Mad dogs and Englishmen
Go out in the midday sun,
The Japanese don't care to.
The Chinese wouldn't dare to,
Hindoos and Argentines sleep firmly from twelve to one.
But Englishmen detest a siesta.
In the Philippines
There are lovely screens
To protect you from the glare.
In the Malay States
There are hats like plates
Which the Britishers won't wear.
At twelve noon
The natives swoon
And no further work is done.
But mad dogs and Englishmen
Go out in the midday sun.

It's such a surprise for the Eastern eyes to see
That though the English are effete,
They're quite impervious to heat,
When the white man rides every native hides in glee,
Because the simple creatures hope he
Will impale his solar topee on a tree.

> Bolyboly bolyboly bolyboly baa,
> Bolyboly bolyboly bolyboly baa,
> Habaninny habaninny habaninny haa,
> Habaninny habaninny habaninny haa.

It seems such a shame
When the English claim
The earth
That they give rise to such hilarity and mirth.

Mad dogs and Englishmen
Go out in the midday sun.
The toughest Burmese bandit
Can never understand it.
In Rangoon the heat of noon
Is just what the natives shun.
They put their Scotch or Rye down
And lie down.
In a jungle town
Where the sun beats down
To the rage of man and beast
The English garb
Of the English sahib
Merely gets a bit more creased.
In Bangkok
At twelve o'clock
They foam at the mouth and run,
But mad dogs and Englishmen
Go out in the midday sun.

Mad dogs and Englishmen
Go out in the midday sun.
The smallest Malay rabbit
Deplores this stupid habit.
In Hongkong
They strike a gong
And fire off a noonday gun
To reprimand each inmate
Who's in late.
In the mangrove swamps
Where the python romps
There is peace from twelve till two.
Even caribous
Lie around and snooze,
For there's nothing else to do.
In Bengal
To move at all
Is seldom, if ever done,
But mad dogs and Englishmen
Go out in the midday sun.

## PLANTERS' WIVES

*from* WORDS AND MUSIC

*Chorus*

The Sun never sets on Government House
For English Might
Selected the site.

No matter how much the Communists grouse
The Sun never sets on Government House.

The Sun never sets on Government House,
The Nation smiles
O'er thousands of miles,
No matter how much we sozzle and souse
The Sun never sets on Government House.

PLANTERS'   Our Husbands deal in Sugar and in Rubber,
WIVES:        Our Husbands deal in Coffee and in Tea,
Whenever we meet the Vicar's wife we snub her
To prove our vast superiority,
We're usually sour and apathetic
In tropical heat,
Nobody who's sweet survives,
We powder and primp
And try to be sympathetic,
Oh dear,
It's queer
That only with men
We're thoroughly energetic,
We're Planters' Wives.


## LET'S SAY GOOD-BYE

*from* WORDS AND MUSIC

Verse   Now we've embarked on this foolish game
Don't let's destroy it with tears.
Once we begin
To let sentiment in
Happiness disappears.

Reason may sleep
For a moment in Spring
But please let us keep
This a casual thing,
Something that's sweet
To remember through the years.

Refrain   Let our affair be a gay thing
And when these hours have flown
Then, without forgetting
Happiness that has passed,
There'll be no regretting
Fun that didn't quite last.
Let's look on love as a plaything.
All these sweet moments we've known
Mustn't be degraded,
When the thrill of them has faded
Let's say, 'Good-bye' and leave it alone.

## THE HALL OF FAME

*from* WORDS AND MUSIC

*Announcement*

Ladies and Gentlemen,
In this peculiar Era
Communal unity
Is daily drawing nearer,
We are indebted to the papers
For thus dispersing of the vapours
Which have hitherto concealed
A lot of simple lives that should have been revealed.
Think what Publicity
Means to the teeming masses,
Think what it signifies
To all those lads and lasses
Who, but for being advertised,
Might have lived all their days unrecognized,
So we and they together bless
The kindly efforts of the Press.

### The Man who caught the Biggest Shrimp

I'm the man who caught the biggest shrimp in the world
And the second biggest prawn as well,
I live at Ryde
And I take great pride
In the tale I have to tell.
The Reporters flock
To examine every rock
And to explore each stretch of sand,
Though why they choose
Me to figure in the News
I shall never understand.

### The oldest Postmistress in England

I'm the very oldest Postmistress in England
And probably the oldest on the Earth,
I've been asked by all the Papers for a statement
So I give you these few facts for what they're worth.
My appetite is absolutely splendid,
There's nothing in the world I can't digest,
I seldom feel uneasy or distended
And I'm never disagreeable or depressed,
I still deliver all the letters daily,
Though my memory is just as good as new
I've a hazy recollection of Disraeli
And I lived in Bray in Eighteen Forty-Two,
I think the Modern Girl is very pretty,
I've never smoked a single cigarette,
I think all this Divorcing is a pity
And I'm sorry that the Nation is upset,
I well recall in Eighteen Thirty-Seven
My parents lived in Weston-Super-Mare,
I'm actually one hundred and eleven
But I cannot see why anyone should care!

### The Man who Rowed Across Lake Windermere in an Indiarubber Bath

For years and years and years and years
I've burned to satisfy
A passionate desire in me
To catch the Public Eye,
When living in obscurity
In Station Road, Penarth,
I thought of crossing Windermere
In an indiarubber bath.

ALL: He rowed across Lake Windermere
In an indiarubber bath!

The Press responded to a man,
I'm known from coast to coast
And eighty lonely women
Have proposed to me by post,
I'm made a lifelong member
Of a most exclusive Club
For I rowed across Lake Windermere
In an indiarubber tub.

ALL: He rowed across Lake Windermere
In an indiarubber tub!

I'm grateful to the *Mirror*
And the *Sketch* for my success
And also to the *Telegraph*,
The *Mail*, and the *Express*.
It doesn't matter now to me
What shadows cross my path
For I rowed across Lake Windermere
In an indiarubber bath.

ALL: He rowed across Lake Windermere
In an indiarubber bath!

### The Holiday Mermaid

I'm a Typist from Putney, and once every year
I stay with my aunt at Torquay
And last time I went there, as no one was near,
I decided to bathe in the sea,
I'd put on me costume and folded me frock
And was tying me 'air in a veil
When two men nipped out from behind a big rock
And gave me this kid with a pail,
Now me face wasn't powdered, me fringe wasn't curled,
And me parents are properly wild
'Cos me photo's been published all over the world
As a 'Holiday Mermaid with Child'!

### The Clergyman Who's Never Been to London

I'm the Clergyman who's never been to London,
I'm the Clergyman who's never been to Town,
An enterprising journalist approached me
And every word I said he jotted down,

I had to face a battery of cameras
And hold an extra service in the snow
And all because I've *never* been to London
And haven't got the *least* desire to go!


### My Life Story

I've been paid by kind Lord Rotherbrook
A very handsome sum
Though I'm stupid and illiterate
And practically dumb.
I cannot really count
How many choruses I've graced
But the story of my life
Is in the very best of taste.
I was on the stage at seventeen
And off at twenty-three
And living with a business man
At Birchington-on-Sea.
My appendix caused me trouble
And in order to survive
I had it taken out three times
In nineteen twenty-five.
In April nineteen twenty-eight
I married Lord St Lyne,
Divorcing him in January
Nineteen twenty-nine.
I've been photographed four hundred times
On foot, and in my car,
And that's the human story
Of how I became a Star!


### Choral Finale

Long live the Press,
Long live the Press,
We're grateful for its subtlety,
Its power and its finesse,
It's brought us from obscurity
To well-deserved success,
Long live the Daily Press!

## MAD ABOUT THE BOY

*from* WORDS AND MUSIC

### *Verse*

SOCIETY
WOMAN:

I met him at a party just a couple of years ago,
He was rather over-hearty and ridiculous
But as I'd seen him on the Screen
He cast a certain spell.
I basked in his attraction for a couple of hours or so,
His manners were a fraction too meticulous,
If he was real or not I couldn't tell
 But like a silly fool, I fell.

### *Refrain*

Mad about the boy,
I know it's stupid to be mad about the boy,
I'm so ashamed of it
But must admit
The sleepless nights I've had about the boy.
On the Silver Screen
He melts my foolish heart in every single scene.
Although I'm quite aware
That here and there
Are traces of the cad about the boy,
Lord knows I'm not a fool girl,
I really shouldn't care,
Lord knows I'm not a schoolgirl
In the flurry of her first affair.
Will it ever cloy?
This odd diversity of misery and joy,
I'm feeling quite insane
And young again
And all because I'm mad about the boy.

### *Verse*

SCHOOLGIRL:

Home work, home work,
Every night there's home work,
While Elsie practises the gas goes pop,
I wish, I wish she'd stop,
Oh dear, oh dear,
Here it's always 'No, dear,
You can't go out again, you must stay home,
You waste your money on that common Picturedrome,
Don't shirk—stay here and do your work.'

Yearning, yearning,
How my heart is burning.
I'll see him Saturday in *Strong Man's Pain*
And then on Monday and on Friday week again.
To me he is the sole man
Who can kiss as well as Colman,
I could faint whenever there's a close-up of his lips,
Though John Barrymore is larger
When my hero's on his charger
Even Douglas Fairbanks Junior hasn't smaller hips.
If only he could know
That I adore him so.

### Refrain

Mad about the boy,
It's simply scrumptious to be mad about the boy,
I know that quite sincerely
Housman really
Wrote *The Shropshire Lad* about the boy.
In my English Prose
I've done a tracing of his forehead and his nose
And there is, honour bright,
A certain slight
Effect of Galahad about the boy.
I've talked to Rosie Hooper,
She feels the same as me,
She says that Gary Cooper
Doesn't thrill her to the same degree.
In *Can Love Destroy?*
When he meets Garbo in a suit of corduroy,
He gives a little frown
And knocks her down.
Oh dear, oh dear, I'm mad about the boy.

### Verse

COCKNEY:   Every Wednesday afternoon
I get a little time off from three to eleven,
Then I go to the Picture House
And taste a little of my particular heaven.
He appears
In a little while,
Through a mist of tears
I can see him smiling
Above me.
Every picture I see him in,
Every lover's caress,

Makes my wonderful dreams begin,
Makes me long to confess
That if ever he looked at me
And thought perhaps it was worth the trouble to
Love me,
I'd give in and I wouldn't care
However far from the path of virtue he'd
Shove me,
Just supposing our love was brief,
If he treated me rough
I'd be happy beyond belief,
Once would be enough.

### Refrain

Mad about the boy,
I know I'm potty but I'm mad about the boy.
He sets me 'eart on fire
With love's desire,
In fact I've got it bad about the boy.
When I do the rooms
I see 'is face in all the brushes and the brooms.
Last week I strained me back
And got the sack
And 'ad a row with Dad about the boy.
I'm finished with Navarro,
I'm tired of Richard Dix,
I'm pierced by Cupid's arrow
Every Wednesday from four till six.
'Ow I should enjoy
To let 'im treat me like a plaything or a toy,
I'd give my all to him
And crawl to him,
So 'elp me Gawd I'm mad about the boy.

### Verse

TART:    It seems a little silly
For a girl of my age and weight
To walk down Piccadilly
In a haze of love.
It ought to take a good deal more to get a bad girl
    down,
I should have been exempt, for
My particular kind of Fate
Has taught me such contempt for
Every phase of love,
And now I've been and spent my last half-crown
To weep about a painted clown.

*Refrain*

Mad about the boy,
It's pretty funny but I'm mad about the boy,
He has a gay appeal
That makes me feel
There's maybe something sad about the boy.
Walking down the street,
His eyes look out at me from people that I meet,
I can't believe it's true
But when I'm blue
In some strange way I'm glad about the boy.
I'm hardly sentimental,
Love isn't so sublime,
I have to pay my rental
And I can't afford to waste much time,
If I could employ
A little magic that would finally destroy
This dream that pains me
And enchains me,
But I can't because I'm mad about the boy.


## JOURNEY'S END

*from* WORDS AND MUSIC

*Announcement*

Ladies and Gentlemen,
Forgive my strange appearance,
Our kindly author has
With splendid perseverance
Worked without stint for your enjoyment
And in this age of unemployment
He decided on a plan
To utilize as many aliens as he can,
For, like Sir Oswald Stoll,
He feels an obligation
To do his level best
To help the German Nation
And if Charell would condescend
To make a spectacle of *Journey's End*
It is our author's little scheme
To show this strange 'Teutonic Dream!'

### Yodelling Song

La dalaito,
La dalaito,
Swift mountain streams
Play the music of dreams,
La dalaito,
La dalaito,
Morning sweet morning
So happily gleams,
La dalaito—la dalaito—etc. etc.

### Kleine Pupchen

Kleine Pupchen,
Boop oop adoop-chen,
You are my own vis-à-vis,
Kleine Pupchen,
Boop oop adoop-chen,
My sweetheart some day you'll be,
So if you leave me
Don't go too far,
Da da un dahda,
This is my firm protocol,
Hold me in your arms a bit,
Display your charms a bit,
There could be no harm in it
For you're my Baby Doll!

### Te Quiero

In an old Spanish Garden I found you,
The hibiscus was shining all round you,
The guitars in the distance were playing
All the love songs I longed to be saying
'Neath the stars that were gleaming above you,
I laid all my dreams at your feet,
Though now I have lost you, I love you
'Te Quiero', my sweet Señorita.

### Duet: A Gondola on the Rhine

BOTH:  You and me in a Gondola,
Just a Gondola
On the Rhine,

SHE:  Gazing without ending
In each other's eyes,

HE:      I shall catch you bending
         On your Bridge of Sighs,

BOTH:    We'll tour all round the Mond-ola,
         We'll abscond-ola,
         Pom, pom!
         And maybe
         One day there will be three
         In our Gondola on the Rhine.

*Love and War*

Love and War,
Those are the games worth playing,
No man could ask any more
When the bugles and trumpets bray.
Love and War
Open Adventure's door,
All that men sigh for,
Live, laugh and die for,
Love and War.

## HOUSEMAIDS' KNEES

### *from* WORDS AND MUSIC

Verse    Pretty little housemaids proper and sedate,
         Um um umum um um,
         We seldom go to bed too early and we rise extremely
             late.
         Um um umum um um um,
         Pretty little housemaids eager to improve,
         Each shining hour by slightly widening our small
             domestic groove.
         We wish to help the Nation
         To forget its pence and pounds,
         Our little innovation
         Is on patriotic grounds.

Refrain  Make England brighter
         That's what we try to do,
         Our clothes are lighter,
         Our skirts are shorter too,
         When there's the slightest breeze
         You see these

Housemaids' knees.
When there's a crisis
Forget it while you can,
Our firm advice is
To every business man
Just take a look at these
Housemaids' knees.
In our domestic and our personal relationships
You must forgive us if our consciousness of 'station'
    slips,
A little beauty
May stop you feeling blue,
We feel our duty
Is to enable you
To gaze at skittish,
Absolutely British,
Housemaids' knees!


## THREE WHITE FEATHERS

*from* WORDS AND MUSIC

Verse 1    I can't help feeling
Fate's made a fool of me rather,
It placed me where I shouldn't be
And really couldn't be by rights;
We lived at Ealing,
Me and me mother and father;
I've scaled the social ladder
And I've never had a head for heights;
We had a pawnshop on the corner of the street,
And Father did a roaring trade.
I used to think those rings and necklaces were sweet,
Now I wouldn't give them to my maid.

Refrain 1    I've travelled a long long way
And the journey hasn't been all jam;
I must admit
The Rolls in which I sit
Is one up on the dear old tram;
I say to myself each day
In definitely Marble Halls,
Today it may be three white feathers,
But yesterday it was three brass balls.

Verse 2   By easy stages
          Though my beginnings were humble
          I've studied each small movement
          Of my self-improvement
          From the start;
          I've toured for ages,
          I'll never falter or stumble;
          I'll give an air of breeding
          And a first-rate reading
          Of the part;
          You must forgive me if I kid myself a bit
          In me tiara and me gown,
          And though my accent may not altogether fit,
          Don't be afraid I'll let you down.

Refrain 2  I've travelled a long long way
          And had a lot of jolts and bumps;
          I'll concentrate
          And be ahead of fate,
          Whichever way the old cat jumps;
          I'll wink as I slyly drink
          To the ancestors who line our halls,
          Today it may be three white feathers,
          But yesterday it was three brass balls.

Refrain 3  I've travelled a long long way
          And now I've found the man I love;
          I'll do my share, so long as he is there,
          To help me with a gentle shove . . .
              (*She stops singing*)
          We're moving.


# DESCRIPTION OF BALLETS

*from* WORDS AND MUSIC

      Ladies and Gentlemen,
      The next scene needs explaining
      And Mr Cochran hopes
      You'll find it entertaining.
      It is his firm determination
      To make you use imagination
      And to gather at a glance
      The charm of ordinary life in terms of dance.

Think of an English Club
On lines of Russian Ballet.
Picture those dear old men
Cavorting musically;
What could be prettier to see
Than angry Colonels in captivity
Pointing the light fantastic toe
As through their daily lives they go!

2 ... See how the 'Dance' can bring to bloom
Even a boarding-house in Ilfracombe.
The Ballet Spirit as portrayed
At number five Marine Parade.

3 ... Now for the sake of our Revue
You'll see a crèche of infants under two.
Note the effect of airy grace
In this clean sanitary place!


## SOMETHING TO DO WITH SPRING

*from* WORDS AND MUSIC

*Verse*

HE:  The Spring is here, dear,
     Oh dear, oh dear, dear,
     Can't you see
     The simply agonizing sheen
     On every angry little tree?

SHE: I must admit it's rather fun
     To think that every single thing
     That Nature ever does is overdone.

HE:  I know exactly what you mean.
     It all looks far too clean—
     A badly painted scene,
     The grass is far too green.

SHE: Perhaps there's something we have missed.

HE:  I never could have kissed
     A sentimentalist.

SHE:   Still there's something in the atmosphere
       That makes me happy here.

HE:    Don't make me giggle, dear.

### Refrain 1

SHE:   The sun is shining where clouds have been—

HE:    Maybe it's something to do with Spring.

SHE:   I feel no older than seventeen—

HE:    Maybe it's something to do with Spring.

SHE:   A something I can't express,
       A sort of lilt in the air,
       A lyrical loveliness,
       Seems everywhere.

HE:    That sheep's behaviour is most obscene.

BOTH:  Maybe it's something to do with Spring.

### Refrain 2

HE:    The dewdrops glitter like diamond links—

SHE:   Maybe it's something to do with Spring.

HE:    They say that rabbits have minds like sinks—

SHE:   Maybe it's something to do with Spring.

HE:    The way that the sows behave
       May seem delightfully quaint.
       But why should the cows behave
       With *no* restraint?

SHE:   I'd love to know what that stallion thinks—

HE:    Maybe it's something to do with Spring.

## THE WIFE OF AN ACROBAT

*from* WORDS AND MUSIC

Verse     Always travelling to and fro
And always packing to go
Is apt to derange one.
I believe I should lose my head
If once I slept in a bed
That wasn't a strange one.
Never topping the Bill at all
In each Variety Hall
We open or close them.
Apart from waving my hand about
When he's finished a trick
I do nothing but stand about
Feeling slightly sick.
Even if I had lovely legs I'm not the type of girl
Who blatantly shows them.
When I look at the pair I've got
It seems a little bit hard
To have to expose them.
People say that a pride in tricks
Every animal feels.
I'd prefer to be one of six
Old performing seals.

Refrain 1  I'm the wife of an Acrobat
And the world has passed me by.
I'm dressed in tights
To play the 'Twice a Nights'
And only God knows why.
What a life!
For an Acrobat
As he flies from hoop to hoop
I have a sort of feeling, when our souls have passed
    away
When giving shows in Heaven, three performances a day,
I'll say what all the angels are expecting me to say,
'Allez OOp—Allez OOp—Allez OOp!'

Refrain 2  I'm the wife of an Acrobat
And our eldest boy's a scout.
I hate the lad
To come and see his dad
Entirely inside out.

Now the wives of the Acrobats
Form a most exclusive group,
You'll seldom see us riding 'Haute École' along the park
And many of us look as if we'd come out of the Ark,
Our conversation meagrely consists of one remark,
'Allez OOp—Allez OOp—Allez OOp!'

Refrain 3 I'm the wife of an Acrobat,
When my old man don't feel well—
To hold each prop
And wonder if he'll drop
Is my idea of Hell.
What a life for an Acrobat!
When I watch him loop and loop
I wonder what he's thinking upside down on the trapeze
And if he's really happy with his head between his knees
And then his face gets crimson
And I know he's going to sneeze!
'Allez OOp—Allez OOp—Allez OOp!'

Refrain 4 I'm the wife of an Acrobat,
When our kids are in their cots
It's kind of sad
To realize their Dad
Is tying himself in knots.
Now the wife of an Acrobat
Is the 'Dead Pan' of the troupe,
I've stood about for twenty years,
My hair is turning grey,
I hear my old man gasping as I watch him swing and
    sway
And if he broke his bloody neck I know I'd only say,
'Allez OOp—Allez OOp—Allez OOp!'


# THE YOUNGER GENERATION

*from* WORDS AND MUSIC

*Verse*

GIRLS:            Mother, tell us, Mother,
                  Have you anything in your heart to tell the four of us,
                  Are you perfectly sure of us,
                  We are eager to know?

MOTHER:        I trust you everywhere you go.

GIRLS:         Mother, tell us, Mother,
               If the dreams that you dreamed in Springtime have come
                   true for you.
               What love promised to do for you
               Did it actually do?

MOTHER:        With Love the whole wide world seems new.

GIRLS:         Teach us to understand this magic flame,
               As you did when at first your lover came,
               What did he bring to you?
               What melodies did he sing to you?

MOTHER:        The same . . .
               Melodies that lovers sing
               Whenever the heart is gay with Spring
               And Youth is there.
               I assure you the truth is there.
               The years hurry for young love is brief,
               Tears follow with the fall of the leaf,
               Age may bring you sadly to grief
               Unless you're wise and realize
               That dignity is the greatest prize
               To guard.

GIRLS:         We'll try so hard.

MOTHER:        Once on a time I was young and fair like you.

GIRLS:         We know.

MOTHER:        Happily dreaming my adolescence through.

GIRLS:         Heigho.

MOTHER:        Then I married your father,
               Gay and handsome and frank,
               But it shattered me rather
               When I found he drank.

GIRLS:         Oh what a shock,
               That was really too too bad!

MOTHER:        So sad,
               Then I took stock
               Of the assets that I had.

GIRLS:        We're glad.

MOTHER:       Ten long years I had sly love,
              Then I whispered to my love,
              Get thee behind me,
              Life has resigned me,
              I'd never stoop to buy love.

                        *Refrain*

              Age calls the tune,
              Youth's over soon,
              That is the natural law.
              There's a Younger Generation
              Knock knock knocking at the door.
              Why sit and fret?
              Vainly regret
              Things that have gone before?
              There's a Younger Generation
              Knock knock knocking at the door.
              Though the world is well lost for love dreams
              There's wisdom above dreams
              To compensate mothers and wives,
              When the days of youth have passed them,
              This should last them
              All their lives.
              I've had my fun,
              All that is done,
              Why should I sigh for more?
              There's a Younger Generation
              Knock knock knocking at the door.

GIRLS:        Dear dear Mamma,
              Your wise advice to us
              Has made us see that the doubts in our hearts were vain.

MOTHER:       Love comes
              But once or twice to us,
              If it is wise love, the memory will remain
              Through the years,
              Have no more fears,
              For Age brings peace,
              Sweet release
              From all
              The fetters that have bound you,
              Call
              Your memories around you,
              All your troubled dreams will cease.

(*spoken*) Marie—Marie—MARIE!
Don't keep me waiting,
Can't you see how very late I am?

MARIE:          May I venture to state, Madame,
                That I answered the bell.

MOTHER: (*speaks*) My dress quickly.
        (*sings*) So aggravating,
                  Can't you see in what a nervous state I am?

MARIE:          It's a quarter to eight, Madame.

MOTHER: (*spoken*) Very well, very well.

                I waste a lot of time on those damned girls,
                I think I'll wear the rubies and the pearls.

MARIE:          They're in the jewel case,
                But hadn't you better do your face
                And hair?

MOTHER:         All right then, there!
                La lala la la lalalala,
                Lalala lala lalala—lalala lala la.

MARIE:          This wig must be sent to be dressed,
                And could I be allowed to suggest
                That before retiring to rest
                You lock the door
                And in this drawer
                Hide every garment that you wore
                From sight.

MOTHER:         All right—all right.
                Who would suppose I was nearly forty-three.
                Ah me!
                I can knock spots off those simpering 'Jeunes Filles'.
                You see
                Virgin charms don't allure men,
                They need something beyond,
                All the wise and mature men
                Need a 'Femme du Monde',
                I can be tender
                And wise and witty too
                It's true
                I don't surrender.

Before surrender's due.
A few—
Lovers may have betrayed me
When my heart disobeyed me
But I've escaped now,
I have them taped now,
Life has indeed repaid me.

Age can be gay,
Age can betray
Destiny's foolish law,
Though the Younger Generation's
Knock knock knocking at the door,
Age is a joke
Planned to provoke
Dreams that the fools ignore,
When the Younger Generation's
Knock knock knocking at the door,
I shall still be gay and attractive,
As long as I'm active,
I'll savour each delicate sin,
Not until my footsteps stagger
And I'm 'Gaga'
I'll give in.
Give me a moon,
Give me a tune,
Give me a dancing floor.
There's a Younger Generation
Knock knock knocking at the door.

# MIDNIGHT MATINÉE
## (Speech in Verse)

### *from* WORDS AND MUSIC

GIRLS: (in masks— Een arrarah ola brure
which makes speech Taala caana effalure
incomprehensible) Tar Apollo nuraling
Jupiter abalching.

Tanger weero avaloy
Burel ammalee to Troy
Baara weether dolaser
Mount Olympus bolaser.

Een arrarah ola brure
Taala caana effalure
Tar Apollo nuraling
Jupiter abalching.

Hola jaaga ammo purtain
Borrodah anula curtain.


# MIDNIGHT MATINÉE
## (Opening Chorus)

*from* WORDS AND MUSIC

We're going to do a Midnight Matinée!
We're going to do a Midnight Show!
We're not *quite* sure
What Charity it's for
But probably the Press will know,
We're going to have a talk on Saturday
To make a list of friends who'll go,
The Season's such a bore,
We haven't had much excitement since the War
And so . . .
We'll do a Midnight Show.

Last year we did a 'Feather Parade',
That was a great success.
But some got bent
And some would break
And a lot got sent
To Melton by mistake.
At Easter we went mad I'm afraid,
We really must confess,
We gave a great—
Big 'Circus Ball'
But forgot the date
So no one came at all.

We're going to do a Midnight Matinée!
We're going to do a Midnight Show!
A sort of 'Masque'
Where everyone will ask
And nobody will *ever* know,

We're going to have a talk on Saturday
To make a list of friends who'll go,
God knows how much we'll fetch
But we shall have all our pictures in the *Sketch*
And so—
We'll do a Midnight Show.


MIDNIGHT MATINÉE
(Pageant of Bygone Enchantresses)

*from* WORDS AND MUSIC

Bygone Loves and bygone Lovers
Live again in History's pages,
As one turns them one discovers
Love's Romance across the Ages.
Diane de Poitiers.

Queen of every fascination,
This Enchantress lives again,
Siren of the Restoration,
Mistress Gwynn of Drury Lane.
Nell Gwynn.

Eastern Stars, your light grows less,
Oh Eastern Moon, your beauty pales
Before this sinister Princess
Salomé of the Seven Veils.
Salomé.

Tragic Queen of Tragic Story,
Memory that haunts us yet,
Here we see you in your glory,
Lovely Marie Antoinette.
Marie Antoinette.

Battle Queen of History,
Gallant Memory, Brave Romance,
Welcome, Welcome, Hail to Thee,
Joan of Arc. The Maid of France!
Joan of Arc.

Beauty rare, and stately calm,
England holds your memory dear,
Queen of Fashion, Queen of Charm,
Lady Blessington is here.
Lady Blessington.

Lady sweet beyond compare,
Strange the legend, strange the deed,
Shielded by your flowing hair,
Riding on your snow-white steed.
Lady Godiva.


## THE PARTY'S OVER NOW

*from* WORDS AND MUSIC

Though we hate
Abominate
Each party we're invited to
To stay out
And dance about
Because we've nothing else to do.
Though every night
We start out bright
And finish with a row
We've been so bored,
Thank the Lord
That the Party's over now!

Verse    Night is over, dawn is breaking,
Everywhere the Town is waking
Just as we are on our way to sleep.
Lovers meet and dance
A little,
Snatching from romance
A little
Souvenir of happiness to keep.
The music of an hour ago
Was just a sort of 'Let's pretend',
The melodies that charmed us so
At last are ended.

Refrain  The Party's over now,
The dawn is drawing very nigh,
The candles gutter,
The starlight leaves the sky.
It's time for little boys and girls
To hurry home to bed
For there's a new day
Waiting just ahead.
Life is sweet
But time is fleet,
Beneath the magic of the moon,
Dancing time
May seem sublime
But it is ended all too soon,
The thrill has gone,
To linger on
Would spoil it anyhow,
Let's creep away from the day
For the Party's over now.

# *Set to Music*

## I'M SO WEARY OF IT ALL

*from* SET TO MUSIC *and* ALL CLEAR (New York)

Verse   People that I sing to
Bring a breath of Spring to
Envy me my gay career.
No one in the city
Has much time for pity,
Nobody can be sincere;
Thousands cheer me and applaud me,
Every one stares.
If they've wounded me and bored me
Nobody cares;
Women at the tables,
Loosening their sables,
Look at me with cruel eyes,
Then a little something in me dies
And cries.

Refrain  Weary of it all,
This getting and spending,
This futile unending
Refrain,
It's driving me insane;
I'm so weary of it all.
Other voices call,
The cattle at twilight,
The birds in the sky light
Of dawn,
Yet here am I forlorn
And so weary of it all.
I miss the wild-wood
I wandered through in childhood
With a heart as light as air,
What would I give once again to be there
With my old, deaf mother!
Night begins to fall,
By memory tortured
I dream of an orchard

In Spring,
The songs I used to sing.
Now I have to swing,
I'm so weary of it all.

Patter   Wake up in the morning
'Round about noon,
A little lunch on a tray,
Shopping without stopping till my senses swoon,
Or else some dreary matinée,
Home at five,
More dead then alive,
Another day nearly gone.
Cocktails to mix,
My face and hair to fix,
The weary round goes on.
Eight or nine,
I have to go and dine
With this or that rich man about town,
Caviar and grouse
In an overheated house,
God, how it gets me down!
Home I go defeated and depressed again,
Only time for just one hour of rest again.
Bright lights,
White lights,
Waiters leering,
Faces sneering,
Laughing, chaffing,
Shouting, cheering,
Weary of it all
This giving and giving,
This life that I'm living in hell.
With broken dreams to sell,
Just an empty shell,
Weary, weary, weary of it all!

# I'VE BEEN TO A MARVELLOUS PARTY

*from* SET TO MUSIC (New York)

Verse 1  Quite for no reason
I'm here for the Season
And high as a kite,
Living in error
With Maud at Cap Ferrat
Which couldn't be right.
Everyone's here and frightfully gay,
Nobody cares what people say,
Though the Riviera
Seems really much queerer
Than Rome at its height,
Yesterday night—

Refrain 1  I've been to a marvellous party
With Nounou and Nada and Nell,
It was in the fresh air
And we went as we were
And we stayed as we were
Which was Hell.
Poor Grace started singing at midnight
And didn't stop singing till four;
We knew the excitement was bound to begin
When Laura got blind on Dubonnet and gin
And scratched her veneer with a Cartier pin,
I couldn't have liked it more.

Refrain 2  I've been to a marvellous party,
I must say the fun was intense,
We all had to do
What the people we knew
Would be doing a hundred years hence.
Dear Cecil arrived wearing armour,
Some shells and a black feather boa,
Poor Millicent wore a surrealist comb
Made of bits of mosaic from St Peter's in Rome,
But the weight was so great that she had to go home,
I couldn't have liked it more!

Verse 2  People's behaviour
Away from Belgravia
Would make you aghast,
So much variety

Watching Society
Scampering past,
If you have any mind at all
Gibbon's divine *Decline and Fall*
Seems pretty flimsy,
No more than a whimsy,
By way of contrast
On Saturday last—

Refrain 3    I've been to a marvellous party,
We didn't start dinner till ten
And young Bobbie Carr
Did a stunt at the bar
With a lot of extraordinary men;
Dear Baba arrived with a turtle
Which shattered us all to the core,
The Grand Duke was dancing a foxtrot with me
When suddenly Cyril screamed Fiddledidee
And ripped off his trousers and jumped in the sea,
I couldn't have liked it more.

Refrain 4    I've been to a marvellous party,
Elise made an entrance with May,
You'd never have guessed
From her fisherman's vest
That her bust had been whittled away.
Poor Lulu got fried on Chianti
And talked about esprit de corps.
Maurice made a couple of passes at Gus
And Freddie, who hates any kind of a fuss,
Did half the Big Apple and twisted his truss,
I couldn't have liked it more.

Refrain 5    I've been to a marvellous party,
We played the most wonderful game,
Maureen disappeared
And came back in a beard
And we all had to guess at her name!
We talked about growing old gracefully
And Elsie who's seventy-four
Said, 'A, it's a question of being sincere,
And B, if you're supple you've nothing to fear.'
Then she swung upside down from a glass chandelier,
I couldn't have liked it more.

## RUG OF PERSIA

*from* SET TO MUSIC (New York)

GIRLS:      Ah—Ah—Ah—etc.

MARSINAH:   Just a rug of Persia,
            Less than the dust,
            Yet it's a woman's art.

GIRLS:      Ah—Ah—Ah—etc.

MARSINAH:   Tread upon it lightly
            If tread you must,
            For in it lies my heart.

GIRLS:      Ah—Ah—Ah—etc.

MARSINAH:   Click clack,
            Click clack
            Goes the needle sharp and bright,
            From early dawn to late at night
            My busy fingers weave.

GIRLS:      Click clack,
            Click clack
            Goes the needle sharp and bright,
            She's at her tricks from morn till night
            With nothing up her sleeve!

MARSINAH:   Until my own true love appears
            I shall sit here for years and years,
            Each stitch is watered by my tears,
            When will he come to me?
            When will he come to me?
            This wondrous prince I see,
            I weave my destiny
            Here on my tapestry,
            This is the forest of my girlhood fancies,
            This is my world of dreams,
            This is the hero of my love romances
            Splashing through lakes and laughing streams,
            Here on the right is the moon of my delight,
            This is a Persian horse,
            This rather deft little object on the left
            Is the Star of the East of course.
            Though you may think I am far too faddy
            My heart belongs to my old Bag-Daddy
            Ah—Ah—Ah—Ah—Ah!

# *Conversation Piece*

## PROLOGUE

*from* CONVERSATION PIECE

SOPHIE:          Ladies and Gentlemen,
A prologue to a play is out of date,
A leisurely technique of past decades.
So please regard us as two friendly shades
Returning down the years to indicate,
More by our presence, than by what we say,
The atmosphere and tempo of this play.

MARTHA: My friend has explained it most concisely,
She always was one to put things nicely!

SOPHIE: We represent the fine but faded flower
Of that old 'Demi-Monde' that used to be
At Vauxhall, and at Brighton by the sea
Before the pure in heart came into power,
Before a great, but sanctimonious Queen
Firmly rang down the curtain on our scene.

MARTHA: Please don't suppose *our* flowers were faded,
Others were pushed, *we* were persuaded!

SOPHIE: The interruptions of my friend are meant
To clarify for you our 'Status Quo',
A social level neither high nor low
With which we were entirely content
And which provides the background, may I say,
Of this polite, but faintly raffish play.

# I'LL FOLLOW MY SECRET HEART

### *from* CONVERSATION PIECE

MELANIE: A cloud has passed across the sun,
The morning seems no longer gay.
With so much business to be done,
Even the sea looks grey.
C'est vrai. C'est vrai.
It seems that all the joy has faded from the day
As though the foolish world no longer wants to play.

PAUL:    (*speaking*) Go and dress.

MELANIE: (*speaking*) What shall I wear? A black crêpe with a little bonnet?

PAUL:    What on earth is the matter with you this morning?

MELANIE: White, white for a bride. But the sun ought to shine on a bride.

PAUL:    You're not a bride yet.

MELANIE: But I shall be soon, shall I not? A very quiet aristocratic bride
with a discreet heart!

*(sings)*
You ask me to have a discreet heart
Until marriage is out of the way
But what if I meet
With a sweetheart so sweet
That my wayward heart cannot obey
A single word that you may say?

PAUL:    (*speaking*) Then we shall have to go away.

MELANIE: (*sings*)
No. For there is nowhere we could go
Where we could hide from what we know
Is true.
Don't be afraid I'll betray you
And destroy all the plans you have made,
But even your schemes
Must leave room for my dreams.
So when all I owe to you is paid
I'll still have something of my own,
A little prize that's mine alone.

I'll follow my secret heart
My whole life through,
I'll keep all my dreams apart
Till one comes true.
No matter what price is paid,
What stars may fade
Above,
I'll follow my secret heart
Till I find love.


## QUARTETTE: REGENCY RAKES

*from* CONVERSATION PIECE

Verse  You may think
     Looking at the four of us
     Food and drink
     Constitute the core of us.
     That may be,
     But still you'll see
     Our names on posterity's page.
     You will read
     Histories galore of us
     Strutting England's stage.
     We represent
     To a certain extent
     The ineffable scent
     Of our age.

Refrain 1 We're Regency Rakes
     And each of us takes
     A personal pride
     In the thickness of hide
     Which prevents us from seeing
     How vulgar we're being,
     Without making us wince,
     We're ruthless and rude
     And boast of a crude
     And lordly disdain
     Both for mind and for brain.
     Though obtuse and slow-witted,
     We're not to be pitied,
     For we follow the Prince,

Every orgy
With our Georgie
Lasts till dawn without a lull.
We can venture
Without censure
To be noisy, drunk and dull!
We revel in Sport,
Madeira, and Port,
And when we pass out
With Sclerosis and Gout
All our children will rue our mistakes,
Roistering Regency Rakes,
Ho! Ho!
Roistering Regency Rakes.

Refrain 2   We're Regency Rakes
And each of makes
A personal issue
Of adipose tissue
But still notwithstanding,
Our stomachs expanding,
We all yearn for romance.
We frequently start
Affairs of the heart,
Sublimely unheeding
That long over-feeding
Has made so disgusting
Our loving or lusting
That girls eye us askance,
Though we wonder
As we blunder
Into this or that bordel,
Whom we know there,
Why we go there,
But we're far too drunk to tell,
Though over-jocose,
Unfunny and gross,
We don't lose a fraction
Of self-satisfaction.
Complacency never forsakes
Roistering Regency Rakes!
Ho! Ho!
Roistering Regency Rakes.

# CHARMING, CHARMING
## (Quartette)

*from* CONVERSATION PIECE

SOPHIE: Charming! Charming! Charming!

ROSE: This gown is for the morning,
When Mademoiselle goes out,
As Madame sees
In the slightest breeze
The feathers float about.

SOPHIE
MARTHA } : Charming! Charming! Charming!

ROSE: This jacket is for driving,
Or strolling beside the sea.

SOPHIE: Pretty as it seems to be
It's a little too full in the sleeves for me.

ALL: Ah la la la—la la—la la.

SOPHIE: Pretty as it seems to be
It's a trifle full in the sleeves for me.

MELANIE: This dress is for the evening,
To wear when I meet my dear,
Whenever that may chance to be.
In the moment that he looks at me
The skies will suddenly clear.
I'll know him then for my destiny,
And so through each changing year
I shall leave him never, for evermore.

ROSE: Don't you think these pinks and blues are sweet?
This stuff is sent especially from France.

MELANIE: Oh, please, please say you think these satin shoes are
sweet,
They make me feel I want to dance.

Danser—danser—la Vie est gaie.
Je me sens libre, abandonnée.
Le chant trouble mon cœur

Qui donc m'envoie ce doux bonheur,
Mon corps, mes pieds, ensorcelés,
Légers, ailés, vont s'envoler.
Tra la la la la—la la la—la la la la la,
Tra la la la la—la la la—lalalalalala—la la.

SOPHIE
MARTHA  } : Look for a love that's gay and sweet.
ROSE
MELANIE

SOPHIE
MARTHA  } : Music to guide your dancing feet.
ROSE
MELANIE

SOPHIE   }   Follow your secret strain
MARTHA  } : And you won't be living in vain,
ROSE     }   Treat your desire by word and deed
             Lightly—lightly—
             And if at first you don't succeed
             Try and try again.

MELANIE:     Mon corps, mes pieds, ensorcelés,
             Légers, ailés, vont s'envoler.
             Tra la la la la—la la la—la la la—la—la,
             Tra la la la—la la la—

             (*ALL rush to window to watch the soldiers go by*)

ROSE:        When I see the soldiers marching by
             With fife and drum
             Beneath a summer sky,

SOPHIE   } : Little dears who love to do and die,
MARTHA

ROSE:        My spirit sings
             And spreads its wings to fly,
             Think of all the battles they have won.

MELANIE:     So brave and strong
             They march along
             Like little boys
             Who play with toys
             For fun.

SOPHIE
MARTHA  }: Little boys who frolic in the sun.

ROSE:      Right—right—right left right,

ALL:      Right—right—right left right left—
March little soldiers, we all adore you,
We'd swoon before you
If we thought that you would care,
What e'er befalls you,
Where duty calls you,
We should love to be there
To share
All your troubles, but we'd never dare,
But we're quite prepared to cheer you to victory,
To joy or despair,
Joy or despair,
That's only fair.
Dear little soldiers,
Should you admire us
And feel desirous
On returning from the fray,
We'd soon surrender,
You'd find us tender
And sublimely unresisting
In assisting
You to spend
Your soldiers' pay pay pay.

## THERE'S ALWAYS SOMETHING FISHY ABOUT THE FRENCH

*from* CONVERSATION PIECE

*Verse 1*

SOPHIE:   A life of Love is curious
But not injurious
If you are wise.

MARTHA: For you get pleasure,
Leisure,
Knowledge to treasure
After the gay life dies;

SOPHIE:   Though men we seldom bind to us
          They're often kind to us,

MARTHA:   And entre nous
          English Gentlemen,
          Spanish Noblemen,
          Indian Merchantmen too,
          Always play the game,
          Never cause us shame.

### Refrain 1

BOTH:     But there's always something fishy about the French!
          Whether Prince or Politician
          We've a sinister suspicion
          That behind their savoir faire
          They share
          A common contempt
          For every mother's son of us.
          Though they smile and smirk
          We know they're out for dirty work,
          We're most polite
          But don't put out the night-light!
          Every wise and thoroughly worldly wench
          Knows there's always something fishy about the French!

### Refrain 2

BOTH:     Oh, there's always something fishy about the French!
          As a race, they're conscientious
          But undoubtedly licentious,
          Though the compliments they pay
          Are gay
          And ever so nice,
          We don't believe a word of them,
          They may kiss our hands
          And talk to us of foreign lands,
          We 'Toi' and 'Moi'
          And watch for 'Je ne sais quoi'—
          Every time their fingers begin to clench—
          Well, we know there's something fishy about the French!

## PROLOGUE—ACT II

*from* CONVERSATION PIECE

SOPHIE:   This play, or let us say, this pantomime,
          Being too small in scope, too tenuous,
          Too personal to illustrate the strenuous
          And glittering excitements of the time,
          We feel it, in a sense, obligatory
          To hint at what goes on *behind* the story.

MARTHA:   My friend, though a trifle too rhetorical,
          Means it should be more historical.

SOPHIE:   We ask you to imagine, if you please,
          That just around the corner of the tale,
          Mrs Fitzherbert and the Prince inhale
          The selfsame air, the same urbane sea breeze.
          Imagine that this world is living still
          And passing just beneath the window-sill.

MARTHA:   You've left out Brummell, the pert impostor,
          And what about Pitt? And the Duke of Gloucester?

SOPHIE:   Picture a little further if you will
          The neat Pavilion Gardens, and the Steyne.
          The little band that orchestrates the scene.
          The Fireworks, the Races, the Quadrille
          And furthermore, the bawdy, merry Hell
          Created by our lordly clientéle!

## ENGLISH LESSON

*from* CONVERSATION PIECE

Verse 1   The tree is in the garden,
          The water is in the pot;
          The little sheep
          On the mountain sleep,
          The fire is very hot.

Refrain     Oh! c'est dur
              Tous ces mots obscurs
              Me rendent triste;
              Rien n'existe
              Que le malheur qui insiste;
              Dieu, je tâche d'apprendre, mais voilà
              Je ne peux pas.

Verse 2     The fire is not in the garden,
              The tree is not in the pot,
              The silly sheep
              On the something sleep
              But whether they do or not,
              I do not care a jot;
              I don't care if they're cold
              Or if they're hot.

Refrain 2    Oh! c'est dur,
              Tous ces mots obscurs
              Me rendent triste;
              Rien n'existe
              Que le malheur qui insiste;
              Dieu, je tâche d'apprendre, mais voilà
              Je ne peux pas.

# THERE WAS ONCE A LITTLE VILLAGE

*from* CONVERSATION PIECE

There was once a little village by the sea,
Where we lived our lives in amiable tranquillity.
We were humble in our ways
And we swam through all our days
As little fishes swim
In immobility;
We watched for gales
In the evening sky
And we trimmed our sails
Till the night went by,
No less, no more,
Than stones on an English shore.

Then whimiscal Fate,
Resenting our state,
Decided to break us
And mould and re-make us;
Our sweet isolation
From civilization
Has all vanished away.
We're urban and proud
Supporting a crowd
Of Doxys and Dandys
And Regency Randys,
Who fiddle and faddle
And piddle and paddle
And turn night into day.
The Pavilion
Cost a million
As a monument to Art,
And the wits here
Say it sits here
Like an Oriental tart!
The dashing 'beau monde'
Has ruffled our pond
And even the turbot
Know Mrs Fitzherbert,
We're richer than ever before
But Brighton is Brighton no more,
No more
Brighton is Brighton no more.


# MELANIE'S ARIA

### *from* CONVERSATION PIECE

MELANIE: Dear Friends,
Will you forgive me, pray.
If many of the words I say
In English may be wrong.

ALL:      She hasn't been in England very long.

MELANIE: A stranger in a foreign land,
I beg that you will understand
How gratefully I find
The gentlemen so very kind,
So very kind.

> *(to the Duke of Beneden)*
> The offer of protection
> That Monsieur le Duc has made
> I set aside,
> For my foolish pride
> Would feel itself betrayed.

ALL: Charming! Charming! Charming!

MELANIE: *(to Lord St Marys)*
Monsieur, my Lord St Marys
Has made me an offer too.
Royal though his scheme may be,
It could never be part of a dream for me.

ALL: Ah la la la—la la—la la.

MELANIE: Handsome though your Prince may be
He is far too broad in the beam for me.

> *(to the Marquis of Sheere)*
> But there is one, one only,
> Who honours me with his heart,
> Although I'm not the wife for him
> I shall cherish all my life for him
> A feeling somehow apart.
> I'd suffer sorrow and strife for him.
> Though we may be lovers never,
> We're friends for ever—for evermore.

MELANIE: C'est assez de mensonge,
Le secret qui me ronge,
Que tout au fond de moi
J'ai tendrement gardé.
Enfin avec franchise
Il faut que je le dise,
Avouant mon secret,
Que tu n'as pas compris
Plus de cœur discret,
C'est toi qui par l'amour,
Toi qui m'as delivrée,
Je suis à toi toujours.
Esclave de mon cœur,
Me rendras-tu la vie
Je t'en supplie, crois-moi,
Lorsque je dis c'est toi
Plus de cœur discret.

C'est toi qui par l'amour,
Toi qui m'as delivrée,
Je suis à toi toujours.
Esclave de mon cœur,
Me rendras-tu la vie.
Je t'en supplie, crois-moi,
Je t'en supplie, crois-moi,
C'est toi.
Parmi le monde entier c'est toi que j'aime.
Je t'en supplie,
Crois-le si même
Tu ne le veux.
Toi,
Parmi le monde entier c'est toi que j'aime,
Je suis à toi toujours.


## MOTHERS AND WIVES

*from* CONVERSATION PIECE

QUARTETTE: In an atmosphere of bawdy jeu d'esprit
We contrive to be tenaciously conventional,
Though intelligent, we hope,
Our imaginative scope
When all is said and done
Is one-dimensional.
Our appearance should be ample guarantee
Of our vigorous and rigorous morality,
We regard our husbands' gout
As a proper and devout
And Godly recompense
For sensuality.
But when we look at our greying hairs
We sometimes sigh as we say our prayers,
Dear Lord, we're bored,
Is virtue enough reward?

# NEVERMORE

*from* CONVERSATION PIECE

Verse   Dear Friend,
If hearts could only be
Content with love and sympathy;
How sweetly we could live,
We both of us have so much love to give.
No matter how our minds conspire,
Imprisoned by our own desire,
We are not free to choose.
What love we gain,
What love we lose,
We cannot choose.

Refrain  Nevermore. Nevermore,
Can life be quite the same.
The lights and shadows change,
All the old familiar world is strange,
Evermore. Evermore,
Our hearts are in the flame.
Others may regain their freedom,
But for you and me,
Never-nevermore.

# *Tonight at 8.30*

## WE WERE DANCING

*from* TONIGHT AT 8.30: WE WERE DANCING

Verse 1   If you can
Imagine my embarrassment when you politely asked me to
    explain
Man to man,
I cannot help but feel conventional apologies are all in vain.
You must see.
We've stepped into a dream that's set us free,
Don't think we planned it,
Please understand it.

Refrain 1  We were dancing
And the gods must have found it entrancing
For they smiled
On a moment undefiled
By the care and woe
That mortals know.
We were dancing
And the music and lights were enhancing
Our desire,
When the world caught on fire,
She and I were dancing.

Verse 2   Love lay in wait for us,
Twisted our fate for us,
No one warned us,
Reason scorned us,
Time stood still
In that first strange thrill.
Destiny knew of us,
Guided the two of us,
How could we
Refuse to see
That wrong seemed right,
On this lyrical enchanted night?
Logic supplies no laws for it,
Only one cause for it.

Refrain 2   We were dancing
And the gods must have found it entrancing
For they smiled
On a moment undefiled
By the care and woe
That mortals know.
We were dancing
And the music and lights were enhancing
Our desire,
When the world caught on fire,
She and I were dancing.


# HAS ANYBODY SEEN OUR SHIP?

*from* TONIGHT AT 8.30: RED PEPPERS

Verse 1   What shall we do with the drunken sailor?
So the saying goes.
We're not tight but we're none too bright,
Great Scott! I don't suppose!
We've lost our way
And we've lost our pay,
And to make the thing complete,
We've been and gone and lost the bloomin' fleet!

Refrain 1   Has anybody seen our ship?
The H.M.S. Peculiar.
We've been on shore
For a month or more,
And when we see the Captain we shall get 'what for'.
Heave ho, me hearties,
Sing Glory Hallelujah,
A lady bold as she could be
Pinched our whistles at 'The Golden Key'.
Now we're in between the devil and the deep blue sea.
Has anybody seen our ship?

Verse 2   What's to be done with the girls on shore
Who lead our Tars astray?
What's to be done with the drinks galore
That make them pass away?
We got wet ears
From our first five beers—
After that we lost control,
And now we find we're up the blinking pole!

Refrain 2  Has anybody seen our ship?
           The H.M.S. Disgusting.
           We've three guns aft
           And another one fore
           And they've promised us a funnel for the next world war.
           Heave ho, me hearties,
           The quarterdeck needs dusting.
           We had a binge last Christmas year,
           Nice plum puddings and a round of beer,
           But the Captain pulled his cracker and we cried, 'Oh
               dear!'
           Has anybody seen our ship?

Refrain 3  Has anybody seen our ship?
           The H.M.S. Suggestive.
           She sailed away
           Across the bay,
           And we haven't had a smell of her since New Year's Day.
           Heave ho, me hearties,
           We're getting rather restive.
           We pooled our money, spent the lot,
           The world forgetting by the world forgot,
           Now we haven't got a penny for the you know what!
           Has anybody seen our ship?


## MEN ABOUT TOWN

*from* TONIGHT AT 8.30: RED PEPPERS

Verse   We're two chaps who
        Find it thrilling
        To do the killing,
        We're always willing
        To give the girls a treat.
        Just a drink at the Ritz,
        Call it double or quits,
        Then we feel the world is at our feet.
        Top hats, white spats
        Look divine on us,
        There's a shine on us,
        Get a line on us
        When we come your way.
        Gad! Eleven o'clock!
        Let's pop into the Troc.
        Ere we start the business of the day.

Refrain 1  As we stroll down Picc-Piccadilly
           In the bright morning air,
           All the girls turn and stare,
           We're so nonchalant and frightfully debonair.
           When we chat to Rose, Maud or Lily
           You should see the way their boy friends frown,
           For they know without a doubt
           That their luck's right out,
           Up against a couple of men about town.

Refrain 2  As we stroll down Picc-Piccadilly
           All the girls say, 'Who's here?
           Put your hat straight, my dear,
           For it's Marmaduke and Percy Vere de Vere.'
           As we doff hats, each pretty filly
           Gives a wink at us and then looks down
           For they long with all their might
           For a red-hot night
           When they see a couple of men about town.


# THEN

*from* TONIGHT AT 8.30: SHADOW PLAY


SIMON:  Here in the light of this unkind familiar now
        Every gesture is clear and cold for us,
        Every yesterday's growing old for us,
        Everything changed somehow,
        If some forgotten lover's vow
        Could wake a memory in my heart again,
        Perhaps the joys that we knew would start again.
        Can't we reclaim an hour or so?
        The past is not so long ago.


VICKY:  Then, love was complete for us,
        Then, the days were sweet for us,
        Life rose to its feet for us
        And stepped aside
        Before our pride.
        Then, we knew the best of it,
        Then, our hearts stood the test of it.
        Now, the magic has flown,
        We face the unknown,
        Apart and alone.

## PLAY, ORCHESTRA, PLAY

*from* TONIGHT AT 8.30: SHADOW PLAY

Listen to the strain
It plays once more for us,
There it is again,
The past in store for us.
Wake
In memory some forgotten song,
To break
The rhythm—driving us along
And make
Harmony again a last encore for us.

Play, orchestra, play,
Play something light and sweet and gay
For we must have music,
We must have music
To drive our fears away.
While our illusions
Swiftly fade for us,
Let's have an orchestra score
In the confusions
The years have made for us,
Serenade for us,
Just once more.
Life needn't be grey,
Although it's changing day by day,
Though a few old dreams may decay,
Play, orchestra, play.

## YOU WERE THERE

*from* TONIGHT AT 8.30: SHADOW PLAY

I

SIMON: Was it in the real world
Or was it in a dream?
Was it just a note from some eternal theme?
Was it accidental
Or accurately planned?
How could I hesitate
Knowing that my fate
Led me by the hand?

*Refrain*

You were there,
I saw you and my heart stopped beating,
You were there
And in that first enchanted meeting
Life changed its tune,
The stars, the moon
Came near to me.
Dreams that I dreamed,
Like magic seemed
To be clear to me, dear to me.
You were there.
Your eyes looked into mine and faltered.
Everywhere
The colour of the whole world altered.
False became true,
My universe tumbled in two,
The earth became heaven, for you
Were there.

2

VICKY: How can we explain it,
The spark, and then the fire?
How add up the total
Of our hearts' desire?
Maybe some magician,
A thousand years ago—
Wove us a subtle spell
So that we could tell
So that we could know—

*Refrain*

You were there,
I saw you and my heart stopped beating,
You were there
And in that first enchanted meeting
Life changed its tune,
The stars, the moon
Came near to me.
Dreams that I dreamed,
Like magic seemed
To be clear to me, dear to me.
You were there,
Your eyes looked into mine and faltered.
Everywhere

The colour of the whole world altered.
False became true,
My universe tumbled in two,
The earth became heaven, for you
Were there.


## DRINKING SONG

*from* TONIGHT AT 8.30.: FAMILY ALBUM

JASPER: Here's a toast to each of us
        And all of us together.
        Here's a toast to happiness
        And reasonable pride.
        May our touch on life be lighter
        Than a seabird's feather;
        May all sorrows as we pass
        Politely step aside.

JANE:   Jasper, my love,
        You ask for too much, I fear,
        What if your hopes
        Should never come true, my dear?
        Best be prepared for sorrow to stay
        At least for a day,
        At least for a day.
        How can we find
        The wisdom you dream for us?
        There must be tears
        In Destiny's scheme for us
        But if at last we're able to smile
        We'll prove it was all worth while!

JASPER: Now I drink to those of us who, happily united,
        Ornament our family and share our joy and pain.
        Charles, my friend, and Edward, too, connubially
            plighted,
        Last, my dears, but always best, my own beloved
            Jane.

JASPER: Harriet married a soldier,
        A man of pleasant birth,
        A man of sterling worth
        And finely tempered steel,

Ready to die for the Empire,
The sun must never set
Upon this brave but yet
Ambiguous ideal.
So now, dear Charles, I am saluting you,
That never-setting sun
Shall call you blest,
If far-off natives take to shooting you
You will at least have done
Your level best.

ALL:      Harriet married a soldier,
May life be bright for him;
May might be right for him
For ever and for aye.
Harriet married a soldier
And in the matrimonial fray,
Despite his glories in the field,
He'll have to honour and obey
And be defeated till Judgement day!

JASPER:   Now we come to Emily whose progress has been
             steady;
Only married two short years and three fat sons
   already.

Emily married a doctor,
A mild and gentle man,
A sentimental man
Of scientific mind.
Doing his best for the nation,
For ever dutiful,
A really beautiful
Example for the rest of us,
A challenge for the rest of us,
The noblest and the best of us combined.

JASPER:   Now then, for my dearest dear
I must ask your kind and grave indulgence for
How then, can I make it clear to you?

JANE:     Sweet love, I appreciate
All these noble sentiments, but time is so
Fleet, love, what's this hesitating for—
Waiting for?

JASPER: You, love,
For ever a part of me,
True love,
Enshrined in the heart of me,
Who cares
What dreams we may lose?
For ever we choose
This lovely illusion.

JANE: After the difficult years have fled
Laughter will mock at the tears we've shed.

BOTH: We hold the future in store
Together for evermore.

ALL: Here's a toast for each of them
And both of them together.
Here's a toast to happiness
And reasonable pride.
May their touch on life be lighter
Than a seabird's feather;
May their sorrows as they pass
Politely step aside.

## PRINCES AND PRINCESSES

*from* TONIGHT AT 8.30: FAMILY ALBUM

Princes and Princesses,
Every rainy day,
In our party dresses
Made a trifle gay
With a rose and a shawl,
We would act a play
In the servants' hall.

Lavvy was the evil Queen
Wickeder than Nero,
Jasper, being just thirteen,
Always played the hero.
Crown and sceptre,
Rose and ring,
Magic charms for everything.
Death, destruction, fire and flame
Was our Sunday game.

Princes and Princesses,
Every rainy day,
In our party dresses
Made a trifle gay
With a rose and shawl,
We would act a play
In the servants' hall.


## MUSIC BOX

*from* TONIGHT AT 8.30: FAMILY ALBUM

ALL:      Let's play a tune on the music box;
Let's play a tune on the music box.

BOYS:     Let the angels guide you,
Be good and brave and true.
Let the angels guide you,
Oh do! Oh do! Oh do!

GIRLS:    Let the angels guide you,
Be good and brave and true.
Let the angels guide you,
Oh do! Oh do! Oh do!

JANE:     Spurn each vile temptation,
Avoid each evil lure.

JASPER:   Keep your conversation
Inordinately pure.

EMILY:    Lift your hearts to heaven
And pray for ultimate grace.

ALL:      Be always virtuous just in case.

JANE:     But of course in this vale of tears
Life may sometimes cheat a bit.
Hearts are prone to beat a bit
Causing great confusion.
When temptation to sin appears
Try to be discreet a bit,
Look well before the leaping,
Dream true awake or sleeping,
Love tears are waste of weeping.
Let reason over-ride you, guide you.

ALL:        Look well before the leaping,
            Dream true awake or sleeping,
            Love tears are waste of weeping.
            Let reason be your guiding star.

JASPER:     Jane, I'm surprised, I'm ashamed of you;
            Such a material point of view.

            Keep your soul's endeavour
            Sufficiently sincere.
            Purity is ever
            An excellent veneer.
            Good may be rewarded
            In some indefinite place.

ALL:        Be always virtuous just in case.

JANE &      Death may have shaken us,
JASPER:     Gloom overtaken us,
            Life may awaken us yet.
            The sable plumes and cypresses
            We might as well forget.

LAVINIA:    Jasper, cry shame on you!
            Decency's claim on you
            Should at this moment prevent
            Such bad, impertinent
            Ungodly argument.

ALL:        Let the angels guide you,
            Be good and brave and true.
            Let the angels guide you,
            Oh do! Oh do! Oh do!
            Spurn each vile temptation,
            Avoid each evil lure.
            Keep your conversation
            Inordinately pure.
            Good may be rewarded
            In some indefinite place;
            Be always virtuous just in case.

# HEARTS AND FLOWERS

*from* TONIGHT AT 8.30: FAMILY ALBUM

JANE:    Hearts and Flowers,
Dreaming hours
Under skies of blue,
Two fond hearts so sweetly beat in tune
'Neath the midnight magic of the moon.
Petals falling,
Love-birds softly calling,
Life begins anew,
When Cupid's dart discloses
The secret of the roses,
Hearts and Flowers and You.

JANE &  Hearts and Flowers,
JASPER: Bygone hours,
How the time has flown!

JASPER: You wore white camellias in your hair;

JANE:    All you did was hold my hand and stare;

BOTH:   Have we altered,
Have our footsteps faltered
Through the years we've known?
When all our days are done, love,
There'll still be only one love,
You and you alone.

# *Operette*

*from* OPERETTE

Ladies and Gentlemen,
With your very kind permission
In accordance with tradition
We appear.
Unsentimental men
May declare us nauseating,
But by clear articulating
We are bent upon creating
Atmosphere.
We represent those carefree days
That still retained a bland hypocrisy
And looked upon Democracy
As quaint—
A certain transitory phase
Which every accurate historian
Has blamed upon Victorian
Restraint.
Our life was gay,
Champagne adorning it,
It passed away
And left us mourning it.
We've run our race
Time can't replace
These years of grace.
Non-temperamental men,
We implore you to surrender
To a mood of gay and tender
Sentiment.
Ladies and Gentlemen,
Though we wish our words were clearer,
If they've brought your memory nearer
To the light Edwardian Era
We're content—
We've said our fill
Without much skill,
But thank you very very much for keeping still.

# THE OPENING CHORUS

*from* OPERETTE: THE MODEL MAID

Hurray! Hurray!
We're ever so gay
And French as French can be,
We say 'Merci'
And 'This is the Vie'
Without exactly proving much.
We might as well be Russian or Dutch
Or Japanese,
Our sole intention is to please;
We're so vivacious
That we carry all before us
Prancing about beside the silver sea.
But goodness gracious
It it wasn't for the Chorus
Dancing about where would the Peerage be?
Hurray! Hurray!
We're ever so gay,
We smile and smirk and grin
Through thick and thin,
We'll never give in.
And though we tear ourselves to shreds
And wear these foolish hats on our heads
And do high kicks,
We all rehearsed with Seymour Hicks
In Trouville—Trouville—Trouville—Nineteen-six.
On the Plage
Where the shady little ladies are at large,
It's Continental Hades
Where you sell your soul for this and that and those,
Spend your money
On milk and honey
And frills and furbelows.
If you're rich
You can take Yvette
To play roulette,
For which
She'll overcharge;
But nevertheless when day is done
A man must have a little fun
And fun is fun at Trouville on the Plage.

## POM-POM

*from* OPERETTE: THE MODEL MAID

Hurrah—Hurrah!
Wherever we are
We'll cheer until we're blue
The famous new
Couturier who,
With velvet, crêpe de chine and lace,
Can help us in the horrible race
To commandeer
The nearest eligible Peer,
So lift your voices up and cheer
For Pom-Pom—Pom-Pom—Darling Pom-Pom's here!

## COUNTESS MITZI

*from* OPERETTE: THE MODEL MAID

### Verse 1

MITZI:    My Father was Hungarian,
          My Mother came from Spain,
          I've several Aunts
          In the South of France
          And a Grandmamma—Maternal Grandmamma
          In the Ukraine.

CHORUS:   She went too far—poor Grandmamma,
          For it's cold in the old Ukraine.

MITZI:    My Uncle is Bavarian,
          I'm quite a pet of his,
          So if I'm not
          A Polyglot
          I should like to know who is!

CHORUS:   If she's not a Polyglot we should like to know who is.

### Refrain

MITZI:    They call me Countess Mitzi,
          But I can't imagine why,
          For my name is really Ludovika
          Anastasie Frederika Isabel Rosa Mariposa Nikinikolai.

CHORUS: We can perfectly well see why
        That to alter it people try;

MITZI:  For they'd rather say 'Countess Mitzi'
        Just a teensy weensy bitsie,
        Than a string of names like Ludovika
        Anastasie Frederika Isabel Rosa Mariposa Nikinikolai.

*Verse 2*

MITZI:  My Grandpapa on Mother's side
        Was far more East than West,
        He spent his life
        With a Chinese wife
        In a mental home—half-Oriental home
        In Bucharest.

CHORUS: What cruel fate!
        We'd simply hate
        To be 'batty' in Bucharest.

MITZI:  My Grandma on the other side
        Was Russian to the core,
        She danced in Kiev
        But came to grief
        In a brawl in Singapore.

CHORUS: Ah, what a blow
        To sink so low
        As a brawl in Singapore.

*Reprise*

MITZI:  Beware of Countess Mitzi,
        The world will tell you why,
        For my name is really
        Ludovika—Anastasie—Frederika
        Isabel—Rosa—Mariposa
        Nikinikolai.
        You can perfectly well see why
        People think I've a naughty eye
        For they'd rather say Countess Mitzi
        Just a teensy weensy bitsie
        Than a string of names like
        Ludovika—Anastasie—Frederika
        Isabel—Rosa—Mariposa
        Nikinikolai!

# DEAREST LOVE

*from* OPERETTE: THE MODEL MAID

JOHN: I saw your face,
Shadows of the morning cleared,
I knew that suddenly
The world had dropped away.

MARY: Somewhere in space
Some new lovely star appeared
To rule our destiny
For ever and a day.

JOHN: I knew, the moment that I touched your hand,
The gods had planned
Our meeting.

MARY: Now in this instant in the whole of Time
Our lovers' rhyme
Is near completing.

JOHN: I saw you turn away and for a while
My poor heart drooped and faltered;
And then I saw your strange elusive smile
And all my life was altered.

BOTH: My dearest dear,
For evermore
The happiness we've waited for
At last is here.

*Refrain*

JOHN: Dearest Love,
Now that I've found you
The stars change in the sky,
Every song is new,
Every note is true,
Sorrows like the clouds go sailing by.

MARY: Here, my Love,
Magic has bound you
To me—ever to be
In my heart supreme,
Dearer than my dearest dream,
The only love for me.

JOHN: Skies that were cloudy are clear again,
        All other people seem
        Like figures in a dream;

MARY: Every song that I loved I seem to hear again,
        Time goes by like a murmuring stream.

JOHN: Love has enchanted the two of us,
        A magic we can share,
        A something in the air,

MARY: Proving that Destiny knew of us
        Now Heaven is at our feet,
        This happiness complete
        Could not be merely chance,
        This exquisite romance

BOTH: For ever has us bound,
        For this that we have found
        No time or tide could sever—ever.

        Dearest Love,
        Now that I've found you
        The stars change in the sky,
        Every song is new,
        Every note is true,
        Sorrows like the clouds go sailing by.
        Here, my Love,
        Magic has bound you
        To me—ever to be
        In my heart supreme,
        Dearer than my dearest dream,
        The only love for me!


### FOOLISH VIRGINS
(Double Sextette)

*from* OPERETTE: THE MODEL MAID

MEN:   Here are ladies,
        Charming ladies,
        A fascinating flock of them—
        Our hearts are taking stock of them;
        No well-respected amorist
        Could be expected to resist

This lovely group
Of femininity,
So we stoop
On bended knee.

GIRLS: Here are gentlemen,
Handsome gentlemen,
Though conscience may be muttering,
Our hearts insist on fluttering;
We feel today our luck is in
But can't betray our genuine
Relief to meet
So much virility
At our feet
In all humility,
None the less
Our gay fragility
They mustn't guess.

MEN: Dear little ladies, we beseech you
Not to be deaf to what we say,
If our romantic thoughts could reach you
Maybe you'd consent to stay
And not be too offended;
We should think it splendid
If you'd just consent to stay.

GIRLS: If we were offended
We'd go away,
But we must not appear too willing
Lest you should think us not quite nice,
Though we admit it might be thrilling
Just for once to sacrifice
Our sense of obligation
To our education,
Which was very strict and stern.

MEN: What is education
If not to learn?
Just a stroll beside the ocean
Might be a notion
More or less acceptable to moral views.

GIRLS: It really would be too ungracious to refuse.

MEN: After that delicious ramble
We might enjoy a little gamble:

GIRLS: Backing your luck may be a thrill
But we prefer a game of skill.

MEN:   Later on with Moët Chandon
You might abandon
All disturbing fears of what Mamma would think.

GIRLS: You surely don't suppose we'd ever take to drink!

MEN:   Later still we might persuade you
To take a swim as Nature made you.

GIRLS: Fie and for shame, you go too far,
Kindly remember that we are:

*Refrain*

One  little
Two  little
Three little
Four little
Five little
Six little
Foolish Virgins
Eager to be some good man's wife
And learn the facts of life.
Neat little
Sweet little
Shy little
Sly little
Meek little
Chic little
Chicks emergin'
Out of the shell that held them fast
At last—at last—at last.
Please excuse our artless prattling,
We're as green as nuts in May,
On the loose and almost rattling
For the matrimonial fray.
We've one little
Two little
Three little
Four little
Five little
Six little ego's urgin'
Any rich man we chance to see
To take us on a spree
With a substantial guarantee,
Foolish Virgins we.

# THE STATELY HOMES OF ENGLAND
## (Quartette)

### *from* OPERETTE

Verse 1    Lord Elderley, Lord Borrowmere,
           Lord Sickert and Lord Camp
           With every virtue, every grace,
           Ah what avails the sceptred race,
           Here you see—the four of us,
           And there are so many more of us
           Eldest sons that must succeed.
           We know how Caesar conquered Gaul
           And how to whack a cricket ball;
           Apart from this, our education
           Lacks co-ordination.
           Though we're young and tentative
           And rather rip-representative,
           Scions of a noble breed,
           We are the products of those homes serene and stately
           Which only lately
           Seem to have run to seed!

Refrain 1  The Stately Homes of England,
           How beautiful they stand,
           To prove the upper classes
           Have still the upper hand;
           Though the fact that they have to be rebuilt
           And frequently mortgaged to the hilt
           Is inclined to take the gilt
           Off the gingerbread,
           And certainly damps the fun
           Of the eldest son—
           But still we won't be beaten,
           We'll scrimp and scrape and save,
           The playing fields of Eton
           Have made us frightfully brave—
           And though if the Van Dycks have to go
           And we pawn the Bechstein Grand,
           We'll stand
           By the Stately Homes of England.

Verse 2    Here you see
           The pick of us,
           You may be heartily sick of us,
           Still with sense

We're all imbued.
Our homes command extensive views
And with assistance from the Jews
We have been able to dispose of
Rows and rows and rows of
Gainsboroughs and Lawrences,
Some sporting prints of Aunt Florence's,
Some of which were rather rude.
Although we sometimes flaunt our family conventions,
Our good intentions
Mustn't be misconstrued.

Refrain 2   The Stately Homes of England
We proudly represent,
We only keep them up for
Americans to rent.
Though the pipes that supply the bathroom burst
And the lavatory makes you fear the worst,
It was used by Charles the First
Quite informally,
And later by George the Fourth
On a journey north.
The State Apartments keep their
Historical renown,
It's wiser not to sleep there
In case they tumble down;
But still if they ever catch on fire
Which, with any luck, they might
We'll fight
For the Stately Homes of England.

Refrain 3   The Stately Homes of England,
Though rather in the lurch,
Provide a lot of chances
For Psychical Research—
There's the ghost of a crazy younger son
Who murdered, in thirteen fifty-one,
An extremely rowdy Nun
Who resented it,
And people who come to call
Meet her in the hall.
The baby in the guest wing,
Who crouches by the grate,
Was walled up in the west wing
In fourteen twenty-eight.
If anyone spots
The Queen of Scots

In a hand-embroidered shroud
We're proud
Of the Stately Homes of England.

*Reprise—Act II*

Verse 3   Lord Elderley, Lord Borrowmere,
Lord Sickert and Lord Camp,
Behold us in our hours of ease,
Uncertain, coy and hard to please.
Reading in Debrett of us,
This fine Patrician quartette of us,
We can feel extremely proud,
Our ancient lineage we trace
Back to the cradle of the Race
Before those beastly Roman bowmen
Bitched our local Yeomen.
Though the new democracy
May pain the old Aristocracy
We've not winced nor cried aloud,
Under the bludgeonings of chance what will be—will be.
Our heads will still be
Bloody but quite unbowed!

Refrain 4   The Stately Homes of England
In valley, dale and glen
Produce a race of charming,
Innocuous young men.
Though our mental equipment may be slight
And we barely distinguish left from right,
We are quite prepared to fight
For our principles,
Though none of us know so far
What they really are.
Our duty to the nation,
It's only fair to state,
Lies not in pro-creation
But what we pro-create;
And so we can cry
With kindling eye
As to married life we go,
What ho!
For the Stately Homes of England!

Refrain 5   The Stately Homes of England,
Although a trifle bleak,
Historically speaking,
Are more or less unique.

We've a cousin who won the Golden Fleece
And a very peculiar fowling-piece
Which was sent to Cromwell's niece,
Who detested it,
And rapidly sent it back
With a dirty crack.
A note we have from Chaucer
Contains a bawdy joke.
We also have a saucer
That Bloody Mary broke.
We've two pairs of tights
King Arthur's Knights
Had completely worn away.
Sing Hey!
For the Stately Homes of England!

# WHERE ARE THE SONGS WE SUNG?

*from* OPERETTE

Verse  Once in a lifetime
When we are very very young—and Love
Comes out to greet us for the first time,
We open wide our arms and say to him
This is the only, and the last time.
That young surrender
We can remember when some little tune
Recalls our hearts to vanished splendour
Like organ music in a sunny street
So sweetly flat—so sadly tender.

And so when Love again rides by
We sometimes sigh:

Refrain 1 Where are the songs we sung
When Love in our hearts was young?
Where, in the limbo of the swiftly passing years,
Lie all our hopes and dreams and fears?
Where have they gone—words that rang so true
When Love in our hearts was new?
Where in the shadows that we have to pass among,
Lie those songs that once we sung?

Refrain 2　Where are the songs we sung
　　　　　When Love in our hearts was young?
　　　　　Can you remember all the foolish things we said,
　　　　　The plans we planned—the tears we shed?
　　　　　Where is it now—that enchanted dawn
　　　　　When Love in our hearts was born?
　　　　　Where, in the shadows that we have to pass among,
　　　　　Lie those songs that once we sung?


# THE ISLAND OF BOLLAMAZOO

*from* OPERETTE: THE MODEL MAID

### *Refrain 1*

ALL:　　　On the Island of Bollamazoo
　　　　　Life is almost too good to be true.

POM-POM:　You can fish on a reef
　　　　　Wearing pearls and a leaf
　　　　　Which at Brighton you never could do.
　　　　　For a few coloured beads from the Penny Bazaar
　　　　　You can buy luscious oysters wherever you are
　　　　　And you don't have to wait for a month with an R
　　　　　On the Island of Bollamazoo.

ALL:　　　On the Island of Bollamazoo
　　　　　Life is almost too good to be true.

POM-POM:　You don't have to care what your neighbours might think
　　　　　If a charming young lady should give you a wink
　　　　　You can buy her outright for the price of a drink
　　　　　On the Island of Bollamazoo.

### *Refrain 2*

ALL:　　　On the Island of Bollamazoo
　　　　　Life is almost too good to be true.

POM-POM:　No one ever gets warm
　　　　　Over Tariff Reform
　　　　　And the thought of Home Rule is taboo.
　　　　　Unlike Campbell-Bannerman's dignified pose
　　　　　The local Prime Minister welcomes his foes
　　　　　With a club in one hand and a ring through his nose
　　　　　On the Island of Bollamazoo.

ALL:        On the Island of Bollamazoo
            Life is almost too good to be true.

POM-POM:    The ladies are dusky, domestic and fair,
            For the suffragette movement they wouldn't much care,
            And they'd think 'Votes for Women' were something to wear
            On the Island of Bollamazoo.


## PROLOGUE ACT II

### *from* OPERETTE

Ladies and Gentlemen,
Though it wasn't our ambition
To succeed the intermission,
Here we are,
Ladies and Gentlemen,
Do not think us too ironic
If we hope you've quenched your chronic
Thirst for Scotch or Gin and Tonic
In the Bar.

We now begin the Second Act
Which we believe will be effectual
And not too intellectual
A bore—
But still we cannot blink the fact
That though you get a little wit through us
It's hard to have to sit through us
Once more.
The only vindication for us is
We're like those classical Greek Choruses
Who made the curse
Of laboured verse
A great deal worse.
Bluff Regimental men
Would—we feel—prefer a frolic
To this rather mock-symbolic
Rhymed refrain.
Ladies and Gentlemen,
Do not think the author cheated,
This effect has been repeated
Once again;
Although we lack
Charm and attack
We thank you very, very much for coming back.

## SING FOR JOY

*from* OPERETTE: THE MODEL MAID

MARY:    Rhapsody—there is rhapsody
In the atmosphere.

CHORUS:    The lady is enchanted.
The lady is enchanted.

MARY:    My dearest wish is granted,
My heart had found wings,
Each moment brings
My lover near.

CHORUS:    Each fleeting moment brings him near.

MARY:    Every note of my song he'll hear,
True and clear,
Love is here,
Love is here,
He'll answer.

Sing for joy,
I will echo it,
Sing for Joy,
Let the music play,
Lifting us away
Beyond retreating,
Lyrically meeting
To the tune that our hearts are beating.
This moment is divine, love,
Yours and mine, love,
This melody enthralling,
Calling—calling.
Sing for Joy,
I will echo it,
Tra la la—tra la la, tra la la—tra la la,
Sing for the joy of love.
Ah ah ah ah
Ah ah ah ah

CHORUS:    Let their heaven last,
The future and the past
Merging in the dream they're sharing.

MARY:      Ah ah ah ah
          Ah ah ah ah.

CHORUS:    Now no matter how the Gods conspire
          This moment is their hearts' desire.

MARY:      Joy is the song I sing to you.
          Ever new,
          Ever true.

          Sing for Joy,
          I will echo it,
          Sing for Joy,
          Let the music play,
          Lifting us away
          Beyond retreating,
          Lyrically meeting
          To the tune that our hearts are beating.
          This moment is divine, love,
          Yours and mine, love,
          This melody enthralling,
          Calling—calling.
          Sing for Joy,
          I will echo it,
          Tra la la—tra la la
          Tra la la—tra la la,
          Sing for the joy of love.


## MY DEAR MISS DALE

*from* OPERETTE: THE MODEL MAID

'My dear Miss Dale,
When you receive this letter
I shall be far away,
And hope you will forgive me when I say
That it is better
For you and I
To say goodbye . . . '

'Trust must prevail
And in our hearts' confusion
Whatever love we give
It's better far that we should learn to live
Without illusion . . . '

What have I done that you should treat me so?
What bitter Fate should wish to cheat me so?
Why should this hour of happiness supreme
Change to despair with the swiftness of a troubled dream?
I only know all my love I gave to you
With happy heart willingly a slave to you,
This foolish heart that you have so cruelly betrayed
I now withdraw from you,
For ever more from you,
For ever more!

# OPERETTE

### *from* OPERETTE: THE MODEL MAID

GIRLS: Tell us, darling Liesl, please,
How you became a star:
Was it hard in the beginning?
Were you sinned against?—Or were you sinning?

LIESL: In reconstructing my career for you
I must make one thing clear for you,
That's only fair.

GIRLS: We'll concentrate with all our might.

LIESL: Be under no misapprehension,
I do not intend to mention
Who my lovers were,

GIRLS: How disappointing, but how right!

LIESL: But all the same
You will agree
An artist's life can never be
Quite free from blame.
But don't forget
And try to see
That everything in life to me
Is Operette.

Ever since a child of tender age
The world has been a stage
For me to dance upon;

Wedding bells could never ring for me,
The only thing for me
Was 'Getting On'.
I made my start
While other girls were having love affairs,
I set my heart
Upon a destiny above affairs,
Throughout my lonely youth
I knew too much reality,
So now my only truth
Is artificiality.
But if some light refrain
Can make me live again
Then you can really clearly see
All that I am or wish to be.

*Refrain*
Something remembered of joy and regret,
That's Operette—that's Operette!
Melodies that call to mind forgotten laughter,
Songs that linger in the memory for ever after,
That was my start,
That is my heart,
Life for me is ever orchestrated,
Everywhere my scene is set,
Singers of songs have the world in their debt.
Memories that Time can never stop,
For ever Operette!

# *Miscellaneous*

## SOMEDAY I'LL FIND YOU

*from* PRIVATE LIVES

Verse 1   When one is lonely the days are long;
You seem so near
But never appear.
Each night I sing you a lover's song;
Please try, try to hear,
My dear, my dear.

Verse 2   Can't you remember the fun we had?
Time is so fleet,
Why shouldn't we meet?
When you're away from me days are sad;
Life's not complete,
My sweet, my sweet.

Refrain   Some day I'll find you,
Moonlight behind you,
True to the dream I am dreaming
As I draw near you
You'll smile a little smile;
For a little while
We shall stand
Hand in hand.
I'll leave you never,
Love you for ever,
All our past sorrow redeeming,
Try to make it true,
Say you love me too.
Someday I'll find you again.

## MOST OF EVERY DAY

Time makes a mess of things,
Oh what a mess of things
Time makes!
Time breaks a lot of things,

Oh what a lot of things
Time breaks!
Now I'm apart from you
Remembering
Joys that we both of us knew
Time keeps on beating,
Repeating, repeating
My heartaches.

Refrain  Most of every day,
Most of every hour of every day
I'm thinking of you,
Lovely one;
When you turned away,
When you smiled that smile and turned away
I knew we were through,
Lovely one.
Still my foolish heart insists on aching,
No release
Asleep or waking,
Most of every day,
Most of every hour of every day
I'm thinking of you.


# I TRAVEL ALONE

Verse    The world is wide, and when my day is done
I shall at least have travelled free,
Led by this wanderlust that turns my eyes to far horizons.
Though time and tide won't wait for anyone,
There's one illusion left for me
And that's the happiness I've known alone.

Refrain  I travel alone,
Sometimes I'm East,
Sometimes I'm West,
No chains can ever bind me;
No remembered love can ever find me;
I travel alone.
Fair though the faces and places I've known,
When the dream is ended and passion has flown
I travel alone.
Free from love's illusion, my heart is my own:
I travel alone.

## MRS WORTHINGTON

Regarding yours, dear Mrs Worthington,
Of Wednesday the 23rd,
Although your baby,
Maybe,
Keen on a stage career,
How can I make it clear,
That this is not a good idea.
For her to hope,
Dear Mrs Worthington,
Is on the face of it absurd,
Her personality
Is not in reality
Inviting enough,
Exciting enough
For this particular sphere.

Refrain 1  Don't put your daughter on the stage, Mrs Worthington,
Don't put your daughter on the stage,
The profession is overcrowded
And the struggle's pretty tough
And admitting the fact
She's burning to act,
That isn't quite enough.
She has nice hands, to give the wretched girl her due,
But don't you think her bust is too
Developed for her age,
I repeat
Mrs Worthington,
Sweet
Mrs Worthington,
Don't put your daughter on the stage.

Refrain 2  Don't put your daughter on the stage, Mrs Worthington,
Don't put your daughter on the stage,
She's a bit of an ugly duckling
You must honestly confess,
And the width of her seat
Would surely defeat
Her chances of success,
It's a loud voice, and though it's not exactly flat,
She'll need a little more than that
To earn a living wage.
On my knees,

Mrs Worthington,
Please
Mrs Worthington,
Don't put your daughter on the stage.

Refrain 3     Don't put your daughter on the stage, Mrs Worthington,
Don't put your daughter on the stage,
Though they said at the school of acting
She was lovely as Peer Gynt,
I'm afraid on the whole
An ingénue role
Would emphasize her squint,
She's a big girl, and though her teeth are fairly good
She's not the type I ever would
Be eager to engage,
No more buts,
Mrs Worthington,
NUTS,
Mrs Worthington,
Don't put your daughter on the stage.

Refrain 4     Don't put your daughter on the stage, Mrs Worthington,
Don't put your daughter on the stage,
One look at her bandy legs should prove
She hasn't got a chance,
In addition to which
The son of a bitch
Can neither sing nor dance,
She's a *vile* girl and uglier than mortal sin,
One look at her has put me in
A tearing bloody rage,
That sufficed,
Mrs Worthington,
Christ!
Mrs Worthington,
Don't put your daughter on the stage.

*The Forties*

# NOTE ON 'THE FORTIES'

When the Second World War began in 1939 I decided, with tight-lipped patriotism, to renounce all creative impulse for the duration and devote myself hook, line and sinker to the service of my country. This gesture, admirable as it appeared to me at the time, turned out on more mature consideration to be a rather silly one. Even at the beginning when I was working in Paris in charge of a Propaganda Office, I was impelled by my inherent passion for making rhymes to write daily verses not only to members of my staff but to my loved ones in England. Later on, after the fall of France, when I set forth on my incessant journeys round the globe, a spate of lyrics gushed out of me. Much of this output was dictated by circumstances, for wherever I went, from Australia to South Africa, from the Gold Coast to the jungles of Assam and Burma, from the blazing heat of the Persian Gulf in August to Malta, Gibraltar, Scapa Flow, Cairo, Jerusalem, Mombasa and India's Coral Strand, there were always troops sweating out the dreary years and starving for entertainment. Accompanying me on many of these trips both corporeally and on the piano was my old friend, Norman Hackforth, who had, years before, appeared in a minor role in *Bitter Sweet*. It was he who cherished and tuned the piano when we were able to travel a piano and he who coped valiantly with the noteless, tuneless horrors we were faced with in camps and messes when we were not able to travel a piano. Rain or shine, drought or monsoon, there was Norman bashing out my accompaniments on those monstrous instruments with as much careless insouciance as if he had been playing on a series of Steinway Grands. During these far-flung peregrinations, when I was called upon to perform solo for an hour and a half, frequently four or five times a day, it was obviously necessary to acquire as large a repertoire as possible. I remember cabling to Cole Porter to ask his permission to re-write 'Let's Do It'. He gave it generously. 'Let's Do It' was not only a great song as he originally wrote it but it happens to have a rhyming scheme which can be utilized indefinitely without destroying the basic metre. I wrote special refrains for the Navy, the Army, the Air Force, hospital nurses, civic receptions, etc., etc. and have continued to use it as a 'finisher' to this day. It has never failed me. In addition to this it was all that convulsive travelling that produced 'Nina', 'Uncle Harry', 'I Wonder What Happened To Him' and countless other lyrics. In fact, from the lyric-writing point of view, 'The Forties', apart from their more obvious disadvantages, were for me exceedingly productive years.

# Sigh No More

## SIGH NO MORE

*from* SIGH NO MORE

Poor mournful ladies
Are you weeping for a dream
Once dreamed?
Are you still listening for some remembered
Theme
That seemed
To promise happiness and love and gentle years
Devoid of fears?
Sweet music starts again
Lift up your hearts again,
And dry, ah, dry those tears.

Refrain   Sigh no more, sigh no more.
Grey clouds of sorrow fill the sky no more.
Cry no more,
Die no more
Those little deaths at parting,
New life and new love are starting,
Sing again, sing again,
The winter's over and it's spring again.
Joy is your
Troubadour,
Sweet and beguiling ladies, sigh no more,
Sigh no more,
Sweet and beguiling ladies, sigh no more.


## THE PARTING OF THE WAYS

*from* SIGH NO MORE

HE:   You're looking just as you used to look,
Almost the same coloured dress,
Nothing is changed
And your hair's still arranged
With that light, unforgotten finesse.

207

Gay lady out of a story book,
I miss that flame-coloured scarf,
You left it behind
When we went out to find
All those bluebells—remember? Don't laugh!
Later we dined and saw a show,
That was a long time ago.

### Refrain 1

We've reached the parting of the ways,
That melancholy phrase is true,
The days we knew
Are ending.
We know that though we may be hurt
The only thing that's certain is
The curtain is
Descending.
Stars have faded,
Our hearts are jaded,
Enchantment loses its glow,
No use pleading
When love lies bleeding
And so heigho.
We know now the ending of our song,
Our love affair was horrid and it lasted far too long.

SHE: You haven't changed, not a little bit,
Same old half-cynical smile,
I see you now,
Overdressed, in the prow
Of that houseboat we hired on the Nile.
Do you remember those exquisite
Oysters we had in Peking?
And the stale caviar
That we ate in the bar
Of the Station Hotel in King's Lynn?
What a sophisticated pair
And what a dull love affair!

### Refrain 2

We've reached the parting of the ways,
One more depressing phase is through,
I gaze at you dumbfounded,
This is our final rendezvous
My little love canoe, my dear,
With you, my dear,
Is grounded.

While we bickered
The love-light flickered
And burned unpleasantly low,
Cupid clocked out,
We've both been knocked out
And so heigho.
There's no sense in waiting for the gong,
Our love affair was horrid and it lasted *far* too long.

## MOTHER AND DAUGHTER

*from* SIGH NO MORE

(The setting is a reproduction of a full page in the
*Illustrated London News* circa 1905)
(The MOTHER and DAUGHTER are posed artistically
in the manner of the day)
(The whole scene is in different shades of black and
white and grey)

MOTHER:     In the broad Edwardian era
            Forty years ago
            Virtue was undoubtedly dearer,
            Marriage had a clearer
            Status Quo

DAUGHTER:  That was very long ago,
           That was very long ago.

MOTHER:     Though young girls about to be mated
            Couldn't pick and choose
            In the *Illustrated*
            *London News*.

DAUGHTER:  Though they couldn't pick and choose
           They were definitely news.
           Fond Mama
           Stiff with pride
           Basking firmly in reflected glory.

MOTHER:     Fond Mama,
            Sweet young bride,
            What a thoroughly successful story,
            Marriage was the crowning glory
            Girls could choose.

DAUGHTER: No—no—no,
No—no—no,
Married bliss was always over-rated
Even in the *Illustrated*
*London News.*

BOTH:     Moments from life that you could never lose
Framed in the *Illustrated London News.*
Mother and daughter both doing well,
Tralalalala—tralalalala—tralalalalalalalalala*lala*,
Elderly doe and timid gazelle,
Tralalalala—tralalalala—tralalalalalalalala—la *lala*.

MOTHER:   Just a mother

DAUGHTER: With her daughter

BOTH:     In a pose triumphant and meek.
Has the mother
Taught her daughter
Any really useful technique?
Tralalalalalalalalalala
Tralalalalalalalalalala
Tralalalalalalalalalala—lalalalala—*la la la.*
Though the mother
Taught her daughter
How to look both modest and shy,
Then the camera
Fairly caught her
With that steely glint in her eye.
Tralala etc., etc.
A most resolute glint in her eye,
And a camera, like Washington, can't tell a lie.

BOTH:     Mother and daughter both doing well,
Fully blown rose and bud.

MOTHER:   Better to laugh
While quaffing Moselle
Than to stay gently mooing
And chewing
The cud.

DAUGHTER: When the heart is young
Sentimental songs are sung,
There are primroses on the ground.

MOTHER:    But when youth is gone
You must base your dreams upon
Something more commercially sound.

BOTH:    Two of a kind
Resolved and refined,
Binding an age-old spell,
Any observer could tell
Mother and daughter both doing well.

BOTH:    Mother and daughter both doing well,
Ah, what a graceful phrase,
Amorous thrill
We're willing to sell
For a nice dividend
To the end
Of our days.
In another class
We should be as bold as brass,
But in High Society—no.
We should miss the bus
If we were promiscuous
It would overcome comme-il-faut,
Ladies who leer
Aren't likely to hear
Chimes of a wedding bell.
Though self-control can be hell,
Mother and daughter both doing well.


# I WONDER WHAT HAPPENED TO HIM

*from* SIGH NO MORE

Verse 1    The India that one read about
And may have been misled about
In one respect has kept itself intact.
Though 'Pukka Sahib' traditions may have cracked
And thinned
The good old Indian army's still a fact.
That famous monumental man
The Officer and Gentleman
Still lives and breathes and functions from Bombay to
    Katmandu.

At any moment one can glimpse
Matured or embryonic 'Blimps'
Vivaciously speculating as to what became of who.
Though Eastern sounds may fascinate your ear
When West meets West you're always sure to hear—

Refrain 1    Whatever became of old Bagot?
I haven't seen him for a year.
Is it true that young Forbes had to marry that Faggot
He met in the Vale of Kashmir?
Have you had any news
Of that chap in the 'Blues',
Was it Prosser or Pyecroft or Pym?
He was stationed in Simla, or was it Bengal?
I know he got tight at a ball in Nepal
And wrote several four-letter words on the wall.
I wonder what happened to him!

Refrain 2    Whatever became of old Shelley?
Is it true that young Briggs was cashiered
For riding quite nude on a push-bike through Delhi
The day the new Viceroy appeared?
Have you had any word
Of that bloke in the 'Third',
Was it Southerby, Sedgwick or Sim?
They had him thrown out of the club in Bombay
For, apart from his mess bills exceeding his pay,
He took to pig-sticking in *quite* the wrong way.
I wonder what happened to him!

Verse 2    One must admit that by and large
Upholders of the British Raj
Don't shine in conversation as a breed.
Though Indian army officers can read
A bit
Their verbal wit—has rather run to seed.
Their splendid insularity
And roguish jocularity
Was echoing through when Victoria was Queen.
In restaurants and dining-cars,
In messes, clubs and hotel bars
They try to maintain tradition in the way it's always been.
Though worlds may change and nations disappear
Above the shrieking chaos you will hear—

Refrain 3    Whatever became of old Tucker?
             Have you heard any word of young Mills
             Who ruptured himself at the end of a chukka
             And had to be sent to the hills?
             They say that young Lees
             Had a go of 'D.T.s'
             And his hopes of promotion are slim.
             According to Stubbs, who's a bit of a louse,
             The silly young blighter went out on a 'souse',
             And took two old tarts into Government House.
             I wonder what happened to him!

Refrain 4    Whatever became of old Keeling?
             I hear that he got back from France
             And frightened three nuns in a train in Darjeeling
             By stripping and waving his lance!
             D'you remember Munroe,
             In the P.A.V.O.?
             He was tallish and mentally dim.
             That talk of heredity can't be quite true,
             He was dropped on his head by his ayah at two,
             I presume that by now he'll have reached G.H.Q.
             I'm sure that's what happened to him!

Refrain 5    Whatever became of old Archie?
             I hear he departed this life
             After rounding up ten sacred cows in Karachi
             To welcome the Governor's wife.
             D'you remember young Phipps
             Who had *very* large hips
             And whose waist was excessively slim?
             Well, it seems that some doctor in Grosvenor Square
             Gave him hormone injections for growing his hair
             And he grew something here, and he grew something
                there.
             I wonder what happened to her—him?

## NEVER AGAIN

*from* SIGH NO MORE and SET TO MUSIC
New York, 1938

> Over now,
> The dream is over now,
> Maybe it really wasn't so important anyhow.
> What's been can't be again
> Reluctantly I see,
> My heart is free again,
> Belongs to me again,
> The brief illusion I lived for has gone.
> No more confusion and tears from now on;
> To start again
> And break my heart again
> If you should ask me to,
> I'd say, 'To hell with you!
> Away with you!'

Refrain  No, never again,
> Never the strange unthinking joy,
> Never the pain;
> Let me be wise,
> Let me learn to doubt romance,
> Try to live without romance,
> Let me be sane.
> Time changes the tune.
> Changes the pale unwinking stars,
> Even the moon,
> Let me be soon
> Strong enough to flout romance—
> And say, 'You're out, romance,'
> Never again!

## THAT IS THE END OF THE NEWS

*from* SIGH NO MORE

Verse 1  We are told very loudly and often
> To lift up our hearts,
> We are told that good humour will soften
> Fate's cruellest darts
> So however bad our domestic troubles may be
> We just shake with amusement and sing with glee.

Refrain 1  Heigho, Mum's had those pains again,
           Granny's in bed with her varicose veins again,
           Everyone's gay because dear cousin Florrie
           Was run down on Saturday night by a lorry,
           We're so thrilled, Elsie's in trouble,
           That hernia she had has turned out to be double,
           When Albert fell down all
           The steps of the Town Hall
           He got three bad cuts and a bruise.
           We're delighted
           To be able to say
           We're unable to pay
           Off our debts,
           We're excited
           Because Percy's got mange
           And we've run up a bill at the vet's.
           Three cheers! Ernie's got boils again,
           Everything's covered in ointment and oils again,
           Now he's had seven
           So God's in His heaven
           And that is the end of the news.


Verse 2    We are told that it's dismal and dreary
           To air our despairs,
           We are told to be gallant and cheery
           And banish our cares
           So when fortune gives us a cup of hemlock to quaff
           We just give a slight hiccup and laugh laugh laugh.


Refrain 2  Heigho, everything's fearful,
           We do wish that Vi was a little more cheerful,
           The only result of her last operation
           Has been gales of wind at the least provocation.
           Now don't laugh, poor Mrs Mason
           Was washing some smalls in the lavatory basin
           When that old corroded
           Gas-heater exploded
           And blew her smack into the news.
           We're in clover,
           Uncle George is in clink
           For refusing to work for the war,
           Now it's over
           Auntie Maud seems to think
           He'll be far better placed than before.
           What fun—dear little Sidney.
           Produced a spectacular stone in his kidney,

He's had eleven
So God's in His heaven
And that is the end of the news.

Refrain 3    Heigho, what a catastrophe,
            Grandfather's brain is beginning to atrophy,
            Last Sunday night after eating an apple
            He made a rude noise in the Methodist chapel.
            Good egg! Dear little Doris
            Has just been expelled for assaulting Miss Morris.
            Both of her sisters
            Are covered in blisters
            From standing about in the queues.
            We've been done in
            By that mortgage foreclosure
            And Father went out on a blind,
            He got run in
            For indecent exposure
            And ever so heavily fined.
            Heigho hi-diddle-diddle,
            Aunt Isabel's shingles have met in the middle,
            She's buried in Devon
            So God's in His heaven
            And that is the end of the news.

# LOCH LOMOND

### *from* SIGH NO MORE

On yon bonny banks, and on yon bonny braes
Where the sun shines bright on Loch Lomond,
Where me and my true love spent many happy days
On the bonny bonny banks of Loch Lomond.

For I'll take the high road,
And you'll take the low road,
And I'll be in Scotland afore ye,
And me and my true love will ever meet again
On the bonny bonny banks of Loch Lomond.

On yon bonny banks, and on yon bonny braes
Where the sun shines bright on Loch Lomond,
Where me and my true love spent many happy days
On the bonny bonny banks of Loch Lomond.

For I'll take the high road,
And you'll take the low road,
The high road is my road,
The low road's a slow road,
And I'll guarantee ya
I'll be there to see ya
On the bonny bonny banks of Loch Lomond!
For me and my honey,
My bonny Hieland laddie,
In his wee bittie kilt
Of Caledonian plaidie,
He's my new love, my true love,
My little sugar daddy,
When we're hiccupping through the heather,
Together we cry:

I'll take the high road,
And you take the low road,
And I'll be in Scotland before ye.
And me and my true love,
(And other friends as well)
Such as Katie, Connie,
Frankie and Johnnie,
Prepared for a roll in the hey-nonny-nonny,
On the bonny bonny bonny banks of Loch Lomond.


## WILLY

### *from* SIGH NO MORE

ANGELS' VOICES:   Willy—Willy—Willy,
Sweet boy secure in innocence,
Give an ear to the Angels' choir,
Steer clear of all incontinence,
Put a curb on all base desire.

Willy—Willy—Willy.

1ST GOOD ANGEL:   Dear little lad unheeding,
Pray give a thought to your immortal soul,
May the path you choose be right,
Let virtue's light become your goal.

    (*spoken*) Over to you.

1ST BAD ANGEL:      That's a dull book you're reading,
                    You're far too old to be so prim and staid,
                    I've some postcards here from France,
                    Just take a glance,
                    Don't be afraid.
                    I'll show you many delightful things
                    If you'll but meet me half way.
                        (*spoken*) Over to you.

1ST GOOD ANGEL:     Pray pay no heed to the frightful things
                    That dreadful creature may say.
                        (*spoken*) Excuse me.

1ST BAD ANGEL:      The really pure always do the spiteful things,
                    They can't endure gaiety and joy.
                        (*spoken*) Over.

1ST GOOD ANGEL:     Turn a deaf ear,
                    Concentrate on rightful things,
                    You're such a dear
                    Pretty little Boy.

                    Willy—Willy—Willy.

                    Try to exert some self-control,
                    Try to be captain of your soul,
                    Virtue's path is hilly,
                    Never look—never look
                    Left or right,
                    Press on gallantly to the light,
                    Pitfalls lie in waiting,
                    Try to avoid them one by one
                    If you would be a man my son,
                    No procrastinating,
                    Think pure thoughts like a nice boy should
                    And try, oh try to be good.

1ST BAD ANGEL:      Willy—Willy—Willy.

                    Don't waste your time with wrongs and rights,
                    There can be more exciting lights,
                    Stroll down Piccadilly,
                    Never mind, never mind what they say,
                    Gather rosebuds while you may,
                    What are you afraid of,
                    Purity can be overdone,

Learn to be gay and have some fun,
That's what boys are made for,
There's no future in 'Good' my lad
So try, oh try to be bad.

2ND GOOD ANGEL: Don't hover on the parapet
'Twixt the hills and the shifting sand.

3RD GOOD ANGEL: Read Bunyan and Dean Farrar, pet,
They will help you to understand.

(*They offer him a small gold halo. He turns it over carefully in his hands, scrutinizes it and hands it back disdainfully*)

ALL GOOD ANGELS: Willy—Willy—Willy—Willy—

1ST BAD ANGEL: (*Producing a smart opera hat*)

Suppose you took
This entrancing opera hat
Which has a sheen to match a raven's wing,
You couldn't look
Anything but smart in that,
Imagine strolling down the Mall in Spring
With, by your side,
Some little lady-love
Smirking with pride
At everyone you meet,
It's very sweet
To have a shady love,
A most discreet
Rosie O'Grady love,
Life's incomplete
And, on the whole, extremely flat
If you go marching down the years without an opera
hat.

1ST GOOD ANGEL: The laws of Right
Are quite immutable,
A robe of white
Would be more suitable,
You'll look a sight
And it will serve you right at that,
Just fancy turning down a halo for an opera hat!

(*Willy puts out his tongue at her, takes the hat, opens and shuts it once or twice, then puts it behind him on the chair. Three Bad Angels dance up to him*)

BAD ANGELS:        Don't throw up the sponge, Willy,
                   Your youth will swiftly fly,
                   Love's a thing to conjure with, Willy,
                   You don't know till you try,
                   Don't retire to a cloister, dear,
                   All the world is your oyster, dear,
                   Don't become a muff, Willy,
                   Just learn to do your stuff, Willy,
                   It's time to take the plunge,
                   Don't throw up the sponge!

GOOD ANGELS:       (*Chanting in counter melody*)

                   All things bright and beautiful
                   Will guide you to the light
                   If you'll just be dutiful
                   And keep the goal in sight.
                   Turn aside from temptation, dear,
                   Give a thought to salvation, dear,
                   Get into your stride, my boy,
                   Don't let down the side, my boy,
                   Hark to the trumpet call
                   And keep your eye on the ball.

                   (*Six of the Bad Angels, who have been sitting round on the
                   floor playing poker, spring to their feet and execute a brisk
                   and saucy 'Can-Can'. Two Good Angels return with the halo
                   to which is attached a packet of milk chocolate. Willy accepts
                   it and places it on the chair with the opera hat*)

ALL:               Willy—Willy—Willy—
                   You can be good or the reverse,
                   There is one thing that's much much worse,
                   That is to be silly,
                   Keep that ever before your eyes
                   And try, oh try to be wise!

                   (*All the Angels Good and Bad circle round him until he is
                   completely obscured from view. Finally he pushes through
                   them. The music and singing stop abruptly*)

WILLY:             (*furiously*) With all these bloody Angels in the house a
                   chap can't get a moment's peace.

                   (*He takes a large bite of chocolate, rams the opera hat on to
                   his head and stamps off*)

# WAIT A BIT, JOE

*from* SIGH NO MORE

Verse     When I was quite a tiny lad
My nurse rehearsed me in a set routine
Of good and bad.
When I grew up my parents would
Unduly emphasize the gulf between
The bad and good.
Aware that Love can be a most destructive force
I try to steer a middle course.

Refrain 1  There's a right way—and a wrong way,
There's a weak way—and a strong way,
Take it easy,
Drive with caution when the road is greasy,
Wait a bit—wait a bit—Joe.
There's an old way—and a new way,
There's a false way—and a true way,
Keep your ears back
And you'll never have to fight the tears back,
Wait a bit—wait a bit—Joe.
Never trust your conscience as a method of defence
When 'Old Adam' bubbles up inside,
On mature reflection you will find that common sense
Is a far more serviceable guide.
There's the wrong life—and the right life,
There's the home life—and the night life,
But whichever direction you go
Wait a bit—wait a bit—Joe!

Refrain 2  There's a right way—and a wrong way,
There's a short way—and a long way,
Let your hair down
But before the thrill begins to wear down
Wait a bit—wait a bit—Joe.
There's a dull way—and a smart way,
There's a head way—and a heart way,
Love may fret you
But before you let the goblins get you
Wait a bit—wait a bit—Joe.
Try to keep your balance and endeavour to create
A design for living at your ease,
If you're ever eager and go snapping at the bait
You will end by giving at the knees.

There's a last love—and a first love,
There's a best love—and a worst love,
If you don't want to lose on the throw
Wait a bit—wait a bit—Joe!


## NINA

*from* SIGH NO MORE

Refrain 1   Señorita Nina
            From Argentina
            Knew all the answers,
            Although her relatives and friends were perfect dancers
            She swore she'd never dance a step until she died.
            She said, 'I've seen too many movies
            And all they prove is
            Too idiotic,
            They all insist that South America's exotic
            Whereas it couldn't be more boring if it tried.'
            She added firmly that she hated
            The sound of soft guitars beside a still lagoon,
            She also positively stated
            That she could not abide a Southern Moon,
            She said with most refreshing candour
            That she thought Carmen Miranda
            Was subversive propaganda
            And should rapidly be shot,
            She said she didn't care a jot
            If people quoted her or not!
            She refused to begin the Beguine
            When they requested it
            And she made an embarrassing scene
            If anyone suggested it
            For she detested it.
            Though no one ever could be keener
            Than little Nina
            On quite a number
            Of very eligible men who did the Rhumba
            When they proposed to her she simply left them flat.
            She said that love should be impulsive
            But not convulsive
            And syncopation
            Has a discouraging effect on procreation
            And that she'd rather read a book—and that was that!

Refrain 2  Señorita Nina
           From Argentina
           Despised the Tango
           And though she never was a girl to let a man go
           She wouldn't sacrifice her principles for sex.
           She looked with scorn on the gyrations
           Of her relations
           Who danced the Conga
           And swore that if she had to stand it any longer
           She'd lose all dignity and wring their silly necks!
           She said that frankly she was blinded
           To all their over-advertised romantic charms
           And then she got more bloody-minded
           And told them where to put their tropic palms.
           She said I hate to be pedantic
           But it drives me nearly frantic
           When I see that unromantic
           Sycophantic
           Lot of sluts
           For ever wriggling their guts,
           It drives me absolutely nuts!
           She declined to begin the Beguine
           Though they besought her to
           And in language profane and obscene
           She cursed the man who taught her to,
           She cursed Cole Porter too!
           From this it's fairly clear that Nina
           In her demeanour
           Was so offensive
           That when the hatred of her friends grew too intensive
           She thought she'd better beat it while she had the chance.
           After some trial and tribulation
           She reached the station
           And met a sailor
           Who had acquired a wooden leg in Venezuela
           And so she married him because he *couldn't* dance!

Coda       There surely never could have been a
           More irritating girl than Nina,
           They never speak in Argentina
           Of this degenerate bambina
           Who had the luck to find romance
           But resolutely wouldn't dance!
           She wouldn't dance!—Hola!!

## THE MERRY WIVES OF WINDSOR

*from* SIGH NO MORE

*Verse*

Here are ladies
Set in tranquillity
Living our lives
In a haze of gentility,
Charming ladies
Secretly yearning
To cherish a burning
Desire.
This decade is
Fiercely Victorian,
Though it has charm
For the modern historian
We despise it
For in our eyes it
Denies us the right to acquire
Full completeness.
In a life that is far too brief at best
All the sweetness,
As you've possibly guessed,
Makes us very repressed.
Though our trade is
Wifely devotion
We long for emotional thrill.
Someone some day
Might lead us astray
But probably nobody will.


MRS MACADOO: Pity us—pity us—pity us, please,
We are living in a tedious age.


ALL:         Mrs Macadoo means
We're might-have-beens
Wilting in a gilded cage.


MRS MACADOO: Nobody—nobody—nobody sees
How admirably bored we feel.


ALL:         Mrs Macadoo means
Our love routines
Are far too damned genteel.

*Refrain 1*

We're The Merry Wives of Windsor,
Of Windsor—of Windsor,
In this grey town
Of fabulous renown
We all reside,
Though our whist is rather pseudo
We're adepts at ludo,
We sit and sew
And hardly ever go
Outside.
As so many men have written sonnets on
Female charm and grace
We've popped our latest shawls and bonnets on
Just in case,
When we watch the soldiers drilling
It's thrilling—too thrilling,
We all assert
That virtue doesn't always pay,
We say
We're The Merry Wives of Windsor
And if good luck comes our way
We shall all be merry Widows
One fine day.

*Refrain 2*

We're The Merry Wives of Windsor,
Of Windsor—of Windsor,
Domestic pets
Whose conjugal duets
Are just off key,
If our better halves, who bore us,
Should pass on before us
We'd like to know exactly when it's going to be,
As we live enclosed by prunes and prudery,
Jaded, faded flowers,
We can't resist a little rudery
Out of hours,
We're extremely comme-il-faut here
But life is so slow here
That if we meet
A reasonably sweet—dragoon
We swoon,
We're The Merry Wives of Windsor
And we ask of Fate one boon
That we'll all be Merry Widows
Fairly soon.

# MATELOT

*from* SIGH NO MORE

Verse 1    Jean Louis Dominic Pierre Bouchon,
True to the breed that bore him,
Answered the call
That held in thrall
His father's heart before him.
Jean Louis Dominic sailed away
Further than love could find him
Yet through the night
He heard a light
And gentle voice behind him say:

Refrain 1    Matelot, Matelot,
Where you go
My thoughts go with you,
Matelot, Matelot,
When you go down to the sea
As you gaze from afar
On the evening star
Wherever you may roam,
You will remember the light
Through the winter night
That guides you safely home.
Though you find
Womenkind
To be frail,
One love cannot fail, my son,
Till our days are done,
Matelot, Matelot,
Where you go
My thoughts go with you,
Matelot, Matelot,
When you go down to the sea.

Verse 2    Jean Louis Dominic Pierre Bouchon
Journeyed the wide world over,
Lips that he kissed
Could not resist
This loving roving rover.
Jean Louis Dominic right or wrong
Ever pursued a new love,
Till in his brain
There beat a strain

He knew
To be his true love
Song:

Refrain 2  Matelot, Matelot,
Where you go
My heart goes with you,
Matelot, Matelot,
When you go down to the sea.
For a year and a day
You may sail away
And have no thought of me,
Yet through the wind and the spray,
You will hear me say
No love was ever free.
You will sigh
When horizons are clear,
Something that is dear
To me
Cannot let me be,
Matelot, Matelot,
Where you go
My heart goes with you,
Matelot, Matelot,
When you go down to the sea.

Refrain 3  Matelot, Matelot,
Where you go
My heart will follow,
Matelot, Matelot,
When you go down to the sea.
When there's grief in the sky
And the waves ride high
My heart to yours will say
You may be sure, that I'm true
To my love for you.
Though half the world away,
Never mind
If you find other charms,
Here within my arms
You'll sleep,
Sailor from the deep,
Matelot, Matelot,
Where you go
My heart will follow,
Matelot, Matelot,
When you go down to the sea.

## THE BURCHELLS OF BATTERSEA RISE

*from* SIGH NO MORE

Verse 1    We are those people who seldom make fusses,
You see us in tubes and in trams and in buses,
We couldn't be classed as 'Noblesse',
Nevertheless
We're not so humble,
Any observer who's really observant
Can see how we flinch at the phrase 'Civil Servant',
The Government fools us,
Bureaucracy rules us,
But still we mustn't grumble,
We're the class that they take for a ride,
Still we say with commendable pride:

Refrain 1    We're the Burchells of Battersea Rise,
We're the backbone of England and proud of the fact,
Though in utter confusion we're frequently hurled
By political views from the *News of the World*
We're supposed to be solid and wise
Though we don't hold with boasting out loud of the fact.
If the workers unite
We'll be Left and quite Right
And cry, 'Oh what a surprise
For the Burchells of Battersea Rise!'

Refrain 2    We're the Burchells of Battersea Rise,
We believe every word that we read in the Press,
When encouraged to argue and stick out our chins
We go off at half-cock and Bureaucracy wins,
We resent and detest and despise
Being talked of as 'This Happy Breed' in the Press,
If the author we meet
We'd be happy to greet
Him with two lovely black eyes
From the Burchells of Battersea Rise.

Verse 2    Though we're fed up with restrictions and strictures
We learn about life from the Press and the Pictures
So all our inaccurate views
You must excuse
And rise above them.

Having survived over five years of war
If the National Government wants an encore
We shall pray that it warms up
And fill some more forms up
To prove how much we love them,
Though we're dead against rocking the boat
Still we hold the majority vote.

Refrain 3   We're the Burchells of Battersea Rise
And we see at least four Double-Features a week,
To American war films we'd rather not go
For we say, 'How by Golly would Hollywood know?'
If they have people in to advise
We can only surmise that their teachers are weak,
Though we've seen many actors
Win through through Max Factor's
We can't hand them a prize
From the Burchells of Battersea Rise.

Refrain 4   We're the Burchells of Battersea Rise
And we've written and written and written again
To some local official who Dad seems to think
Might concede us a permit to build a new sink,
We've already had several tries,
It's as bad as the Battle of Britain again,
Though we've drawn up the plans
We shall sit on our cans
Till the old bastard replies
To the Burchells of Battersea Rise.

Refrain 5   We're the Burchells of Battersea Rise
And we all believed firmly in 'Peace-in-our-time',
We heard speeches from Germans and Eyeties and Frogs,
No one knew what they meant so we went to the dogs
And the Government told us such lies,
We've heard plenty of cackling old geese in our time,
We were mugs to agree
But in future we'll see
That they don't capitalize
On the Burchells of Battersea Rise.

Extra Refrains   We're the Burchells of Battersea Rise
And when foreigners murmur, 'We hope you're all right,'
How we wish that they'd buzz off and leave us alone
For we live chock-a-block in an occupied zone
With the land full of alien spies.
Poor old England's a bleeding Utopia all right,

We've got Bishops and Peers
Who will burst into tears
If the Huns won't fraternize
With the Burchells of Battersea Rise.

We're the Burchells of Battersea Rise
And we're faced with a dismal selection again,
We may find if we swallow the Socialist bait
That a simple head cold is controlled by the State,
Though we know Winston Churchill is wise
And we'd love him to win the election again,
If he's forced to say 'Yes'
To the Beaverbrook press
There'll be loud animal cries
From the Burchells of Battersea Rise.


## JAPANESE SPIES

*from* SIGH NO MORE

Verse 1     Can you guess who we are?
            It will take you some time to discover.
            Can you guess what we do?
            We're telling you.
            We're fearfully secret agents who unwisely undertook
            To continue our activities in Asia.
            This simple explanation will account for why we look
            Like a rather old production of *The Geisha*.
            We're adepts at deciphering and learned a lot of tricks
            From a sweet old couple in Spain.
            We tried to take up sabotage in nineteen-thirty-six
            But we had to drop it again.
            We've mastered lots of secret codes and since the War began
            We've been on a special training course in Eire
            And now we're on our way to see the Emperor of Japan
            With a note of introduction from Valera.

Refrain 1   Two little Japanese spies are we,
            Eager to do some undermining,
            Off on a gay subversive spree
            Hoping the Rising Sun's still rising.
            The language we have never known
            But still we take no risks,
            We practise with a Linguaphone
            And twelve delightful discs.

We have been told by the C.I.D.
That the Mikado's simply pining
Just to utilize
Two little Japanese spies.

Verse 2   Our training in the early days was really rather fun,
With our darling old professor in Geneva
We had to learn disguises and our repertoire would run
From the Sultan of Johore to Little Eva.
You have to be resourceful and you have to use your brains
When you're drugging somebody's drink
And you have to keep your temper when you're scrubbing out
    the stains
Of that damned invisible ink.
You're taught to swallow documents no matter where you are
And *if* you bring them up again they cane you.
One evening in a restaurant we went a bit too far
And ate two *Daily Workers* and the menu.

Refrain 2   Two little Japanese spies are we,
Wine in the wood and not quite mellowed,
Off for a voyage across the sea
Under-equipped but over-yellowed.
We said to the authorities
'An exit permit, please,'
But all the 'A' priorities
Were taken by M.P.s.
One day an eminent C. in C.
Gave us a look and fairly bellowed,
'Pardon my surprise—pardon my surprise,
You're not Bulgarian,
Not Roumanian,
Not Bavarian,
Not Albanian,
Not Hungarian,
Not Ukrainian,
Far too alien
For Australian,
Suddenly it's struck me like a blow between the eyes
That's a great disguise,
You're two little Japanese spies.'

Extra lines   We've mastered loads of secret codes
And since the War we've been
In County Kerry brushing up our blarney,
We've learnt to sing in Japanese
'The Wearing of the Green',
'The Minstrel Boy' and 'Lily of Killarney'.

# *Pacific 1860*

## FAMILY GRACE

*from* PACIFIC 1860

For what we have received
May the Lord fill our hearts with gratitude
And through the coming day
We humbly pray
With appetites relieved
In this remote, most eccentric latitude
That He, with tolerance of all small mistakes,
May walk beside us
And, in His understanding, guide us.
For what we have received
Accept, O Lord, in your serene beatitude
Today and all our days
Our thankful praise
For tropic fruits
And bamboo shoots,
For tender roots—incredible
And fortunately edible—
And also for the boon
Of most delicious fish from the lagoon.
This morning prayer
Represents our attitude
Please fill our hearts,
Instil our hearts
With gratitude.
Amen—amen.

## IF I WERE A MAN

*from* PACIFIC 1860

HENRIETTA: If I were a man I would marry a wife
Who would help me to lead an exemplary life
And the house that I'd build
Would be pleasantly filled
With children belonging to me,

232

It would also command
Several acres of land
And an excellent view of the sea,
A most excellent view of the sea.

CAROLINE:  If I were a man I would sail away
To the uttermost ends of the earth,
And I would return a millionaire
With jewels of fabulous worth.
Diamonds and rubies beyond compare
Ropes of pearls for my true love's hair
And I'd guarantee on that happy day
That, unlike us, she need never say
That she hadn't a thing to wear!

LOUISE:  If I were a man I would make up my mind
To be wise, understanding and gentle and kind.
I wouldn't catch fish and I wouldn't kill birds,
I wouldn't shoot poor defenceless rabbits
Nor would I use inelegant words
And I'd try to control my annoying habits.
I wouldn't play jokes and make apple-pie beds,
Get drunk and stagger upstairs,
Nor steal people's pencils and break off the leads,
And leave grease on the backs of the chairs.
I wouldn't be sly and get money from Mother,
If I were a man,
If I were a man,
I would not be my brother!

CAROLINE:  We can't all be noble and good, Louise,
And I'm not at all sure that we should, Louise,
For think of your miserable plight, Louise,
If everyone else were as right, Louise,
And true, Louise,
As you, Louise.

GEORGINA:  If I were a man I'd go out in the dawn
And I'd gaze at the curve of the bay
And I'd write in a book
How the mountains look
At the beginning of day.
If I were a man
I should wish to be born
With a dream that would set me apart
And I'd search the world over
To find my true lover
And give her my passionate heart!

TWINS:          If we were a man we'd be dashing and bold
                And exceedingly witty and cruel.
                Our hearts would be warm but our eyes would be cold,
                And the legend for hundreds of years would be told
                How we died for the honour we'd lived to uphold,
                In the Bois de Boulogne—

ALL:            Why the Bois de Boulogne?

TWINS:          In the Bois de Boulogne in a duel.


## DEAR MADAME SALVADOR
### (Letter Song)

*from* PACIFIC 1860

Dear Madame Salvador,
Although this note may seem absurd to you
I feel impelled to run the risk of your disdain.
In writing thus a warning word to you,
My one desire is but to spare you pain.
Poor Madame Salvador—
Poor Madame Salvador,
I do not know if you're aware or not
Of the malicious, foolish things that people say,
I gravely doubt whether you care or not,
But all the same—in a quite humble way,
Dear Madame Salvador.
Your name and reputation I am eager to defend,
So count on me, I beg of you, sincerely as your friend.


## MY HORSE HAS CAST A SHOE

*from* PACIFIC 1860

ELENA:   My horse has cast a shoe,
         A careless thing to do.
         Although he has apologized
         And shown that he is most upset,
         For conduct so uncivilized
         I cannot quite forgive him—yet.

KERRY: Of course—of course.
      There is nothing so incautious as a horse.

ELENA: My horse has cast a shoe
      So I appeal to you,
      I meet you by a happy chance
      In this untimely circumstance,
      Pray tell me what to do.

KERRY: To be able to assist Madame Salvador
      Is an honour that I shan't forget,
      I will drive you safely home
      In my father's wagonette.

ELENA: You are so kind
      I'll be ever in your debt
      For your chivalry combined
      With your father's wagonette.
      Who could foretell
      That a most obliging fate
      Would arrange for what befell
      To befall me just exactly by your gate?
      Who knows
      What magic power guides the hearts
      Of those
      Who drive about in little carts?

KERRY: Often in dreams
      I have known about this meeting
      And awakened to the beating
      Of my too romantic heart,
      Although it seems
      Too ridiculous to mention
      My intolerable tension
      Has been lightened by a little horse and cart.
      I know
      My dreams are fated to come true,
      And so
      Your horse discreetly cast a shoe.

BOTH: Who knows—what magic power guides the hearts
      Of those—who drive about in little carts?

      Who could have known
      We should feel this lovely glow?
      We were strangers and alone
      Such a little while ago.

Fate set the course
And decided to unbend
By arranging that my horse
Should have led me to the finding of a friend.
Who knows
What magic power guides the hearts
Of those
Who drive about in little carts?

### Reprise

ELENA: My horse had cast a shoe,
A careless thing to do,
Then Kerry smiled and sympathized
And said that all could be arranged
And suddenly I realized
That everything in life had changed.

ROSA: Of course—of course
I could murder that annoying little horse!

ELENA: Then when Kerry whispered 'Dear Madame Salvador'
I discovered that my eyes were wet
And he drove me safely home in his father's
Wagonette.
How could I know
What incalculable force
Had impelled that rather slow
But beguiling little horse?
How can I wait
Till the evening shadows fall
To go through that little gate
And to find, in him, the answer to it all?
That cart led me to him and now I know
My heart will never never let him go.

## I WISH I WASN'T QUITE SUCH A BIG GIRL

### *from* PACIFIC 1860

#### *Verse 1*

PENELOPE: I was told
When not very old
That if my will were strong enough
And if I tried for long enough
The wish that I wished would come true.

GIRLS:      Penny dear,
            We're pining to hear
            Just how and when and where you built
            Those castles in the air you built
            And whether or not they vanished—or they grew.

PENELOPE:   Sad to relate
            A cruel fate
            Disdained my plea
            And mocked at me
            For the only wish I ever made
            Was doomed, biologically, to fade.

GIRLS:      Tell us, please, we're all on fire
            To hear of this frustrated heart's desire!

*Refrain*

PENELOPE:   I wish I wasn't quite such a big girl,
            It's not a very nice thing to be,
            I've prayed to be more delicate and suffer from migraines,
            But even with a temperature my appetite remains.
            I wish I wasn't sturdy and healthy
            To such an unromantic degree.
            Nobody even in joke
            Would ever lay down his cloak
            For a big girl—like me.

*Verse 2*

GIRLS:      Penny dear,
            No really sincere
            True love would ever mind a bit
            If you stuck out behind a bit
            Provided your heart was for him.

PENELOPE:   That, dear friends,
            Entirely depends
            On snatching opportunity
            And in this small community
            The chances of finding true love—are rather dim.

GIRLS:      That may be so
            But still you know
            You'll never win
            If you give in.
            The only thing for you to do
            Is take a more optimistic view.

PENELOPE:   I know you're right, but come what may
            I must continue wistfully to say:

*Refrain 2*

I wish I wasn't quite such a big 'girl!
It's such a very dull thing to be.
I fell into the water once when playing on the brink,
But no one paid attention for they knew I couldn't sink.
I never really eat all I want to,
But still I seem to grow like a tree.
Nobody quite understands
The strange irresolute glands
Of a big girl—like me.

*Refrain 3*

I wish I wasn't quite such a big girl!
I wish I could be more 'petite fille'—
I'm rather good at guessing games because I'm not a
    dunce,
But if I'm playing hide-and-seek I'm always found at once!
When Papa used to come into the nursery
He'd never let me sit on his knee—
The stars may blaze above
But no one ever makes love
To a big girl—like me.

## SAMOLAN SONG (KA TAHUA)

*from* PACIFIC 1860

| Samolan | English Translation |
|---|---|
| AYANO AND SERVANTS: | |
| Ka tahua aoana una | Now Spring love brings, |
| Ka tuhua silo | Now Spring appears, |
| Tango mero ha anu anu | Life beautiful becomes, |
| Saalo-lala belo | Skies are blue, |
| Seu unyea | All the earth |
| Apra lalua | Has flowers, |
| Seu alani umpalo | All the stars ride, |
| Ka tahua aouna una | Now Spring love brings, |
| Ka tahua aouna una | Now Spring love brings, |
| Saalo-lai belo | Skies are blue, |
| Tahali belo. | Happy blue. |
| | |
| Lapuana a seu alani | The moon and all the stars |
| Jinga pralo tahali yani. | Dance with happy laughter. |

## BRIGHT WAS THE DAY

*from* PACIFIC 1860

KERRY: This morning when I woke, the light was clear in the sky,
A sweet wind murmured through the trees.
A singing bird was singing very near in the sky,
And in the breeze
Which drove the clouds so gaily by
I thought I heard a different note—a little sigh
Which seemed to say
This is your day,
Be careful, please,
Be careful, please!
Don't let this light enchantment fade away,
This is your day.

ELENA: This morning when I woke I seemed to know in my heart
That some new happiness was near.
I waited for this unexpected glow in my heart
To disappear.
But strange to say it would not go
And as the moments hurried by it seemed to grow.
If, as you say,
This is your day,
Kind cavalier,
Kind cavalier,
We'll try to let this brief enchantment stay
Just for today—
This is your day.

KERRY: Though we—may never meet again,
There'll never be a day so sweet again.
Deep in my heart, no matter what the troubled years may bring,
A secret voice—will ever sing.

### Refrain

Bright was the day when you came to me,
Someone had whispered your name to me.
Someone had told me how fair you were,
Then at last—there you were!
Light was the music that played for me,
You were the song Destiny had made for me,
I heard the melody start
Delicately—delicately—in my heart.

ELENA: Here in the sunshine I came to you,
Someone had whispered my name to you,
Some potent magic impelled me here,
Touched my heart—held me here!
Dreams long forgotten revive again,
Suddenly life seems to be alive again,
I heard the melody too—
Beckoning me—beckoning me—here to you!

*Reprise*

Bright was the day when you came to me,
Shyly you whispered your name to me,
I knew the theme of your song before,
Far away—long before,
Sweet was the music that played for me
Part of a dream that can never fade for me,
I heard the melody start
Passionately—passionately—in my heart.


## INVITATION TO THE WALTZ

*from* PACIFIC 1860

GIRLS: This is the high—
Light of the year for us,
Dressed to the nines
Up to our chins,
Stars in the sky,
Moonlight is clear for us,
Candlelight shines
And the music begins.

MEN: Social event
Reeking with quality,
Gentlemen bow,
Ladies advance,
We represent
Stately frivolity,
Youth's at the prow
And so on with the dance.

When we say, 'How good the floor is—
Providential
Circumstance,'

GIRLS:   We shall blush
         And reply,
         'What a crush!
         Really we'll swoon
         If they play one more tune!'

MEN:     'Music,' we'll say, 'furthermore is
         So essential
         To romance!'

GIRLS:   What seems a terrible bore is
         That you'd far rather talk than dance!

         This is the high—
         Light of the year for us.

MEN:     Gentlemen bow,
         Ladies advance.

ALL:     Stars in the sky,
         Moonlight is clear for us,
         Youth's at the prow
         And so on with the dance.

MEN:     Ladies—dear ladies—beguiling and sweet—

GIRLS:   Gentlemen—gentlemen—please try to be discreet.

MEN:     Ladies—dear ladies—be kind to our—
         Blind to our—
         Faults.
         One waltz
         Need not sweep you off your feet,
         Though we may gasp at your beauty
         Sense of duty
         Will prevail.
         We represent
         To a large extent
         The purely domestic male.
         Strong emotions and desires
         Training has taught us to check.

GIRLS:   What if you unbanked the fires?

MEN:     God forbid. We'd get it in the neck!
         Ladies—dear ladies—how charming you are.

GIRLS: Gentlemen—gentlemen—don't think us too bizarre,
Though we're prepared to be kind to your—
Blind to your
Faults,
One waltz
Will not get us very far!


# HIS EXCELLENCY REGRETS

*from* PACIFIC 1860

GIRLS: Oh, tell us please
Entirely confidentially
How A.D.C.s
Are trained in social grace.
It's awfully brave
Daily to be called upon to save
His Excellency's face!

MEN: Any explanations
Of the duties of an A.D.C.
Prove the complications
That are rife at Government House.
Certain situations
We could never let a lady see,
There are strange vibrations
In the life at Government House.
Truth is often sacrificed for reasons of diplomacy.

GIRLS: That of course we understand
But all the same it must be grand
To be
So suave, so calm, so dignified!

MEN: If you knew what all that signified—we—
Who break the Ninth Commandment every day
Would hang our heads in shame and say
Forgive—we have to live
Officially on feet of clay.
Every minute
We're made to sin it
Is really very depraved,
But to Hell
With the lies we tell,
His Excellency's honour must be saved.

REFRAIN 1: His Excellency regrets
That owing to an attack of Gout
He really dare not venture out
On Saturday to dine.
His Excellency regrets
That owing to doctor's orders he
Cannot attend the Mission tea
And also must decline
Your kind invitation
For Wednesday week.
A slight operation
And poor circulation
Combined with a weedy physique
Has made him unable to speak.
All this in addition to what
The Doctors describe as a 'Clot'
Which may disappear
By the end of the year
But may, very possibly, not!
His Excellency regrets
That owing to his exalted state
He can no more associate
With amiable brunettes.
Walk up—walk up—we're willing to take your bets
That that's one of the principal things His Excellency
     regrets!

GIRLS: So now we know
About the Diplomatic Corps,
How it can so
Corrupt the soul of youth.
What happens if
Some day you give the waiting world a whiff
Of plain, unvarnished truth?

REFRAIN 2 MEN: His Excellency regrets
That, failing a better alibi,
He must admit he'd rather die
Than open your Bazaar.
His Excellency regrets
That, lacking enough official scope,
He can't disband the Band of Hope
No matter where they are.
He frankly despises
The people he rules,
His gorge also rises

When giving the prizes
At co-educational schools
To rows of illiterate fools.
And if you should write in the book
He'll give you a murderous look.
For it ruins his day
To be taken away
From his rod and his line and his hook!
His Excellency regrets
He hasn't enough to run the house
Or pay the staff—or feed a mouse
Upon the pay he gets.
Heigho—heigho—he's up to his ears in debts
But that's one of the least of the things His Excellency
    regrets!


# THE PARTY'S GOING WITH A SWING

### *from* PACIFIC 1860

There's something about a family rout
That thrills us,
We like to observe our elders on the sly.
We have to repress the urge to laugh which nearly kills us
But nevertheless we try,
Observing every action
And recording every clue
We notice with satisfaction
What some claret cup can do.
The stately advance
Of uncles and aunts
In dozens
Is something to be remembered till we die.
It's often a strain to be polite to all our cousins
But nevertheless we try.
When gossiping and scandal has the party in its grip
The only way to handle it is just to let it rip.

Refrain 1  The party's going with a swing, with a swing,
Gay abandon seems to be the thing.
We can say sincerely
That it's really really really
Very pretty to see our elders have an adolescent fling.
Dear old Mrs Giles
Having driven thirty miles

Has an appetite that wouldn't shame a horse,
Having tucked away
Nearly all the cold buffet
She shows every inclination that she's going to stay the
    course.
We're all so glad that Cousin Maud,
Thank the Lord,
Hasn't yet been prevailed upon to sing.
Though dear Miss Scobie's principles forbid her to carouse
She's apt to get flirtatious when the atmosphere allows
But it's hard to be seductive when there's junket on your
    blouse.
The party's going with a swing.

Refrain 2  The party's going with a swing, with a swing.
           Mrs Drew quite took away our breath,
           She remarked with candour
           Sitting out on the verandah
           That as far as she knew old Mr Drew had drunk himself to
               death.
           Pretty Mrs Bowles
           Having had five sausage rolls
           Was compelled to leave the ball room at a bound.
           Also Colonel Blake,
           Rather gay on tipsy cake,
           Emitted first a hiccup then a more peculiar sound.
           We can't say what the Vicar did,
           God forbid,
           But we can blame the moonlight and the Spring,
           With hearty joviality he started playing 'Bears',
           He pounced on Mrs Frobisher and took her unawares,
           We had to cut her laces at the bottom of the stairs.
           The party's going with a swing.

Refrain 3  The party's going with a swing, with a swing,
           All the old folks hand in hand with youth.
           Mrs John Macmallard
           Bit an almond in the salad
           Which completely removed the stopping from her one
               remaining tooth.
           Dear old Mrs Spears
           Who's been mad for several years
           And believes she has the gift of second sight
           Went into a trance
           Just before the supper dance
           And let loose a flood of language which was highly
               impolite.

We're glad Aunt May who's deaf and dumb
Couldn't come
For she does put a blight on everything.
When Mrs Edward Pratt arrived Papa was scandalized,
To dance in her condition is a little ill-advised,
If we get her through the Lancers we'll be very much
    surprised.
The party's going with a swing.
Mrs Rogers did some conjuring which held us all in thrall,
She cleverly produced a lot of rabbits from her shawl!
But after that the rabbits did the neatest trick of all.
The party's going with a swing.


## BIRTHDAY TOAST

*from* PACIFIC 1860

MR STIRLING: Dear friends, forgive me pray
             If as your host
             I should seem importunate,
             But my paternal pride
             Can't be denied,
             My daughters' natal day
             Demands a Toast,
             Which is very fortunate
             For though the lemonade and cup's all right
             No wine has flowed yet,
             I haven't heard a cork explode yet.

ALL:         How charming—how appropriate—what perfect
                 rectitude!
             Dear Mr Stirling never says a word that might be
                 misconstrued.

MR STIRLING: Allow me to express
             My cheerful mind
             In this refined community
             And say with what delight
             I see tonight
             Our friend the Dean
             And Mrs Green
             Accompanied by Oliver
             And dear Miss Ruxton-Bolliver.
             I also must extend

To Canon Banks
My ardent thanks
For bringing Jane and Harriet
And also Mr Marryot,
Our ever faithful friend
Who never leaves a party till the end.

So now, my dearest Twins,
Pray make the most
Of this opportunity,
This evening you may frolic with impunity.

In Faith be strong
Refrain from wrong
And may your lives be both enjoyable and long.


# MAKE WAY FOR THEIR EXCELLENCIES

*from* PACIFIC 1860

Make way for Their Excellencies,
Make way for Their Excellencies,
Make way for Their Excellencies,
Make way for Their Excellencies,
Kindly step aside,
They are a symbol representing
Sceptre and Crown and Mighty Race,
Gently but firmly ornamenting
This remote but pleasant place—
Over the ocean's far horizon
Proudly the Ruler of the State
Keeps her astute and watchful eyes on
Every wandering delegate.
Hail to this pair whose steely nerve is
Equal to tasks that others fear.
Hail to the Diplomatic Service
Which, so discreetly, sent them here.
Make way for Their Excellencies,
Make way for Their Excellencies,
Make way for Their Excellencies.
Welcome them with pride.

## FUMFUMBOLO

*from* PACIFIC 1860

Ages ago when the world was dawning,
Early in Time—in the beautiful years,
Bolo—the water God of Samolo
Was dying
And on the sands were lying
A million weeping fishes
To hear his final wishes
And watch his soul depart.
Out on the reef there were turtles mourning,
Fumfum, the Goddess of fire, was in tears.
Bolo—the dying God of Samolo
Perceiving
His enemy was grieving
Put out the flames around her
And, though it nearly drowned her,
He took her to his heart.
Then a mountain rose from the sea
And its summit was wreathed in flame
And that is the fabulous history
Of how the volcano came.

Fumfumbolo—Fumfumbolo
Dua kopala—Dua kopala
Fumfumbolo—Fumfumbolo
Bumbumbala—Bumbumbala

When Fumfumbolo lights the sky
No monkeys chatter—no parrots fly,
No flying fishes skim the bay
And every sea-bird hides away.
The salamander leaves the sand,
Even the turtles understand
When God is angry, they move inland.
First the hills seem to crumble,
A deep rumble
Proclaims
That danger is nigh,
From the top of the mountain
A strange fountain
Of flames
Disfigures the sky,
Eagles take flight,
Little lizards and snakes

Creep away out of sight
When our Fire Mountain wakes.
And the surf on the reef
Sings of sorrow and grief
And the birds of the air
On the wings of a prayer
Flying by
Cry to the sky through the smoke and the glare
Fumfumbolo!—Beware!
Crocodiles on sandy banks
Immediately break their ranks
And slide away in fear.
Kinkajous in sore distress
Refuse to venture out unless
A hideaway is near.
Tadpoles and toads
Obstruct the roads
Seeking for shelter.
Oysters retire
Into the mire
Down on the delta.
In the hills
All the whip-poor-wills
Are wailing—wailing.
From far and near
You only hear
The sounds of fear,
The sounds of fear,
The island quivers and quakes,
Shivers and shakes.
Whenever Fumfumbolo wakes!
When Fumfumbolo lights the sky
No monkeys chatter—no parrots fly
No parrots fly—no parrots fly
And that is why!

*English—Samolan translation*

NATIVES:

| | |
|---|---|
| Jolan haliya a abu | The world bewares and hides away, |
| Keya Kopla lalilu | When Gods awake |
| Li saalo-lali tori foom | The sky rains fire |
| A twa alani abadum | And all the stars fall down, |
| Twa nawa juka pralo kwi | All little creatures with a shriek |
| Abu koganu tariki | Hide fearfully their faces, |
| Kopala toonga—Kopala kai | The Gods are angry—the Gods are athirst. |

Doka jinga doka jinga                Devils dance, devils dance,
Upa bana upa bana                    On the sands, on the sands,
Hola pui kriza                       The milk turns sour,
O klabonga o klabonga                No love-making—no love-making,
Apu tali apu tali                    Under the trees—under the trees,
Twadidi luma                         Everything is sad,
Luma solali a luma solaba            Sad night and sad day,
Twa tali yololu a tola lalua         All trees weep and flowers die,
Twa luma solali a luma solaba        All sad night and sad days,
Ka Kopala toonga ka Kopala toonga    Now the Gods are angry, now the
                                       Gods are athirst,
Ka Kopala toonga                     Now the Gods are angry,
Ka Kopala kai. Haliya!               Now the Gods are athirst—Beware!


## ONE TWO THREE

*from* PACIFIC 1860

Verse          A brand new dance
               Invaded France
               In April Eighteen Forty,
               Through every street
               The rhythm beat,
               It swept beyond
               The demi-monde
               And though some people hissed it
               They couldn't long resist it.
               The Right bank fell,
               The Left bank fell
               And though the Court was haughty
               They took the floor
               When some old bore
               Declared the dance was naughty.
               Sur le pont d'Avignon
               People cried, 'C'est bon,'
               As they twirled in the magic of the moon
               All the world and his wife
               Seemed to take a new life
               From that absurd—hurdy-gurdy little tune.


Refrain 1      There is nothing so beguiling as a One Two Three,
               A One Two Three and a hop,
               The music sets you buzzing like a bumble bee,
               Oh dear me,
               You dance until you drop.

Old folks can't abide the One Two Three,
The reason's easy to see,
Every beat for them
Spells defeat for them,
One Two Three.
But of course for flaming youth
It's quite a different affair,
They maintain with perfect truth
That nothing can compare
With the fascinating rhythm of the One Two Three,
It makes them shining and free.
Point your toe,
Off you go,
One Two Three.

Refrain 2　There is nothing so exciting as a One Two Three,
A One Two Three and a hop,
It definitely épaters the bourgeoisie,
Oh dear me,
Their eyes begin to pop,
Missionaries frown upon the One Two Three,
Deacons dither with fear,
Grave anxiety
Racks society,
When they hear
Those scandalous audacious strains
They give a terrible cry,
They fear that such flirtatious strains
Are bound to lead to—My! My! My!
So when anybody shudders at the One Two Three
We just say 'Fiddlededee!'
Arms out straight,
Tête-à-tête,
One Two Three.


# THIS IS A NIGHT FOR LOVERS

*from* PACIFIC 1860

The clouds are following the moon,
The night will be over soon,
The silver pathway fades from sight,
Across the still lagoon
The mountains stand against the sky
Watching the little clouds pass by,

Watching the shadows grow,
Watching the shadows grow
On the sleeping world below.

This is a night for lovers,
A night to be set apart
For ever in somebody's heart,
This is a moment for ever and above,
This is a night for love.
Soon when the dawn discovers
Secrets the night conceals
There'll be bright new hills and a coloured sea
Instead of the delicate mystery
The moon only half reveals.

When dawn is lighting up the sky
The air will be shrill with birds,
The magic of love will gently die
Along with its foolish words.
The mountains stand against the sky.
Watching the little clouds pass by,
Watching the shadows grow,
Watching the shadows grow
On the sleeping world below.

This is a night for lovers
Set between yesterday's fears
And tomorrow's most probable tears,
This is a moment for ever and above,
This is a night for love.

## I NEVER KNEW

*from* PACIFIC 1860

KERRY &   I never knew
ELENA:    That love could be so sweet before,
          I never knew
          That life was incomplete before,
          I never knew—this tremulous ecstasy
          That seems like a dream to me
          Could yet be true.
          How could I guess, dearest, that within my heart
          All other loves apart

There would be you?
How could I know
That I should love you so,
I never knew—I never knew.

KERRY:

The dearest love I ever knew
To hold for ever and for ever,
Though this moment sweet
May with its magic fade away,
It is complete for us
For ever and a day.
Our hearts will beat alone
No more—asleep or waking
This is our own,
This happiness we've known,
This lovely moment is our own,
All other loves forsaking.
I never knew,
I never knew you could love me,
I never knew.

ELENA:

Dear love, let this be true,
Dear love to last for ever,
Though the magic of tonight
May fade away
We'll remember it
For ever and a day.
No more asleep or waking,
This is our own,
This loveliness our hearts have
Never known,
This is our own,
All other loves forsaking,
Dear love, I never knew
Love—could be so true,
Love—I never knew.

KERRY & 
ELENA:

I never knew
Such happiness could be—before,
I never knew
Such colours in the sea—before,
I never knew those mountains were dear to me
Until you were near to me
And made it true,
I feel that now every bird sings to me,
Will lend its wings to me
To bear me through
Each weary day
That I'm away from you.
I never knew.
I never knew.


# THIS IS A CHANGING WORLD

*from* PACIFIC 1860

The world was young
So many many years,
The passage of time must show
Some traces of change,

Love songs once sung,
Much laughter, many tears,
Have echoed down the years,
The past is old and strange.
Each waning moon,
All dawns that rise, all suns that set,
Change like the tides that flow across the sands,
Each little tune
That fills our hearts with vague regret,
Each little love duet
Fades in our hands,
Don't stray among the moments that have fled,
New days are just ahead,
New words are still unsaid.

Refrain 1   This is a changing world, my dear,
New songs are sung—new stars appear,
Though we grow older year by year
Our hearts can still be gay,
Young love at best is a passing phase,
Charming and foolish and blind,
There may be happier, wiser days
When youth is far behind.
Where are the snows of yesteryear?
When Winter's done and Spring is here
No regrets are worth a tear,
We're living in a changing world, my dear.

Refrain 2   This is a changing world, my dear,
New dreams are dreamed,
New dawns appear,
Passion's a feckless cavalier
Who loves and rides away,
Time will persuade you to laugh at grief,
Time is your tenderest friend,
Life may be lonely and joy be brief
But everything must end.
Love is a charming souvenir,
When day is done and night draws near
No regrets are worth a tear,
We're living in a changing world, my dear.

Reprise   This is a changing world, my dear,
The clouds have gone—the skies are clear,
What is there in the atmosphere
That lifts my heart away?
Can you not hear it, that lovely tune,

Urgent, entrancing and sweet,
Telling me clearly how soon,
How soon my love and I will meet?
This that I feel will always be,
This voice that calls is Destiny,
Can't you hear it—can't you see
That love has changed the changing world for me?


# COME BACK TO THE ISLAND

*from* PACIFIC 1860

Come back to the island,
Please leave your heart behind you,
Heartache
Is a keepsake
That will haunt you and remind you,
Keep faith—and remember,
Keep faith—and we'll find you,
Come back to the island,
Come back to your heart.

Soon—the shore will fade,
The pounding surf you will not hear,
The mountain tops will disappear
And be a memory
Beyond the empty sea,
Here—the sun and shade,
The green lagoons, the gleaming sand
Of this benign and loving land
Still will be
Your certainty.

Come back to the island,
Please leave your heart behind you,
Heartache
Is a keepsake
That will haunt you and remind you,
Keep faith—and remember,
Keep faith—and we'll find you,
Come back to the island,
Come back to your heart.

# GIPSY MELODY
## (Trio)

*from* PACIFIC 1860

SOLANGE    Tell us pray what made you become so clinical?
& TRUDI:   Did your head persuade you to count the cost
           Though your love betrayed you and made you cynical?

ROSA:      I'll sing a song to you, both sad and true,
           About a highly born Hungarian,
           Although the husband she was married to
           Was far removed from a barbarian
           She loved a proletarian
           In a valley far away,
           A Gipsy minstrel came to play
           A serenade,
           Everyone from far and near
           Collected in the woods to hear the tune he played.

           Wild and free
           That haunting melody
           Enchanted maid and man,
           Young and old
           Believed the tales he told
           And joined his caravan,
           A most impulsive, foolish plan.

           Their troubles then began.
           The rain soon drove them home again
           No longer wild and free,
           Snow and hail had made that nightingale
           Sound very much off-key,
           A sorry tale you will agree.
           What fools these mortals be.

           But one poor lady left her heart behind
           And from that moment life was sad for her,
           Naught could bring comfort to her troubled mind
           Which, on the whole, was very bad for her.

           That is why
           To any Gipsies passing by
           She'll always sigh:

*Refrain*

ROSA:      Play me
           A Gipsy melody from far away,
           An echo wild and gay
           From some forgotten yesterday,
           My lonely heart can still remember
           Those magic nights beneath the open sky,
           So Gipsy play for me
           That song I'll love until the day I die.

SOLANGE    Play me
& TRUDI:   A Gipsy melody from far away,
           An echo wild and gay
           From some forgotten yesterday,
           My lonely heart can still remember
           Those magic nights beneath the open sky,
           So Gipsy play for me
           That song I'll love until the day I die.


# THIS IS THE NIGHT

*from* PACIFIC 1860

This is a night
Made for posterity,
Here on this isle
Weddings are rare,
We can, with slight
    Lack of sincerity,
Greet with a smile
This most fortunate pair.

Here without doubt
Nature can grin again,
Men can be slow,
Men can be sly,
Girls who come out
Have to go in again
Principally owing to lack of supply.

Please do not think we are jealous
Or disgruntled or aggrieved,
We can sigh,
We can coo,
We can cry,

'Really it's too—
Too too good to be true!'
All social instincts compel us
To be joyful and relieved,
Still we'd like someone to tell us
How this marriage has been achieved.

This sublime and Christian rite
Aims to replenish the stock,
But of course the bridal night
Frequently—is something of a shock!

Life we believe
Really requires some
Sine qua non
Neatly defined,
Owing to Eve
Having been tiresome
Man must go on
Reproducing mankind.


## MOTHER'S LAMENT

*from* PACIFIC 1860

Here in the twilight of our days
From all maternal bondage freed
We've earned this sweet repose no doubt
But still it's dull to sit about
And watch the sands of time run out
With such indecent speed.

Now, as our eyes begin to glaze,
We peer from our domestic cage,
Here in the sere and yellow leaf
Our task is done, our time is brief,
We know that we should feel relief
But all we feel is rage.

Being at last put out to graze
Like cows that are too old to breed
We know that by maternal pride
Our spirits should be fortified
But all the same we're mortified
And very cross indeed.

## PRETTY LITTLE BRIDESMAIDS

*from* PACIFIC 1860

We humbly and devoutly pray
That some kind gentleman some fine day
Will fling all gnawing doubts away
And cordially invite us
To stroll along some shady path
And there to offer us home and hearth
Remarking, as an aftermath,
That the Church should first unite us.

We long to bear the heavy weight
Of the matrimonial halter,
We're tired of following friends we hate
Sedately to the altar.

We're sick of being pretty little bridesmaids,
We're weary of the fussing and the fume,
We dread the awful destiny that guides maids
Unwanted and unmarried to the tomb,
We long to lose our purity
And plump for the security
A wedding-ring undoubtedly provides,
We're sick to death of being pretty little bridesmaids
Instead of being pretty little brides.

We're bored with all those brooches made of seed pearls,
We hate each insignificant bouquet,
We'd like to feel that should we ever need pearls
We could earn them in a more attractive way.

We'd face with equanimity
The intimate proximity
Of someone snoring loudly by our sides,
For we're sick to death of being pretty little bridesmaids
Instead of being pretty little brides.

We shudder every time we see the vicar,
We shrink from orange blossom and champagne,
It's such a very acid-making liquor,
No sooner down than up it comes again.
There's nothing very nice about
Relations throwing rice about,
But that we'd bear and other things besides,
If just for once instead of pretty little bridesmaids
We might be being pretty little brides.

We can't enjoy those roguish implications
Concerning the approaching bridal night,
Nor share the strange, vicarious sensations
In which our elder relatives delight,
If ever we are married off
We pray that we'll be carried off
To where no eager family presides,
For we'd loathe to think of all our beastly little
    bridesmaids
Imagining us pretty little brides!

## I SAW NO SHADOW

*from* PACIFIC 1860

I saw no shadow on the sea,
No warning star appeared,
The skies were free,
No vagrant gipsy told me
Of a fascinating stranger,
Gave no hint of where the danger
Might be.

Then came that strange, disturbing day
That love that I so desired,
The sun and the moon conspired
Above me,
Now like a ghost I watch my happiness depart,
The light of love has cast a shadow on my heart.

All through my life I have wandered,
Ambition my compass and my chart,
Moments I heedlessly squandered
Now return to haunt me—mocking at my heart.
Love, with its lovely illusions,
I neatly, discreetly set aside,
Fear kept me safe from confusion
Leaving me with only
Loneliness and pride,
Cold was the starlight above me,
Time in its passing was slow,
I had no need of a lover to love me
But oh—
That was long ago.

I saw no shadow on the sea,
No voices called to me,
My life was free,
How could I open wide my arms
To the paradise around me
When no love had ever found me
The key?
And then I dreamed some foolish dreams
And, leaving my world behind,
I gaily set out to find
My lover.
Now, in a moment, all those dreams are torn apart,
The light of love has cast a shadow on my heart.


## WEDDING TOAST

*from* PACIFIC 1860

Your Excellencies—Ladies and Gentlemen—
Dear Friends—in this sweet circumstance
When all the air around us and above
Is charged with tenderness and early love
And that enchantment which is called Romance,
I beg of you to lift your glasses up
And drink to those we love—a loving cup.

No one can vouch for love—none can be sure
How long its ardent magic may endure,
No one can order love—all we can do
Is, in our deepest hearts, to keep it true.

To you we love—to you we hold so dear
I drink to here and now and ever after,
May every tear you shed dissolve in laughter,
May joy be yours through every changing year.
I drink to you with certainty and know
That Destiny could never never part
Two lovers when they love each other so.

And oh I envy you with all my heart.

# UNCLE HARRY

### *from* PACIFIC 1860

Verse 1    We all of us have relations,
           Our crosses in life we bear,
           A gloomy group of uncles, cousins and aunts,
           We meet them in railway stations,
           In Harrods or Chester Square,
           And always on the Channel boat to France.
           We have to be polite to them,
           They sometimes send us pheasants,
           We always have to write to them
           To thank for Christmas presents.
           These family obligations
           Admittedly are a bore
           But I possess one uncle that I positively adore.

Refrain 1   Poor Uncle Harry
            Wanted to be a missionary
            So he took a ship and sailed away.
            This visionary,
            Hotly pursued by dear Aunt Mary,
            Found a South Sea Isle on which to stay.
            The natives greeted them kindly and invited them to dine
            On yams and clams and human hams and vintage coconut wine,
            The taste of which was filthy but the after-effects divine.
            Poor Uncle Harry
            Got a bit gay and longed to tarry.
            This, Aunt Mary couldn't quite allow,
            She lectured him severely on a number of church affairs
            But when she'd gone to bed he made a get-away down the stairs,
            For he longed to find the answer to a few of the maiden's prayers.
            Uncle Harry's not a missionary now.

            Poor Uncle Harry
            After a chat with dear Aunt Mary
            Thought the time had come to make a row,
            He lined up all the older girls in one of the local sheds
            And while he was reviling them and tearing himself to shreds
            They took their Mother Hubbards off and tied them round their
                heads.
            Uncle Harry's not a missionary now.
            He's awfully happy
            But he's certainly not a missionary now!

Verse 2    Now Uncle was just a 'seeker',
A 'dreamer' sincerely blest,
Of this there couldn't be a shadow of doubt.
The fact that his flesh was weaker
Than even Aunt Mary guessed
Took even her some time to figure out.
In all those languid latitudes
The atmosphere's exotic,
To take up moral attitudes
Would be too idiotic,
Though nobody could be meeker
Than Uncle had been before
I bet today he's giving way
At practically every pore!

Refrain 2    Poor Uncle Harry
Having become a missionary
Found the native's morals rather crude.
He and Aunt Mary
Quickly imposed an arbitrary
Ban upon them shopping in the nude.
They all considered this silly and they didn't take it well,
They burnt his boots and several suits and wrecked the Mission
    Hotel,
They also burnt his mackintosh, which made a disgusting smell.
Poor Uncle Harry
After some words with dear Aunt Mary
Called upon the chiefs for a pow-wow.
They didn't brandish knives at him, they really were awfully
    sweet,
They made concerted dives at him and offered him things to eat,
But when they threw their wives at him he had to admit defeat.
Uncle Harry's not a missionary now.

Poor dear Aunt Mary
Though it were revolutionary
Thought *her* time had come to take a bow.
Poor Uncle Harry looked at her, in whom he had placed his trust,
His very last illusion broke and crumbled away to dust
For she'd placed a flower behind her ear and frankly exposed her
    bust.
Uncle Harry's not a missionary now.
He's left the island
But he's certainly not a missionary now.

# *Miscellaneous*

## THERE HAVE BEEN SONGS IN ENGLAND

A nation's music belongs to the Race
Through the slow time changes
And the rhythm of moving years.
Our nation's songs are its pride and its grace
Evermore and after,
Though the shape of the world may alter,
In our songs the laughter
Blends the tears.
From the past
We hear the echo of the songs that proved us free,
They are bequeathed to you and me
For ever and ever.

Refrain   There have been songs in England
Since our island rose from the seas,
As the dry land lay on that early English day
A sea wind rustled through the trees,
Very soon the birds appeared,
Later, lyric words appeared,
Later on the people sang,
Still they're singing free.
There have been songs in England
And songs there will always be.

## LET'S DO IT

(With acknowledgements to Cole Porter)

Verse 1   Mr Irving Berlin
Often emphasizes sin
In a charming way.
Mr Coward we know
Wrote a song or two to show
Sex was here to stay.
Richard Rodgers it's true
Takes a more romantic view
Of that sly biological urge.
But it really was Cole
Who contrived to make the whole
Thing merge.

Refrain 1   He said that Belgians and Dutch do it,
            Even Hildegarde and Hutch do it,
            Let's do it, let's fall in love.
            Monkeys when ever you look do it,
            Aly Khan and King Farouk do it,
            Let's do it, let's fall in love.
            The most recherché cocottes do it
            In a luxury flat,
            Locks, Dunns and Scotts do it
            At the drop of a hat,
            Excited spinsters in spas do it,
            Duchesses when opening bazaars do it,
            Let's do it, let's fall in love.

Refrain 2   Our leading writers in swarms do it,
            Somerset and all the Maughams do it,
            Let's do it, let's fall in love.
            The Brontës felt that they must do it,
            Mrs Humphry Ward could just do it,
            Let's do it, let's fall in love.
            Anouilh and Sartre—God knows why—do it,
            As a sort of a curse
            Eliot and Fry do it,
            But they do it in verse.
            Some mystics, as a routine do it,
            Even Evelyn Waugh and Graham Greene do it,
            Let's do it, let's fall in love.

Verse 2     In the Spring of the year
            Inhibitions disappear
            And our hearts beat high,
            We had better face facts
            Every gland that overacts
            Has an alibi,
            For each bird and each bee,
            Each slap-happy sappy tree,
            Each temptation that lures us along
            Is just Nature elle-même
            Merely singing us the same
            Old song.

Refrain 3   Girls from the R.A.D.A. do it,
            B.B.C. announcers may do it,
            Let's do it, let's fall in love.
            The Ballet Jooss to a man do it,
            Alfred Lunt and Lynn Fontanne do it,

Let's do it, let's fall in love.
My kith and kin, more or less, do it,
Every uncle and aunt,
But I confess to it,
I've one cousin who can't.
Critics as sour as quince do it,
Even Emile Littler and Prince do it,
Let's do it, let's fall in love.

Refrain 4   The House of Commons en bloc do it,
Civil Servants by the clock do it,
Let's do it, let's fall in love
Deacons who've done it before do it,
Minor canons with a roar do it,
Let's do it, let's fall in love.
Some rather rorty old rips do it
When they get a bit tight,
Government Whips do it
If it takes them all night,
Old mountain goats in ravines do it,
Probably we'll live to see machines do it,
Let's do it, let's fall in love.


LET'S FLY AWAY

(Music by Cole Porter)

Verse 1   I so despise civilized existence
Which is why I say
I long to take the line of least resistance
And break away.
The Twentieth Century Blues have got me,
This rat-race may appeal to you but not to me,
I'm fed up with reading in Sunday papers
The private lives of adolescent rapers,
I candidly confess my spirit retches
At snaps of Tiny Tots with dogs on beaches,
There's only one solution, dear,
Let's firmly disappear.

Refrain 1   Let's fly away
To where no threats of war obsess us
And where the Press does not depress us
Every single day.

Let's fly away
From diplomatic, static missions
To where the feet of politicians
Are not of China clay.
Let's leave the milk-bar snacks,
'Perms' and breakfast foods
To those girls in plastic macs,
Slacks and pixie hoods.
Let's start today
For somewhere gayer, warmer, dryer,
England's too damp for us,
Let's fly away.

Refrain 2  Let's fly away
From photographs of battered boxers
And sex-besotted bobby-soxers
Assaulting Johnnie Ray.
Let's fly away
From all that roguish imprecision
Of Parlour Games on television
Which ends our Sabbath day.
Let's find a peaceful spot
Taking care to choose
Where Rita Hayworth's not
Always in the news.
Let's kneel and pray
To Mister Thomas Cook Esquire,
Let's pack our bags today
And fly away.

Verse 2  If modern life must be democratic.
Be that as it may,
Without desiring to be too dogmatic
I frankly say
I tear up each paper that publicises
The rather uninspiring enterprises
Of truck-drivers' wives who win competitions
By photographing birds in odd positions,
I don't care if a widow in Thames Ditton
Plunged into a well to save her kitten
And if three mothers swam Loch Ness
I just could not care less.

Refrain 3  Let's fly away
In any aeroplane or glider
Before the movie screens get wider,
We can't afford to stay,

Let's not delay,
For lots of larger, longer, duller
Biblical films in Technicolour
May be on the way,
We're sick of crimped and curled
Over-coloured sex,
Let's face the brave new world
Minus 3-D specs.
Let's firmly say
To Messrs Metro-Goldwyn-Mayer,
'You've had it chums. Okay! Let's fly away.'

Refrain 4　Let's fly away
Before they send us any more girls
Like those ubiquitous Gabor girls,
Alas alack-a-day,
Let's frankly say
We won't discuss the qualche-cosa
Possessed by Mr Rubirosa,
We'd better not delay,
Let's plan to spend La Vie
In some Paradise
Where we're not asked to see
*War and Peace* on ice.
Let's see today
If helicopters are for hire
And gaily say, 'Hey, hey, Let's fly away.'


# LONDON PRIDE

1　London Pride has been handed down to us.
London Pride is a flower that's free.
London Pride means our own dear town to us,
And our pride it for ever will be.
Woa, Liza,
See the coster barrows,
Vegetable marrows
And the fruit piled high.
Woa, Liza,
Little London sparrows,
Covent Garden Market where the costers cry.
Cockney feet
Mark the beat of history.

Every street
Pins a memory down.
Nothing ever can quite replace
The grace of London Town.

Interlude There's a little city flower every spring unfailing
Growing in the crevices by some London railing,
Though it has a Latin name, in town and countryside
We in England call it London Pride.

2 London Pride has been handed down to us.
London Pride is a flower that's free.
London Pride means our own dear town to us,
And our pride it for ever will be.
Hey, lady,
When the day is dawning
See the policeman yawning
On his lonely beat.
Gay lady,
Mayfair in the morning,
Hear your footsteps echo in the empty street.
Early rain
And the pavement's glistening.
All Park Lane
In a shimmering gown.
Nothing ever could break or harm
The charm of London Town.

Interlude In our city darkened now, street and square and crescent,
We can feel our living past in our shadowed present,
Ghosts beside our starlit Thames
Who lived and loved and died
Keep throughout the ages London Pride.

3 London Pride has been handed down to us.
London Pride is a flower that's free.
London Pride means our own dear town to us,
And our pride it for ever will be.
Grey city
Stubbornly implanted,
Taken so for granted
For a thousand years.
Stay, city,
Smokily enchanted,
Cradle of our memories and hopes and fears.
Every Blitz
Your resistance

Toughening,
From the Ritz
To the Anchor and Crown,
Nothing ever could override
The pride of London Town.


# IMAGINE THE DUCHESS'S FEELINGS

Verse 1 The Duchess had manner
    For dignity lurks
    In the shadow of Debrett
    But fate threw a spanner
    Smack in the works
    Tarnishing her coronet.
    Three large sons were born to her
    But one sad morn to her
    There came a horrid moment of regret,
    Said the Duchess,
    'Well!
    Something doesn't jell!'
    Said the Duchess, 'Well—Hell!'

Refrain 1 Imagine the Duchess's feelings
    When she had hatched out her brood
    To find her first son was weak though well mannered,
    Her second rather stupid and her third plain rude.
    Her eldest son when in trouble went white,
    Her second soon looked blue and hung his head,
    But imagine the Duchess's feelings
    When her youngest son went Red!

Verse 2 She sent them to Eton,
    Traditional youth
    Was theirs whatever else they got,
    But nothing could sweeten
    The bitterest truth
    That baby wasn't quite so hot!
    High life gave no joy to him,
    The Hoi Polloi to him
    Provided something that his peers did not,
    Said her Grace, aghast,
    'Is it going to last?'
    Said her Grace, aghast—'Blast!'

Refrain 2  Imagine the Duchess's feelings,
              You could have pierced her with swords
              When she discovered her pet lamb liked Lenin
              And sold the *Daily Worker* near the House of Lords.
              Her eldest son went to Boodle's and White's,
              Her second joined the Blues his father led,
              But imagine the Duchess's feelings
              When her youngest son went Red!

Refrain 3  Imagine the Duchess's feelings,
              Her overwhelming despair
              To find her third son hobnobbed with the butler
              And sang the 'Internationale' in Belgrave Square.
              Her first son's debts bled the family white,
              Her second son blued everything and fled,
              But imagine the Duchess's feelings
              When her youngest son went Red!


# DON'T LET'S BE BEASTLY TO THE GERMANS

Verse 1  We must be kind—
           And with an open mind
           We must endeavour to find
           A way—
           To let the Germans know that when the war is over
           They are not the ones who'll have to pay.
           We must be sweet—
           And tactful and discreet
           And when they've suffered defeat
           We mustn't let
           Them feel upset
           Or ever get
           The feeling that we're cross with them or hate them,
           Our future policy must be to reinstate them.

Refrain 1  Don't let's be beastly to the Germans
           When our victory is ultimately won,
           It was just those nasty Nazis who persuaded them to fight
           And their Beethoven and Bach are really far worse than their bite,
           Let's be meek to them—
           And turn the other cheek to them
           And try to bring out their latent sense of fun.
           Let's give them full air parity—
           And treat the rats with charity,
           But don't let's be beastly to the Hun.

Verse 2    We must be just—
And win their love and trust
And in addition we must
Be wise
And ask the conquered lands to join our hands to aid them.
That would be a wonderful surprise.
For many years—
They've been in floods of tears
Because the poor little dears
Have been so wronged and only longed
To cheat the world,
Deplete the world
And beat
The world to blazes.
This is the moment when we ought to sing their praises.

Refrain 2  Don't let's be beastly to the Germans
When we've definitely got them on the run—
Let us treat them very kindly as we would a valued friend—
We might send them out some Bishops as a form of lease and lend,
Let's be sweet to them—
And day by day repeat to them
That 'sterilization' simply isn't done.
Let's help the dirty swine again—
To occupy the Rhine again,
But don't let's be beastly to the Hun.

Refrain 3  Don't let's be beastly to the Germans
When the age of peace and plenty has begun.
We must send them steel and oil and coal and everything they
need
For their peaceable intentions can be always guaranteed.
Let's employ with them a sort of 'strength through joy' with
them,
They're better than us at honest manly fun.
Let's let them feel they're swell again and bomb us all to hell again,
But don't let's be beastly to the Hun.

Refrain 4  Don't let's be beastly to the Germans
For you can't deprive a gangster of his gun
Though they've been a little naughty to the Czechs and Poles
and Dutch
But I don't suppose those countries really minded very much.
Let's be free with them and share the B.B.C. with them.
We mustn't prevent them basking in the sun.
Let's soften their defeat again—and build their bloody fleet again,
But don't let's be beastly to the Hun.

# COULD YOU PLEASE OBLIGE US WITH A BREN GUN?

Verse 1    Colonel Montmorency who
Was in Calcutta in ninety-two
Emerged from his retirement for the war.
He wasn't very pleased with what he heard and what he
    saw.
But whatever he felt
He tightened his belt—
And organized a corps.
Poor Colonel Montmorency thought,
Considering all the wars he'd fought,
The Home Guard was his job to do or die;
But after days and weeks and years
Bravely drying his manly tears
He wrote the following letter to the Minister of Supply:

Refrain 1    Could you please oblige us with a Bren gun?
Or, failing that, a hand grenade would do.
We've got some ammunition
In a rather damp condition,
And Mayor Huss
Has an arquebus
That was used at Waterloo.
With the Vicar's stirrup pump, a pitch-fork and a spade
It's rather hard to guard an aerodrome;
So if you can't oblige us with a Bren gun—
The Home Guard might as well go home.

Verse 2    Colonel Montmorency planned
In case the enemy tried to land
To fling them back by skill and armoured force.
He realized his army should be mechanized, of course;
But somewhere inside
Experience cried:
'My kingdom for a horse'—
Poor Colonel Montmorency tried
At infinite cost of time and pride
To tackle his superiors again—
Having just one motor bike,
Fourteen swords and a marlinspike,
He couched the following letter in the following urgent
    strain:

Refrain 2    Could you please oblige us with a Bren gun?
We're getting awfully tired of drawing lots.

Today we had a shipment
Of some curious equipment—
And just for a prank
They sent us a tank
That ties itself in knots.
On Sunday's mock invasion Captain Clarke was heard to say
He hadn't even got a brush and comb;
So if you can't oblige us with a Bren gun—
The Home Guard might as well go home.

Refrain 3  Could you please oblige us with a Bren gun?
We need it rather badly I'm afraid.
Our local crossword-solver.
Has an excellent revolver;
But during a short
Attack on a fort
The trigger got mislaid.
In course of operations planned for Friday afternoon
Our Orders are to storm the Hippodrome;
So if you can't oblige us with a Bren gun—
The Home Guard might as well go home.

Refrain 4  Could you please oblige us with a Bren gun?
The lack of one is wounding to our pride.
Last night we found the cutest
Little German parachutist
Who looked at our kit
And giggled a bit,
Then laughed until he cried.
We'll have to hide that armoured car when marching to
    Berlin,
We'd almost be ashamed of it in Rome.
So if you can't oblige us with a Bren gun—
The Home Guard might as well go home.


## ALWAYS BE NICE TO THE GENTLEMEN

Verse 1   A mother and her daughter were strolling hand in hand,
The primroses and violets were carpeting the land,
A lark on high
Caressed the sky
With Spring's eternal lullaby,
The young girl gave a little sigh
And said, 'By God, it's grand!'

Her mother smiled benignly
And wiped away a tear,
'You put things so divinely,
I'm proud of you, my dear!'
The daughter sniffed the evening breeze,
And gallantly controlled a sneeze,
Then gave her mother's hand a squeeze
And whispered in her ear:

Refrain 1   'Hey Momma, hey Momma,
Now that I am twenty-one,
The urge to have a bit of fun
Is bubbling up inside.
Say Momma, say Momma,
I am awfully keen to know
How far a nice young girl should go.'
Her mother then replied:
'My daughter, bear in mind
That God has given you
One remarkable gift;
Although it's not refined
To talk too much about it,
Don't forget, my daughter, that the race is to the swift!'
'Hey Momma, hey Momma,
What am I to say
If one fine day
I find that I've been led astray?'
Her mother said, 'Oh pooh!
Always be nice to the gentlemen,
Consider them your whole life through;
For if you are nice to the gentlemen,
And kind,
You'll find
That if you keep them half as happy as your mother used
    to do
They'll probably be nice to you!'

Verse 2   The mother and her daughter pursued their way along
To where the village church bells were tolling evensong.
Upon the green
A local Dean
Imparted glamour to the scene.
The mother smiled, 'This might have been
The place where I went wrong!'
Her daughter roared with laughter,
And looked at her askance,
'Was that before or after

You ran that house in France?'
Her mother gave the girl a clout
And said, 'All dirty cracks are out,
You may do better, though I doubt
You'll ever get the chance.'

Refrain 2  'Hey Momma, hey Momma,
Is there any guarantee
That pure unsullied girls like me
Will never be beguiled?
Say Momma, say Momma,
Is to be a model wife
The ultimate reward in life?'
Her mother said, 'My child,
Although a moral lapse
Is reprehensible,
Boys, you know, will be boys!
You may amuse the chaps,
But if you're sensible
Whatever else you sacrifice hang on to social poise!'
'Hey Momma, hey Momma,
Where can I apply
If by and by,
I find that I'm left high and dry?'
Her mother shouted, 'Whoops!
Always be nice to the gentlemen,
For that's the stuff to give the troops!
For if you are nice to the gentlemen,
And smart, sweetheart,
If you can hook 'em, and then rook 'em like your mother
        used to do,
They'll probably be nice to you!'

Refrain 3  'Hey Momma, hey Momma,
Though I am so innocent,
You've helped me to a large extent
To formulate a creed.
Say Momma, say Momma,
What the hell am I to do
If I should make a slip or two
By following your lead?'
Her mother said, 'Don't fuss,
Just face realities,
You're no longer at school.
I really can't discuss
Such trivialities,
You'll have to face the music if you're such a bloody fool!'

'Hey Momma, hey Momma,
What am I to think
If some old gink
Should really put me on the blink?'
Her mother said, 'Oh nuts!
Always be nice to the gentlemen,
And never mind the "ifs" and "buts",
For if you are nice to the gentlemen,
And gay,
Hey! Hey!
If you can keep the bastards guessing like your mother used
    to do,
They'll probably be nice to you!'

# The Fifties

# NOTE ON 'THE FIFTIES'

In 'The Fifties' I emerged, to my own and every one else's astonishment, as a highly successful cabaret entertainer. True, when I first appeared at the Café de Paris, a captious journalist announced recklessly that I 'massacred' my own songs. If I did I can only say it was the most triumphantly efficient massacre since Saint Bartholomew's Eve. I appeared for four seasons at the Café de Paris and later agreed for what, to my mind, was a rather excessive salary, to appear for a month at the Desert Inn in Las Vegas. The prospect of this engagement filled me with misgivings because, although I had proved that my sophisticated songs and apparently even more sophisticated personality could go down all right with the crème de la crème of London Café Society, I doubted that the less urbane cross-section of Americans who frequented Las Vegas with the main object of gambling would understand and appreciate the essential 'Englishness' of my material and my performance. My fears however were unfounded. From the first 'dinner show' onwards, when I made my entrance with brisk outward assurance and inward panic, the audiences in that strange desert playground received me twice nightly with the utmost generosity, attention and enthusiasm. Although I found it rather a strain singing every evening at 9.15 and 12.15 for nearly fifty minutes, Sundays included, it was one of the most gratifying and stimulating experiences of my life. I do not believe, however, that I would have been the success I was had I not served the invaluable apprenticeship of performing during the war years to the troops. Singing to troops is a tricky business. As audiences they are unpredictable. In the front line and in far away places when they are starved for entertainment they are wonderful and heartwarming but in transit camps, for instance, when they are either going on leave or returning from leave, they could be, and often were, dull, unreceptive, and, on occasion, definitely hostile. In any case, an exclusively male audience is always more difficult to dominate than a mixed one, particularly for a male performer. However, I am as grateful to the unco-operative troop audiences as I am to the wildly enthusiastic ones. Perhaps more so because they taught me some sharp lessons, the most important of which was never to betray irritation, temper or dismay, and to press on firmly with my programme for so long as they allowed me to do so.

My seasons at the Café de Paris necessitated renewal of my material as often as possible. Among the many songs I wrote at that time were 'Time And Again', a group of burlesque numbers under the heading 'These I Have Loathed', which included 'The Spinning Song', 'Devon', 'Paris', 'An Irish Ballad', etc. I also wrote at that time 'Don't Make Fun of the Festival' which is, I think, one of my best. Sadly, however, from the 'posterity' point of view it stands little chance of survival. It belonged so very much to its particular moment. The Café de Paris audiences, to whom I sang it nightly, loved it and I can only hope that the casual reader, despite the fact that he will miss the jaunty little tune, will enjoy it too.

# 'Ace of Clubs'

## TOP OF THE MORNING

*from* ACE OF CLUBS
(Part of Club Floor Show)

Verse    On my way
Walking along the street,
Noticing the expressions
Of the people that I meet,
I seem to feel a sort of gay beginning
To a brand new lovely summer day beginning,
Come what may
Winter is on the wing,
I can't prevent myself from singing—

Refrain    Top of the morning to you!
Top of the morning to you!
The sun is high,
The summer sky
Is clear and gay
And I've just heard from the B.B.C.
There won't be rain today.
London is shining and free,
That is, as free as a Democracy can be.
Though your cares distract you,
Though your boss has sacked you,
Though your dad has cracked you
On the jaw—
Yesterday's
As hazy as a far-off shore,
Top of the morning
After the night before!

# MY KIND OF MAN

*from* ACE OF CLUBS
(Part of Club Floor Show)

Verse    In me you see a lonely girl
Though certainly not the only girl
Whose love-life is as cold as driven snow,
I can't explain why passion chills me so,
I only know—

Refrain 1  I want to find my kind of man,
My heart has designed my kind of man,
He may be—a gay hussar,
A movie star,
A gentleman of renown,
But when we meet I'll never let him down,
I want to find my kind of man
And I shall do the best I can
Not to meet or mate or marry
Tom, Dick or Harry,
Till I find my kind of man.

Refrain 2  I want to find my kind of man,
I've never defined my kind of man,
He may be—a copper's nark,
A City clerk,
Or even a gigolo—
But when we meet I'll never let him go.
I want to find my kind of man,
And I shall do the best I can
Not to fall for any stinker
Hook line and sinker
Till I find my kind of man.

Refrain 3  I want to find my kind of man,
My dreams have designed my kind of man,
He may be a country type
With tweeds and pipe
Or merely a London spiv—
But when we meet, I'll give and give and give.
Until I find my kind of man,
I'll keep my heart so spick and span,
All decked out in love's apparel,
Lock stock and barrel,
When I find my kind of man.

When I find my kind of man,
We'll start a five year—jive year plan,
Maybe tinker—maybe tailor,
Soldier—or sailor,
But I'll find my kind of man.


# THIS COULD BE TRUE

*from* ACE OF CLUBS

Verse    Chance brought us both together
In a strange, unconventional way,
Here in the starlight with the night all round us
Destiny seems to have caught and bound us.

Refrain 1  This could be true,
This could be true,
Let's both be terribly careful
What we say or do
We may find—shadows on the stairway
When we try to climb too high,
We may find—hazards on the fairway,
Niggers in the woodpile,
Daring us to try—but—
This could be right,
Love at first sight,
Let's take particular pains

To keep the flame alight,
Let's face the fact
That wonderful—wonderful moments in life are few,
Let's defy those niggers in the woodpile, darling,
This could be true.

Refrain 2  This could be true,
This could be true.
Maybe the ultimate goal
Our lives were leading to,
Let's take care—people may resent us,
Laugh at us and call us fools,
Let's beware—time is only lent us,
Stick to regulations,
Follow all the rules—for
This could be sweet,

Gay and discreet,
If you will give me your hand
The future's at our feet.
This is the most—
Incredible, magical moment we ever knew,
So to Hell with rules and regulations, darling,
This must be true!

# NOTHING CAN LAST FOR EVER

### *from* ACE OF CLUBS

Verse Why should I mind?
   Why should I weep for him?
   Love as frail as ours could never last.
   A little time will pass
   And everything we've said and done
   Will lie forgotten in the past.
   Yesterday
   Swiftly fades away,
   Now it is over there's nothing to say,
   Early or late,
   Guided by Fate,
   Passion will lie to you,
   Love say goodbye to you
   And when that moment comes
   It's wise to face the truth,
   The best of it belongs to youth.
   Why should I mind?
   My heart will keep for him
   Some of the love he left behind.

Refrain Nothing can last for ever,
   Love is a lost endeavour,
   Foolishly I
   Would plan and scheme,
   Foolishly try
   To hold my dream,
   Dreading the hour of waking,
   Dreading the moment of breaking,
   Now it is dead
   And buried in the past,
   Nothing can ever last.

## SOMETHING ABOUT A SAILOR

*from* ACE OF CLUBS

Verse 1   The songs they sing of the rollicking deep
Are rather out of key
But one thing you'll agree—is true,
That men who work for the women who weep
Acquire a roving eye
Nobody in their senses would deny.

Refrain 1   There's always something about a sailor,
Nobody's ever able to define,
There's a gay—salty sort of tang about
His devil-may-care,
His nautical air
Of brawn and brine,
When wives and sweethearts are told the fleet's in
Most of them have a perm and tuck the sheets in,
Girls in Gosport hit an all-time high,
Wives in Weymouth have a spree,
Brides in bridal veils
Will vault the altar rails
To follow—the fellow who follows the sea.

Verse 2   The course is set for original sin
On every man-of-war
As everyone ashore—well knows.
Yo-ho my lads, and a bottle of gin
Inspires the happy thought
Of somebody else's wife in every port.

Refrain 2   There's always something about a sailor,
Every time he sets his foot ashore
All the pubs—do a roaring trade until
Each swaggering Jack
Goes staggering back
To sea once more.
So hang the flags out and throw confetti,
Liberty boats are heading for the jetty,
Tarts are tearful when the anchor's weighed,
Geishas grumble on the quay,
Every courtesan
From Tyne to Turkestan
Will follow—the fellow who follows the sea.

## I'D NEVER KNOW

*from* ACE OF CLUBS

Verse     I met a boy—an ordinary character,
A little shy, a bit reserved,
Until that day—my heart had known no trespasser,
I put my trust in Fate,
I knew my path was straight,
But now my path has swerved
And I'm alone in time and space,
Now the whole world is quite a different place.

Refrain 1  Why is the summer giving
London this lovely glow?
What is this joy of loving?
Without him—I'd never, never know—
I'd never, never know.
Why do I feel excited
Each time he says 'Hallo'?
Why do the streets seem lighted?
Without him—I'd never, never know—
I'd never, never know.
He wouldn't please the highbrows
Or drive Alan Ladd from the screen,
But when he lifts his eyebrows
I blush like a girl of fifteen.
Soon it will all be over,
He'll say goodbye and go—
I love him so—
But will he ever know?
Will he ever, ever know?

Refrain 2  Why do I like 'Torch numbers'
Crooned on the radio?
Why do they haunt my slumbers?
Without him—I'd never, never know—
I'd never never know.
Why do I sing quite loudly
Hurrying through Soho?
Why do I walk so proudly?
Without him—I'd never, never know,
I'd never, never, know.
I'd never quite surrender,
I wasn't cut out for a slave,
But when his voice goes tender,

My heart has a permanent wave.
When he's 'in front' I tremble,
Can't hardly play the show,
I love him so—but will he ever know?
Will he ever, ever know?


# THREE JUVENILE DELINQUENTS

*from* ACE OF CLUBS

Verse 1   Three juvenile delinquents,
Juvenile delinquents,
Happy as can be—we
Waste no time
On the wherefores and whys of it;
We like crime
And that's about the size of it.
People say that films demoralize us,
Lead us to a life of shame.
Mental doctors try to civilize us,
Psycho-analyse us,
Blimey what a game!
They don't know how to treat us,
For if they should beat us
That would never do.
When they say, 'Go steady!'
We've the answer ready:
———————— And the same to you!

Verse 2   Three juvenile delinquents,
Juvenile delinquents,
Happy as can be—we
Hit and run
For the thrill and the sport of it;
Nice clean fun
And that's the long and short of it.
Dear old ladies often get the vapours
When we meet them after dark—whoo!
Then next day we read about our capers
In the daily papers,
Blimey what a lark!
We thrill the Sunday readers,
But the silly bleeders
Haven't got a clue.

When the judge says 'Chokey'
We say 'Okey-dokey'
———————————— And the same to you!

Verse 3    Three juvenile delinquents,
Juvenile delinquents,
Happy as can be—we
Lick our chops
When we read what they write of us.
All the cops
Hate the bloody sight of us.
Once we pinched a Cadillac and drove her
From the Marble Arch to Kew;
Hit a fat old geezer in a Rover,
Fairly bowled her over,
Blimey what a do!
We said, 'You mustn't fuss, dear,
There's a lovely bus, dear,
Number twenty-two.
If we've bruised your bonnet,
Stick a plaster on it.'
———————————— And the same to you!

Verse 4    Three juvenile delinquents,
Juvenile delinquents.
Every now and then—when
Kind old cranks
Mention angels of light to us
We say, 'Thanks,
Don't forget to write to us.'
Nowadays the younger generation
Never has to face brute force.
Some old judge, instead of flagellation,
Puts us on probation!
Blimey what a sauce!
Last night we got an earful
From a rather tearful
Clergyman we knew.
When he turned the sobs on
We replied, 'With knobs on'
———————————— And the same to you!

Verse 5    Three juvenile delinquents,
Juvenile delinquents,
Happy as can be—we
Break our backs
To achieve popularity;

Three sharp whacks,
Faith and Hope and Charity.
Once we knocked a pair of silly sluts out
Just behind the 'Horse and Plough',
Dragged them round to where the railing juts out,
Bellowing their guts out,
Blimey what a row!
We had to cosh 'em proper,
Then we saw a copper
Starting to pursue.
Then we cried vibrato,
'How's your old Tomato?'
———————— And the same to you!


## SAIL AWAY

*from* ACE OF CLUBS

Verse 1   When a sailor goes to sea,
Though he leaves his love behind,
Time and tide will set him free
From the grief inside him.
Sea and sky will ease his heart,
Regulate his troubled mind,
Every sailor has a chart
And a star to guide him—home.

Refrain 1  When the storm clouds are riding through a winter
sky,
Sail away—sail away.
When the love-light is fading in your sweetheart's
eye,
Sail away—sail away.
When you feel your song is orchestrated wrong,
Why should you prolong
Your stay?
When the wind and the weather blow your dreams
sky-high,
Sail away—sail away!

Verse 2   Love is meant to make us glad,
Love can make the world go round,
Love can drive you raving mad,
Torment and upset you.

Love can give your heart a jolt
But philosophers have found
That it's wise to do a bolt
When it starts to get you—down.

Refrain 2 When your life seems too difficult to rise above,
Sail away—sail away.
When your heart feels as dreary as a worn-out glove,
Sail away—sail away.
But when soon or late
You recognize your fate,
That will be your great, great day,
On the wings of the morning with your own true
love,
Sail away—sail away—sail away!


# JOSEPHINE

*from* ACE OF CLUBS
(Part of Club Floor Show)

Verse 1 The lady was beautiful,
The lady was dark,
She wasn't too dutiful
But still left her mark
On volumes of history
And thousands of cheques
And all through the mystery
Of 'Ole Debbil Sex!'

Refrain 1 Josephine—Josephine
From the first was rather chic,
As a tot
She would trot
Through the island of Martinique,
Her fortune was told by an aged crone
Who prophesied fame and romance,
And who hissed in her ear
The outrageous idea
That she'd also be Empress of France!
Josephine—Josephine
Had, with men, a set routine
And the people who thought
Her technique was self-taught
Didn't know—Josephine.

Verse 2    Whatever she nearly did
From five to fifteen
We know that she really did
Begin the Beguine.
On first meeting Bonaparte
She murmured, 'Hell's bells!'
You let down the tone, apart
From anything else!

Refrain 2    Josephine—Josephine
Very seldom lost control
Though her wit
Was a bit
Over-seasoned with 'Sauce Créole'.
She very soon married this short young man
Who talked about soldiers all day
But who wasn't above
Making passionate love
In a coarse, rather Corsican way.
Josephine—wasn't keen
And she made an ugly scene,
Until Bonaparte said,
'We must rumple the bed!
Just for show—Josephine!'

Refrain 3    Josephine—Josephine
Though a Queen remained at home
While her lord
Was abroad
Sending postcards, in code, from Rome.
He often appeared
With a three-day beard
From Austria, Poland or Spain,
And one dreadful night
He arrived, rather tight,
Having balled up the Russian campaign.
Josephine—turning green—
Cried, 'Whatever does this mean?'
Then Napoleon said, 'Whoops!
I have lost all my troops
In the snow, Josie—
Oh, Josie,
Snow—Josephine!'

# WOULD YOU LIKE TO STICK A PIN
# IN MY BALLOON?

*from* ACE OF CLUBS
(Part of Club Floor Show)

Would you like to stick a pin in my balloon, Daddy?
Would you like to stick a pin in my balloon?
Just make a grab
When you hear the melody stop,
One little jab
And you'll hear a beautiful pop,
If you'll only suit the action to the tune, Daddy,
You'll be bound to get the hang of it soon,
All the boys I know can do the trick,
So, Daddy, Daddy, won't you stick
A pin in my balloon?


# IN A BOAT, ON A LAKE, WITH MY DARLING

*from* ACE OF CLUBS
(Part of Club Floor Show)

Verse    In my dreams, I often get a
Vision that's divine
Of a very still lagoon
With you in white
And me in blue
Alone in quite
A safe canoe.
Failing this what could be better
Than the Serpentine
On an afternoon
In Love, in June?

Refrain  In a boat, on a lake, with my darling
In the heat of a sweet summer day,
There's the sound of the breeze
In the green willow trees
And the noise of the town fades away
Letting time flutter by like a starling

As we gaze into
The infinite blue
Above
Hand in hand,
Heart to heart,
Just a moment apart
In a boat, on a lake, with my love.


# I LIKE AMERICA

*from* ACE OF CLUBS

GIRLS: Tell us, sailor,
       Tell us, please,
       For we're terribly keen to know
       What it's like to be fancy free,
       Footloose on the rolling sea?
       China girl chop-chop,
       Gay Maltese,
       Hot Mommas from Mexico—

HARRY: If you'll forgive a crude remark
       And don't resent a rude remark
       I'll let you into a secret—

GIRLS: Well?

HARRY: They're all alike in the dark!

GIRLS: There must have been
       Some place you've seen
       Superior to the rest?

HARRY: As a matter of fact
       With political tact
       I like America best.

GIRLS: There's a good time a-comin on de ole plantation
       For a jolly Jack Tar
       Has just confessed
       That he likes America best!

*Verse 1*

HARRY: I don't care for China,
Japan's far too small,
I've rumbled the Rio Grande,
I hate Asia Minor,
I can't bear Bengal
And I shudder to think
Of the awful stink
On the road to Samarkand.

GIRLS: The heat and smell
Must be sheer hell
On the road to Samarkand.

HARRY: I like America,
I have played around
Every slappy-happy hunting ground
But I find America—okay.
I've been about a bit
But I must admit
That I didn't know the half of it
Till I hit the U.S.A.
No likely lass
In Boston, Mass.
From passion will recoil.
In Dallas, Tex.
They talk of sex
But only think of oil.
New Jersey dames
Go up in flames
If someone mentions—bed.
In Chicago, Illinois
Any girl who meets a boy
Giggles and shoots him dead!
But I like America
Its Society
Offers infinite variety
And come what may
I shall return some day
To the good old U.S.A.

*Verse 2*

I've loathed every acre
From Cannes to Canton,
I also deplore Bombay,
I've jeered at Jamaica
And seen through Ceylon,

And exploded the myth
Of those Flying Fith
On the Road to Mandalay.

GIRLS: We'll never mith
Those blasted fith
On the Road to Mandalay.

HARRY: But I like America,
I have travelled far
From Northumberland to Zanzibar
And I find America—okay.
I've roamed the Spanish Main
Eaten sugar-cane
But I never tasted cellophane
Till I struck the U.S.A.
All delegates
From Southern States
Are nervy and distraught.
In New Orleans
The wrought-iron screens
Are dreadfully overwrought.
Beneath each tree
In Tennessee
Erotic books are read.
And when alligators thud
Through the Mississippi mud
Sex rears its ugly head.
But—I like America,
Every scrap of it,
All the sentimental crap of it
And come what may
Give me a holiday
In the good old U.S.A.

# WHY DOES LOVE GET IN THE WAY SO?

### *from* ACE OF CLUBS

Verse 1    Suddenly my world has altered,
Suddenly my step has faltered,
Common sense has flown,
Here I am alone
Coping with these new sensations,
Dark despairs and wild elations,
Eros with his bow—has laid me low.

Refrain 1 Why does love get in the way so?
What have I done
That the son-of-a-gun
Should pick on me?
A little while ago my heart was serene and bright,
Everything seemed all right,
Now I've been struck by a charge of dynamite,
Why does love lead one astray so?
Tell me why
I want to laugh,
I want to cry?
I was gay as a sparrow
Till Cupid's arrow
Punctured this perfect day,
Why does love—get in the way?

Verse 2    Everything is blown to blazes,
Ordinary familiar phrases
Seem to mean much more
Than they did before.
Colours look a great deal brighter,
Black is blacker, white is whiter,
Every sight and sound
Has changed around.

Refrain 2 Why does love get in the way so?
Why should it fret
And completely upset
My peace of mind?
A little while ago my heart was serene and gay,
Everything seemed okay,
And now I suddenly find—I've lost my way.
Why does love lead one astray so?
Why the hell
Should I be caught within its spell?
Life was quite un-enchanted,
All that I wanted,
Now it's a Passion Play!
Why does love get in the way?
Why does love get in the way?

## EVENING IN SUMMER

*from* ACE OF CLUBS

Verse    After the heat of the day is done
Everyone
Who has a garden likes to sit in it and dream
Or read the paper—while the noises of the distant
    traffic seem
Remote and gentle
Sentimental variations on a theme
That comes and goes,
Only London knows
This sweet repose.

Refrain    Evening in summer,
London in June,
Sparrows from roof-tops calling,
Two streets away
You hear a barrel-organ tune,
Night will very very soon
Be falling,
Ships on the river
Londoners hear
Suddenly near,
Sweet to the ear,
Twilight is fading,
Stars shining down,
Evening in summer,
Evening in summer,
Summer in London town.

## BABY'S BOTTLE

*from* ACE OF CLUBS
(Part of Club Floor Show)

Refrain 1    When it's time for Baby's bottle
Give her a bottle of scent.
Sweet perfume
Leads to love in bloom,
So that's—money well spent.
You can fill her Christmas stocking
Full of emeralds and pearls

But some Schiaparelli 'Shocking'
Is the way to get the girls.
When it's time for Baby's bottle
Give her a bottle of scent!

Verse 1    My lady's boudoir, satin, silk
And foamy laces cast aside,
A pair of shoulders white as milk,
A woman's glory and her pride,
A tendril here, a dimple there,
The flutter of a painted fan
Can catch a fellow unaware,
Can make a fool of any man,
Yet, lovely ladies, if by chance
To challenge you I should presume
I vow the essence of romance
Lies in the magic of perfume.

Refrain 2   When it's time for Baby's bottle
Give her a bottle of scent,
Fragrant perfume
Leads to Love in bloom
And that's money well spent.
You can fill her Christmas stocking
With emeralds and pearls
But Schiaparelli 'Shocking'
Will always get the girls.
When it's time for Baby's bottle
Give her a bottle of scent.

Refrain 3   When it's time for Baby's bottle
Give her a bottle of scent,
Soir de Paris
Makes her say 'Oui oui'
Without Father's consent,
She may come a social cropper
And really go too far
If you'll just pull out the stopper
Of Chypre or Shalimar,
When it's time for Baby's bottle
Give her a bottle of scent.

Interlude   At night to greet the Eastern Star
My Lady's drenched in Shalimar,

Another Spring has come to pass
Full of the fragrance of Blue Grass,

When Evening breeze the branches stir
My heart responds to Quelques Fleurs,

A Water Nymph beside the Loire,
Her melody is Narcisse Noir,

A shaded light, a Kiss unseen,
A night of love and Crêpe de Chine,

Two throbbing hearts neath passion's sway,
Ladies beware it's Indiscret,

The Seine, Montmartre and you, chérie,
Toujours, l'amour, Soir de Paris,

Two roguish eyes serenely mocking,
A whispered promise—that is Shocking.

Verse 2    Any wolf who's any good
Pounces on Red Riding Hood
But today—he will not get away with it.
Modern maids are mellowed in the wood.
If you find that cheek to cheek
Dinner dances twice a week
Don't get quick results
You'll get slick results
With my new technique. . . .


## CHASE ME, CHARLIE

*from* ACE OF CLUBS
(Part of Club Floor Show)

Verse 1    When it's late
And the world is sleeping
Our little black cat
No bigger than that
Has a date
Which she's keen on keeping,
No use dissuading her
She's serenading her—beau
In the garden below,
She sings, 'Oh, won't you—

Refrain 1   Chase me, Charlie,
            Chase me, Charlie,
            Over the garden wall?
            I'd like to wander for miles and miles
            Wreathed in smiles
            Out on the tiles with you.
            Chase me, Charlie,
            Chase me, Charlie,
            Don't be afraid to fall,
            Love in the moonlight can be sublime,
            Now's the time,
            Charlie, I'm
            Bound to give in if you'll only climb
            Over the garden wall.

Verse 2     Every night
            At about eleven
            Our little black cat knows,
            Our little black cat goes
            Quick as light
            To her private heaven,
            No use restraining her,
            She's set on gaining her—prize
            With her amorous cries
            Hypnotizing him.

Refrain 2   Chase me, Charlie,
            Chase me, Charlie,
            Over the garden wall.
            Who gives a damn if the neighbours yell?
            Let's rebel
            Just for the hell of it,
            Chase me, Charlie,
            Chase me, Charlie,
            Maybe I'll give my all!
            Won't you come out and be gay with me,
            Play with me,
            Stay with me?
            Just try a roll in the hay with me
            Over the garden wall.

Refrain 3   Chase me, Charlie,
            Chase me, Charlie,
            Over the garden wall.
            Why not give in to the joys of Spring,
            Have a fling,
            Why are you lingering?

Chase me, Charlie,
Chase me, Charlie,
This is my final call.
Pussy-cat, pussy-cat don't be shy,
This is my
Alibi,
Nature intends us to multiply
Over the garden wall.

# 'After the Ball'

## OH WHAT A CENTURY IT'S BEEN

*from* AFTER THE BALL

Oh what a century it's been,
From George the Third to Queen Victoria
We've never had to sing 'Sic transit Gloria',
Oh what a century it's been.

Unhappy foreigners with jealous eyes
Can only gaze at us in awed surprise
For how indeed—ah how indeed
Could any lesser, lower breed
Be even vaguely guaranteed
To understand
This tomb of kings, this earth, this dear dear land,
This race so certain of its quality
And so convinced of its innate superiority.

Oh what a century it's been,
None can deny the upward trend of it
And though we've very nearly reached the end of it
What innovations we have seen,
A British transformation scene.

We've seen the birth of Queen Victoria
And the death of William Pitt
And then we won the battle of Waterloo
Which gave our island story a
Certain lift you must admit
And if you don't, we do.
We've seen the National Gallery open
And the Houses of Parliament burn
The introduction of Income Tax
Which gave us quite a turn,
We've seen the late Prince Consort on a magic-lantern
    screen.

What a happy and glorious,
Most meritorious
Century it has been.

We've read *The Daisy Chain* and *Romany Rye*
And passionately clung
To Walter Scott and Emily Brontë too,
We're rather cross that so many buy
The works of Charlotte Yonge
But none the less—they do,
We simply worship Christina Rossetti
And we're mad about Tennyson's 'Maud',
We love to be up an apple tree
With Mrs Humphry Ward,
From William Blake to Kipling,
With the Brownings in between.

What an unsupersedable,
Wonderfully readable,
Drinkable, feedable,
This happy breedable,
Follow my leaderable,
Oh yes indeedable
Century this has been.


## WHAT A CENTURY

*from* AFTER THE BALL

### *Reprise*

We've praised the works of Frederick Leighton
      and hurled
Abuse at Holman Hunt
For he invites Pre-Raphaelites to tea
And if they hung 'The Light of the World'
Completely back to front
We shouldn't even see.
We only care to go shootin' and huntin'
On chestnuts and fillies and roans,
We're sick to death of Watts-Dunton
And we'd like to burn Burne-Jones.
We much prefer the pictures in a weekly magazine.

What a Royal Academy,
Too Alma-Tademy,
Practical, mystical,
Over-artistical,
Highly pictorial,
Albert Memorial
Century this has been.

We've made the most exhaustive scrutiny
Of the cause of England's might,
Convinced that every Britisher's born to boss,
We thought the Indian Mutiny
Was extremely impolite,
It made us feel quite cross,
We then embarked on a war in Crimea
With egos a little enlarged
And cheered the charge of the Light Brigade
No matter why they charged,
And then those swine in China made a most disgusting
    scene,
What an uneconomical,
Tragical, comical
Century this has been.

What a quite irresistible,
Oliver Twistable,
Woman in White-able,
Wuthering Height-able,
Mill on the Flossible,
Frankly impossible
Century this has been.

We've been brought up on dear Kate Greenaway
And a little while ago
Amelia Bloomer came to promote her cause,
She threw her crinoline away
While the public cried, 'What Ho!'
And walked about in drawers.
We've had to hear Evangelical preachers
But we couldn't believe in them quite
For such hysterical creatures
Couldn't spread the slightest light,
Old William Booth has bawled at us and banged his
    tambourine.

What a pompous, erroneous,
Too sanctimonious
Century this has been.

What a pompous, erroneous,
Too sanctimonious,
Praise-able, Laudable,
Madame Tussaudable,
Lovable, laughable,
Too good by halfable
Century this has been.

# I KNEW THAT YOU WOULD BE MY LOVE

*from* AFTER THE BALL

### Verse 1

LORD WINDERMERE: Summer sings its songs to me,
The lark pours rapture from the skies
And all the world belongs to me
As more and more I realize
That love was never blind to me,
He shot his arrow straight and true,
Destiny was kind to me
And led my heart to you.

### Refrain

I knew that you would be my love
So long, so long ago,
Before we met
The moment was set
And the time drew near
Year by year,
I dreamed the same enchanted dream
That you were dreaming too,
I had no doubt of it, neither had you,
Deep in our hearts we knew.

### Verse 2

LADY WINDERMERE: In all the early years I wandered through
Each step I took was leading me to you
And then, and then, and then
There came the moment when
I found my vision had come true.

### Refrain

I knew that you would be my love
So long, so long ago,
Before we met
The moment was set
And the time drew near
Year by year,
I dreamed the same enchanted dream
That you were dreaming too,
I had no doubt of it, neither had you,
Deep in our hearts we knew.

## MR HOPPER'S CHANTY

*from* AFTER THE BALL

MR HOPPER:    My Grandpa landed from a convict ship
              On the beach of Botany Bay.

OTHERS:       Haul away; haul away; how peculiar people are,
              Fancy landing Grandpapa
              On the beach of Botany Bay.

MR HOPPER:    He didn't strike oil and he didn't strike gold
              But he lived to be very very very very old
              In a rather disgusting way.

MR GRAHAM:    What a curious thing to say!

MR HOPPER:    My Grandma's meeting with this gay young rip
              Was achieved on the very first day.

OTHERS:       Haul away; haul away; having travelled all that far
              Fancy meeting Grandmama
              On a beach on the very first day!

MR HOPPER:    She happened to be, when he landed there,
              Combing her fuzzy-wuzzy blue-black hair
              And he sprang at her straight away.

MR DUMBY:     Steady, old man, Fair Play!

MR HOPPER:    They lay on the sand of that alien land
              Where the wallabys gaily frisk
              And plighted their troth, in a way that was both
              Effective and fairly brisk.

MR GRAHAM:    He ran an appalling risk!

MR HOPPER:    And the net result of the whole affair
              You can perfectly plainly see
              By my coloured skin and kinky hair
              That I'm half aboriginee.

MR DUMBY:     What a socially regrettable, un-Debrettable,
              Maddening thing to be!

MR HOPPER:   It's a solemn thought for a son and heir
             To know who his forebears really were
             And whether or not you know or care
             Before my Dad was a millionaire
             We lived . . .

OTHERS:      Where?

MR HOPPER:   In our family tree!

OTHERS:      Haul away; haul away;
             My goodness gracious me!

MR HOPPER:   I can see my brothers and sisters now
             Swinging about from bough to bough
             On the very, very top . . .

OTHERS:      For heaven's sake stop!

MR HOPPER:   The top of our family tree!


## SWEET DAY

### *from* AFTER THE BALL

Refrain   Sweet day, remain for me
          Clear in my memory,
          When my heart's chilled by the snows of December,
          Let me remember
          Let me remember
          Sweet day
          That seems to be
          Made up of dreams for me
          But when they've faded away
          Let me remember today.

Verse     No melancholy dream,
          No shadow on my heart,
          No transitory gleam
          Of danger in the sky,
          Why should such happiness fill me today,
          Why must such loveliness fade away,
          Why must these magic moments fly
          Just as the leaves of summer fall and die?

No melancholy dream,
No shadow on my heart
Excepting that I know perfection cannot stay,
This has not been in vain
This I will not betray
When summer comes again
I shall remember . . .

Refrain  Sweet day, remain for me
Clear in my memory,
When my heart's chilled by the snows of December,
Let me remember
Let me remember
Sweet day
That seems to be
Made up of dreams for me
But when they've faded away
Let me remember today.

## SWEET DAY

*from* AFTER THE BALL

Reprise  This melancholy dream,
This shadow on my heart,
This bitter disillusion
That has blown away
All that I held so true,
Love that was here to stay,
All I believed I knew
Has now betrayed me.

Sweet day, how brief you were
Sweet day, what grief you bear
Never again shall I say
Let me remember today.

Sweet day, that seems to be
Made up of dreams for me
But when they've faded away
Let me remember today.

# STAY ON THE SIDE OF THE ANGELS

*from* AFTER THE BALL

Stay on the side of the angels,
Keep all your illusions enshrined,
But, Lady Windermere, dear Lady Windermere,
Do not forget to be kind.

The lilies and the languors of virtue,
Though rather oppressively 'nice',
As Swinburne implied,
Can be elbowed aside
By the roses and raptures of vice.

Stay on the side of the angels
But in the stern life that you live,
Lady Windermere, dear Lady Windermere,
Do not forget to forgive.

Those other less fortunate mortals
Who find to their infinite pain
That love, when unjust,
Is more cruel than lust,
Forgive me for quoting again.

Stay on the side of the angels,
Secure and remote and apart,
But, Lady Windermere, dear Lady Windermere,
Keep a compassionate heart.

# CRÈME DE LA CRÈME

*from* AFTER THE BALL

Ladies and Gentlemen, pillars of London Society,
Never in doubt that our blood is impeccably blue,
Any summery afternoon
In the months of July and June
From the bridge on the Serpentine to Rotten Row
Backwards and forwards we go—so
Aristocratically free from financial anxiety,
Blandly aware we belong to the privileged few,

Though the Socialists fume and fight,
To our houses we don't invite
Anybody who dares to claim
The Crème de la Crème
Isn't quite, quite right.
Natural laws
Kindly provide for us
And set aside for us
All the top drawers.
Such metaphors,
Though they are fiction,
Uphold our conviction
That, born to applause,
True to the old routine
Several gold spoons were seen
Clenched in our jaws
Which was because
Nature selected us,
Perfected us,
Expected us to be
Ladies and Gentlemen, born to eternal prosperity,
Firmly convinced our position is really unique,
We believe in the status quo
Because deep in our hearts we know
That though social reformers try to queer our pitch
God's on the side of the rich—which
Leads us to mention with more than a touch of asperity
Heaven can wait if it's only concerned with the meek,
If the angels are really bright
And decide on a plebiscite
They'll discover that, praise or blame,
The Crème de la Crème
Has been quite-quite-right.


## LIGHT IS THE HEART

### *from* AFTER THE BALL

Years of discretion strike a bargain with the past,
Ships that sailed the troubled seas find anchorage at last,
The far horizon clears
And all the ecstasies and all the tears
That in our youth we knew,
That in our youth we shed,

Die like the winds that blew
The clouds from overhead,
Years of discretion strike a bargain with the mind,
Middle age is chivalrous when youth has been unkind,
Seek in Autumn for the happiness that Spring has undermined
And you will find . . .

Light is the heart that has learned to surrender
Dreams that we dreamed in the Spring of the year,
Though we awoke from them
Time can evoke from them
Music that only our memories hear,
Gone are the visions of passionate splendour,
Calm are the waves of the turbulent sea,
Pity the rover
Whose journeys are over
But envy the heart that is free.

Light is the heart that discreetly remembers
Words that were spoken and far away tears,
Memory grieves for them,
Sentiment weaves for them
Colours and meanings that fade with the years,
Though we may still feel a glow from the embers,
Love cannot be what we hoped it would be,
Pity the lover
Who fails to discover
The peace of a heart that is free.


## MAY I HAVE THE PLEASURE

*from* AFTER THE BALL

MR HOPPER: May I have the pleasure of a dance, Lady Agatha,
Are you free by any chance, Lady Agatha,
To oblige me with a One, two, three, One, two, three,
One, two, three-fold miracle.
Magical, lyrical
Waltz, Lady Agatha.
I may have faults, Lady Agatha,
But I can dance all night and never tire,
Every note of music sets my heart on fire
To go, Lady Agatha,
Please don't say No.

DUCHESS OF      Really, Mr Hopper,
BERWICK:        This is really most improper,
                You must learn to be more discreet.
                Frankly, Mr Hopper,
                You will come a social cropper
                If you try to sweep debutantes off their feet.

MR HOPPER:      I can't look at other debutantes, Lady Agatha,
                You're the heart of my romance, Lady Agatha,
                For to me you're more than One, two, three, One, two, three,
                One, two, three times prettier,
                Lovelier, wittier,
                So, Lady Agatha,
                Come weal, come woe, Lady Agatha,
                Let's let the music of the violins
                Hold us both together till the dawn begins
                To glow, Lady Agatha,
                Please don't say No.

DUCHESS OF      Really, Mr Hopper,
BERWICK:        This is really most improper,
                Your Colonial ways are quaint.
                Frankly, Mr Hopper,
                You will come a social cropper
                If you cannot learn, candidly, self-restraint.

MR HOPPER:      None the less I beg you for a dance, Lady Agatha,
                I am truly in a trance, Lady Agatha,
                Please don't say No.

# I OFFER YOU MY HEART

*from* AFTER THE BALL

LORD DARLINGTON:    I offer you my heart
                    And everything I own,
                    I offer you my life
                    And yet you spurn it.

LADY WINDERMERE:    What can you hope to gain
                    By offering your love
                    To someone else's wife
                    Who can't return it?

LORD DARLINGTON:    Are you so sure, so sure that this is true
                    And not an empty phrase, a barricade
                    Built to prevent the world from hurting you,
                    Built to prevent my arms from holding you,
                    Because you are afraid?

LADY WINDERMERE:    Leave me alone, I beg of you, and go;
                    Speak not the words your passion bids you say;
                    For if you truly love me you must know
                    Why I must say goodbye to you—and so
                    I beg you to go away.

LORD DARLINGTON⎱ :   I offer you my heart
LADY WINDERMERE⎰     You offer me your heart

LORD DARLINGTON⎱ :   And everything I own,
LADY WINDERMERE⎰     And everything you own,

LORD DARLINGTON:    I offer you my love,

LORD DARLINGTON⎱ :   Don't turn my love away.
LADY WINDERMERE⎰     I beg you go away.


## WHY IS IT THE WOMAN WHO PAYS?

*from* AFTER THE BALL

Pity three wives in the world of fashion,
Pity three lambs into the slaughter led,
Tied for their lives to their husband's passion
Not for themselves, but for others instead,
What disillusion,
Shame and confusion
Goes with the marriage bed.

Refrain 1   Why are men permitted to sin and sin again,
            Say they're sorry and then begin again?
            Have they certain glands that automatically combust?
            Why is it accepted that they just must lust?
            It isn't fair to their relations,
            Kind to wife or child,
            Though it gives dramatic situations
            And a cynical glaze
            To the plays
            Of Oscar Wilde.

When a girl has gritted her teeth and tried to be
All a husband expects a bride to be,
Why, to coin a phrase,
Must it be the woman who pays and pays
And pays and pays and pays
To the end of her days?

She quickly learns what utter hell it is
To face the fact that men are hunters,
She hears her husband's infidelities
Served up with strawberries at Gunter's.
If she complains, there'll be a scene, of course.
So she remains niminy-piminy
Though she's aware that really he has been of course
Down to Brighton with Miss Thingummy.
But when she is old and grey and full of sleep
What harvest will she reap?
The answer's—none,
There she'll sit, depressed and weary,
Thumping out a rather dreary
Chopin Polonaise—
Proving it's the woman who pays and pays
And pays and pays and pays
To the end of her days.

Refrain 2   Why are men permitted to smile and smirk again,
Say they're sorry, and go berserk again?
We can guess, when they are clasping pearls around our
   necks,
All they've been indulging in is sex—sex—sex!
It isn't right, it isn't moral,
We'd agree to be
Hung with beads of imitation coral
If it weren't a bribe
To our tribal loyalty,
Why are men acquitted of social treachery
When we women, with one light lechery,
Set our world ablaze?
Why is it the woman who pays and pays
And pays and pays and pays
To the end of her days?

She will be treated with contumely,
She'll have to live on the Riviera,
She will be seen parading gloomily
Along the front at Bordighera.
She will be hounded from society

And, growing daffier and daffier,
She may achieve some local notoriety
By wearing sandals made of raffia.
Maybe she'll have one dull German maid with her,
Old friends who've played with her
Will cut her dead.
She will murmur, 'Faites attention'
As she sadly eats the pension
Salmon Mayonnaise.
Portrait of a woman who pays and pays
And pays and pays and pays
To the end of her days.


# LETTER SONG

*from* AFTER THE BALL

Accept, dear Lady Windermere,
This letter from a libertine
Whose love for you for many a year
Will still be true,
Regard this as a souvenir,
An echo of what might have been,
For now I know all hope has gone,
That all my dreams were based upon
The shifting sands of make-believe,
The fabric that all lovers weave,
And though my heart for ever will grieve
I'll love you still.

Beloved, do not blame me for adoring you,
Forgive me with your all-forgiving smile,
Also forgive me, dearest, for imploring you
To hold me in your memory awhile,
This letter is the last I'll ever write to you,
My heart is bleaker than a winter sky,
And so, dear love, I write the words 'Good night' to you,
And so, dear love, I write the words 'Good night' to you,
Because I cannot bear to say 'Goodbye'.

## LADY WINDERMERE'S ARIA

*from* AFTER THE BALL

I feel so terribly alone,
He should be here
To calm the beating of my heart
And still the fear,
The anguish tearing me apart,
He should have known
That, by this folly, I have thrown away,
Renounced for ever,
Home and honour and the pride of living,
This I know to be beyond forgiving,
Shall we walk in shadows until we die
My love and I?
What hope for future years,
What gifts have I to tender to him?
Chill hands and bitter tears,
These only I surrender to him,
What have I left to repay him,
How can I honour, love and obey him?
My lifeless heart will betray him,
This I know,
Too late I know.

I feel so terribly alone and so afraid,
A love that cannot be repaid
Must swiftly fade,
Too soon, too soon, when eager passion dies away,
High romance flies away
And disenchanted, we shall stare
Into the future that the wrong we've done
Forces us to share.
How can I bear,
How can I bear
Such dark despair?

I must return to where my duty lies
And leave him free,
This ardent lover who would compromise
His life for me,
How could I ever repay him,
How could I honour, love and obey him?

My lifeless heart would betray him,
This I know,
At last—I know.

I feel so terribly alone.
Lost, and alone.


## GO, I BEG YOU GO

*from* AFTER THE BALL

MRS ERLYNNE:       Go, I beg you go,
                   For you must never know
                   The tears, the sorrow and the blame
                   That lie in wait for you,
                   It's not too late for you
                   To fly from the shame
                   That threatens your name.

LADY WINDERMERE:   What can it mean to you
                   That I should remain or go
                   And would you dare to say
                   To me, his wife,
                   What he has been to you,
                   The husband I trusted so,
                   It's you who led his love away
                   And broke my life.

MRS ERLYNNE:       The only love he bears, he bears for you,
                   In heaven's name believe that this is true.

LADY WINDERMERE:   His traitor's love means nothing to me,
                   I'm not so blind that I cannot recognize
                   All this implies,
                   Why should you think that I could not see
                   The truth behind all your lies?

MRS ERLYNNE:       Once long ago
                   A woman innocent as you
                   Decided to throw
                   Her happiness away,
                   You cannot know
                   What misery it led her to,
                   I swear this is so,
                   I swear that this is true.

LADY WINDERMERE:                    MRS ERLYNNE:

Why should you think I'd undergo       Once long ago
The same dishonour?                    A woman innocent as you
What has this woman that you know      Decided to throw
To do with me?                         Her happiness away,
Why should her degradation be          You cannot know
Quoted thus to show                    The dark despair it led her to,
What price is paid?                     I swear this is so,
Why should I care? My choice is        I swear that this is true.
  made.

MRS ERLYNNE:        If you take this foolish step you contemplate
                    No love will compensate
                    For all you lose.

LADY WINDERMERE:    Say no more,
                    Say no more,
                    Leave me, for
                    My heart alone must choose.

MRS ERLYNNE:                           LADY WINDERMERE:

Go, I beg you go,                      Now I know that I must go
For life can hurt you so               For if life should hurt me so
As once it hurt me long ago,           As it hurt you long ago
To realize one day                     I'd realize one day
You've thrown true love away,          I'd thrown true love away,
That ultimate woe                      That ultimate woe
You never must know.                   I never must know.


## LONDON AT NIGHT

*from* AFTER THE BALL

*Verse*

SEXTETTE:  When summer twilight fades away
           And darkness falls and night begins
           There ends another dusty day
           With all its dreary disciplines
           That have tied us to
           The work we do
           Until the evening gives us ease
           To wander for an hour or two
           Beneath our London trees.

*Refrain 1*

London at night
With the gas lamps alight
Is a wonderful sight
For the eye to see
With its clubs and pubs and bars
And the sleepy Thames reflecting the stars,
London at night
Whether sober or tight
Is a sight
That Americans die to see,
From the naptha flares that glow
In the markets of Soho
To the far less exotic
And more patriotic
Restraint of Pimlico,
London's a place
That your heart can embrace
If your heart is free
And prone to be
Receptive to delight,
Rome was once gay
In a decadent way
But we're sure that it never was quite
Like London at night.

*Refrain 2*

London at night
With the gas lamps alight
Has an air of sublime unreality
When the moon has thrown
Her grace
On the shadowed stone
Of Hamilton Place,
Though Shepherd Market
Looks nice in the dark it
Is rather a vulgar locality,
On an even lower scale
Are the streets of Maida Vale
Where nocturnal behaviour
Compared with Belgravia
Is quite beyond the pale,
Blue blood we know
Is entitled to flow
In between Mayfair
And Onslow Square,

But by some oversight
Low class and high class
Contrive to defy class
And brightly, politely unite
In London at night.


*Reprise*

London at night
With the gas lamps alight
Is renowned for its moral fragility
From ornate, sedate Pall Mall
To the dark romance of Regent's Canal.
Girls in large hats
Outside Boodle's and Pratt's
Lie in wait for the younger nobility
And they frequently compel
Some inebriated swell
To hop into a hansom
And shout through the transom,
'Drive home—drive home like hell!'
Men who survive
Piccadilly alive
And can take the air
In Leicester Square
And not be put to flight
Earnestly say
That Port Said and Bombay
Are a great deal more prim and upright
Than London at night.

London at night
With the gas lamps alight,
Though it wasn't laid out continentally,
Read the words that Wordsworth wrote
And you can't avoid a lump in your throat,
Creaking four-wheelers
And certainly 'Peelers'
If only they're viewed sentimentally
Have a reassuring charm
Quite unlike the French Gendarme
Who, by shrieking such graphic
Instructions to traffic,
Inspires profound alarm.
Here in our city
We're all of us pretty
Well sure that vice

Will in a trice
Be bundled out of sight,
Old men in lobbies
With dubious hobbies
Can still get the deuce of a fright
In London at night.


## CLEAR BRIGHT MORNING

*from* AFTER THE BALL

Now in the clear bright morning
When the shadows of night
Are dispelled by the light
I can see at last
How my youth and my pride
Swept me away on the tide.

Now in the clear bright morning
With my pride in the dust
I must win back the trust
And the tender love I so nearly betrayed.
How can such love be repaid?

Now in the clear bright morning
When the fear and the dread
And the darkness have fled
I can see at last
How my pride and my youth
Led me so far from the truth.


## ALL MY LIFE AGO

*from* AFTER THE BALL

Once when I was young
A song was sung,
A song of love too passionate to last,
All my life ago,
Among the shadows of the past,
Now I try in vain
To hear again

The echo of that far away refrain,
Once it hurt me so
But that was all my life ago.

Now the future's clear to me,
I cannot say, I can't explain
Why you will be for ever near to me,
Though we may never meet again,
Time has paid its debt to me
And though I know that I must say goodbye,
Oh, my dear, if only you'll remember me
I shall be grateful till I die.

# OH WHAT A SEASON THIS HAS BEEN

### *from* AFTER THE BALL

Oh what a season this has been,
We find our nerves are simply worn to shreds,
We've not a thing to wear that isn't torn to shreds,
Our gloves are smelling of benzine.

The social world has whirled us off our feet,
Too much to drink and far too much to eat,
We feel the lure—we feel the lure
To give up 'Beurre' and 'Petits Pains'
And take our aches to Aix-le-Bains
And do a cure,
We're sick of other people's recipes,
We're not surprised by Soufflés en surprise,
We'd loathe to pay a single call again
And rather die than be invited to a ball again.

Oh what a season this has been,
We just despise the very thought of it
And if you want to know the long and short of it
Rather than start the same routine
We'd gladly face the guillotine,
Oh what a season this has been.

## FAREWELL SONG

MRS ERLYNNE: Don't ever think me ungrateful,
What you have said has made me very proud.

LORD AUGUSTUS: Farewells and partings are hateful,
'Goodbye' for us must never be allowed,
Ah, promise me,
Ah, promise me
That somewhere in the future there may be
A distant day,
A distant day
When you and I can meet again and say
Although no tears between us flowed,
Our eyes were dry, our words discreet,
This foolish little episode
Was really very sweet.
Though I may not claim your hand and heart, my dear,
And we must part, my dear.
It's not the end,
Where you are,
Near or far,
Count on me for ever as your friend.

## SOMETHING ON A TRAY

Advancing years may bring about
A rather sweet nostalgia
In spite of rheumatism and gout
And, certainly, neuralgia.
And so, when we have churned our way
Through luncheon and a matinée,
We gratefully to bed retire
Obsessed with an acute desire
To rest our aching, creaking vertebrae
And have a little something on a tray.

Some ageing ladies with a groan
Renounce all beauty lotions,
They dab their brows with eau-de-Cologne

And turn to their devotions,
We face the process of decay
Attired in a négligé
And with hot bottles at our toes
We cosily in bed repose
Enjoying, in a rather languid way,
A little 'eggy' something on a tray.

Advancing years that many dread
Still have their compensations,
We turn when youth and passion have fled
To more sedate sensations,
And when we've fought our weary way
Through some exhausting social day
We thankfully to bed retire
With pleasant book and crackling fire
And, like Salome in a bygone day,
Enjoy a little something on a tray.

When weary from the fray
Something on a tray
Sends weariness away,
Something on a tray,
Thank God, thank God we say,
For something on a tray.

## FARAWAY LAND

*from* AFTER THE BALL

Refrain 1   I come from a far away land
            Beyond the rim of the sea
            Where the North is hot and the South is cold
            And nothing is more than a few years old
            Except the mountains and desert sand
            And the eucalyptus tree.
            I come from a far away land
            Beyond the rim of the sea.

Verse       I have seen your country in the gentle English light,
            Hedges and farms and cornsheaves in a row,
            I have seen your quiet woods and meadows under white
            Counterpanes of snow.

I have smelt the tang of wood-smoke in the Autumn air,
Listened to a barrel-organ in a London square,
There is so much of England that I know
Almost as though I'd lived here long ago.

Refrain 2   I come from a far away land
Below the arc of the sky,
A land where Englishmen blazed the trails
From Nullarbor Plain to New South Wales,
And conifer trees like sentries stand
On the road to Gundagai.
I come from a far away land
Below the arc of the sky.

Refrain 3   I come from a far away land
On the other side of the world,
A land that's primitive, crude and brave,
Where no one's master and no one's slave,
Yet one and all of us primly stand
When the English flag's unfurled.
I come from a far away land
On the other side of the world.
The journey's long and the seas are wide
But it's sweet to know that there's English pride
On the other side of the world.

# *Miscellaneous*

## TIME AND AGAIN

Verse 1   Life is what you make it
As someone once observed,
A phrase that sounds a trifle glib,
But whoever thought it out
Had clearly never sorted out
The vexing problem of Adam's spare rib.
Chastity, I take it,
Is specially reserved
For those possessing moral fibres,
Mine fail me all the time
And maybe that's the reason I'm
A Baa Baa Black Sheep—calling all subscribers.

Refrain 1  Time and again
I make good resolutions
But somehow they don't seem to stay,
Just when I think I've got the whole thing sewn up
I must own up
Everything gets blown up.
Sex and Champagne
As social institutions
Stampede me and lead me astray,
I begin Beguine-ing
And my Spring cleaning
Is ditched—bitched—bundled away.
All my instincts respond
To an amiable blonde
Which is fatal.
And if some brisk brunette appears
Old Adam cheers,
Back go my ears,
Maybe it's all pre-natal.
How can I train
My hormone distributions
To be less aggressively male?
Time and again I try,
Time and again I fail.

Verse 2    Moralists disparage
           A variable heart
           And say that it should be fenced in
           But they never think about
           Effective means of casting out
           That dear old Die-Hard, Original Sin.
           Table d'hôte is marriage,
           Free love is à la carte,
           And once you've crossed forbidden fruits off
           You merely find that you've
           Unwittingly set out to prove
           The age-old saying,
           'It's better with your boots off!'

Refrain 2  Time and again
           I'm tortured by contrition
           And swear that I'm sorry I've sinned,
           Then when I've lashed myself with whips and scourges
           Sex emerges,
           Out pop all the urges.
           Freud could explain
           My curious condition
           And Jung would have certainly grinned.
           When I meet some sly dish
           Who looks like my dish
           I'm drunk—sunk—gone with the wind.
           How can I start afresh
           When the sins of the flesh
           Override me?
           Maybe some psycho-analyst
           Might slap my wrist
           And give a twist
           To what goes on inside me.
           If I could feign
           The glandular transition
           I'd settle for taking the Veil.
           Time and again I try,
           Time and again I fail.

Refrain 3  Time and again
           I've tried to form a 'credo'
           But somehow I don't seem to learn,
           Just when I think my Guardian Angel's winning
           I go spinning
           Back to the beginning.
           I can't refrain
           From firing a torpedo

Abaft or ahead or astern,
If I hit my quarry
I can't feel sorry,
I'm hooked—cooked—done to a turn.
Though I frequently wish
I could curb my conditioned
Reflexes
I'll be damned if I'll sacrifice
Sugar and spice,
To be precise
Nothing's as nice as sex is.
I can't restrain
My lecherous libido
From slipping and tipping the scale.
Time and again I try,
Time and again I fail.


## THREE THEATRICAL DAMES

Sung once at *Night of a Hundred Stars*, London Palladium.
John Mills, Kenneth More and Peter Ustinov

Verse 1    I started from scratch
           In a house with a thatch
           With two very unpleasant old ladies.
           My parents were dead
           So I finally fled
           And appeared in a tent
           Outside Burton-on-Trent
           In a very small part in *Quo Vadis*.
           I toured in *East Lynne*
           And *The Wages of Sin*
           Till I couldn't tell one from the other,
           Then a rich friend
           And achieved the West End
           In a farce called *She Did It For Mother*.

Refrain 1  Three theatrical Dames,
           Eminent and respectable,
           Our accents are undetectable
           And though we've achieved our aims
           If they knew what we'd done
           In Eighteen Ninety-One
           They certainly wouldn't have made us Dames.

Verse 2　　My very first step
　　　　　　Was Shakespearian 'rep'
　　　　　　Where an awful old 'Ham' used to train us.
　　　　　　I'd nothing to do
　　　　　　In *The Dream* and *The Shrew*
　　　　　　But I carried a spear
　　　　　　In *King John* and *King Lear*
　　　　　　And a hatchet in *Coriolanus*.
　　　　　　I ranted for years
　　　　　　In pavilions on piers
　　　　　　Till my spirits were really at zero,
　　　　　　Then I got a small role
　　　　　　Of a Tart with a soul
　　　　　　In a play by Sir Arthur Pinero.


Refrain 2　Three Theatrical Dames,
　　　　　　Models of prim propriety,
　　　　　　Accepted by High society
　　　　　　Because of our famous names,
　　　　　　If they'd asked us to tea
　　　　　　In Eighteen Ninety-Three
　　　　　　They certainly wouldn't have made us Dames.


Verse 3　　I made my début
　　　　　　In a canvas canoe
　　　　　　In a horrid American drama.
　　　　　　It wasn't a hit
　　　　　　So I left the 'Legit!'
　　　　　　And I got myself backed
　　　　　　In a musical act
　　　　　　Called 'A night in the Garden of Karma'.
　　　　　　An agent called Klein
　　　　　　Said, 'I'm willing to sign
　　　　　　Whoever that girl who unveils is'
　　　　　　So I got my first chance
　　　　　　With a Biblical dance
　　　　　　In a flop at the Old Prince of Wales's.


Refrain 3　Three theatrical Dames,
　　　　　　Each of our houses we adorn
　　　　　　With photographs of the highly-born
　　　　　　In elegant silver frames,
　　　　　　If they'd caught us in Crewe
　　　　　　In Eighteen Ninety-Two
　　　　　　They certainly wouldn't have made us Dames.

Refrain 4  Three theatrical Dames,
              Prominent high and mighty girls,
              The fact that we once were flighty girls
              Our manner today disclaims,
              If they'd seen our high kicks
              In Eighteen Ninety-Six
              They certainly wouldn't have made us Dames.

# THERE ARE BAD TIMES JUST AROUND THE CORNER

## (English Version)

Verse 1  They're out of sorts in Sunderland
            And terribly cross in Kent,
            They're dull in Hull
            And the Isle of Mull
            Is seething with discontent,
            They're nervous in Northumberland
            And Devon is down the drain,
            They're filled with wrath
            On the Firth of Forth
            And sullen on Salisbury Plain,
            In Dublin they're depressed, lads,
            Maybe because they're Celts
            For Drake is going West, lads,
            And so is everyone else.
            Hurray—hurray—hurray!
            Misery's here to stay.

Refrain 1  There are bad times just around the corner,
            There are dark clouds hurtling through the sky
            And it's no good whining
            About a silver lining
            For we know from experience that they won't roll by,
            With a scowl and a frown
            We'll keep our peckers down
            And prepare for depression and doom and dread,
            We're going to unpack our troubles from our old kit
               bag
            And wait until we drop down dead.

Verse 2    From Portland Bill to Scarborough
They're querulous and subdued
And Shropshire lads
Have behaved like cads
From Berwick-on-Tweed to Bude,
They're mad at Market Harborough
And livid at Leigh-on-Sea,
In Tunbridge Wells
You can hear the yells
Of woe-begone bourgeoisie.
We all get bitched about, lads,
Whoever our vote elects,
We know we're up the spout, lads,
And that's what England expects.
Hurray—hurray—hurray!
Trouble is on the way.

Refrain 2    There are bad times just around the corner,
The horizon's gloomy as can be,
There are black birds over
The greyish cliffs of Dover
And the rats are preparing to leave the B.B.C.
We're an *un*happy breed
And very bored indeed
When reminded of something that Nelson said.
While the press and the politicians nag nag nag
We'll wait until we drop down dead.

Verse 3    From Colwyn Bay to Kettering
They're sobbing themselves to sleep,
The shrieks and wails
In the Yorkshire dales
Have even depressed the sheep.
In rather vulgar lettering
A very disgruntled group
Have posted bills
On the Cotswold Hills
To prove that we're in the soup.
While begging Kipling's pardon
There's one thing we know for sure
If England is a garden
We ought to have more manure.
Hurray—hurray—hurray!
Suffering and dismay.

Refrain 3    There are bad times just around the corner
And the outlook's absolutely vile,

There are Home Fires smoking
From Windermere to Woking
And we're *not* going to tighten our belts and smile
    smile smile,
At the sound of a shot
We'd just as soon as not
Take a hot water bottle and go to bed,
We're going to *un*tense our muscles till they sag sag sag
And wait until we drop down dead.

Refrain 4   There are bad times just around the corner,
    We can all look forward to despair,
    It's as clear as crystal
    From Bridlington to Bristol
    That we can't save democracy and we don't much care
    If the Reds and the Pinks
    Believe that England stinks
    And that world revolution is bound to spread,
    We'd better all learn the lyrics of the old 'Red Flag'
    And wait until we drop down dead.
    A likely story
    Land of Hope and Glory,
    Wait until we drop down dead.

## THERE ARE BAD TIMES JUST AROUND
## THE CORNER
### (American Version)

Verse 1   They're nervous in Nigeria
    And terribly cross in Crete,
    In Bucharest
    They are so depressed
    They're frightened to cross the street,
    They're sullen in Siberia
    And timid in Turkestan,
    They're sick with fright
    In the Isle of Wight
    And jittery in Japan,
    The Irish groan and shout, lads,
    Maybe because they're Celts,
    They know they're up the spout, lads,
    And so is everyone else.
    Hurray! Hurray! Hurray!
    Trouble is on the way.

Refrain 1   There are bad times just around the corner,
            There are dark clouds hurtling through the sky
            And it's no use whining
            About a silver lining
            For we KNOW from experience that they won't roll by,
            With a scowl and a frown
            We'll keep our spirits down
            And prepare for depression and doom and dread,
            We're going to *un*pack our troubles from our old kit bag
            And wait until we drop down dead.

Refrain 2   There are bad times just around the corner,
            The horizon's gloomy as can be,
            There are black birds over
            The greyish cliffs of Dover
            And the vultures are hovering round the Christmas tree.
            We're an *un*happy breed
            And ready to stampede
            When we're asked to remember what Lincoln said,
            We're going to *un*tense our muscles till they sag sag sag
            And wait until we drop down dead.

Verse 2     They're morbid in Mongolia
            And querulous in Quebec,
            There's not a man
            In Baluchistan
            Who isn't a nervous wreck,
            In Maine the melancholia
            Is deeper than tongue can tell,
            In Monaco
            All the croupiers know
            They haven't a hope in Hell.
            In far away Australia
            Each wallaby's well aware
            The world's a total failure
            Without any time to spare.
            Hurray! Hurray! Hurray!
            Suffering and dismay.

Refrain 3   There are bad times just around the corner,
            We can all look forward to despair,
            It's as clear as crystal
            From Brooklyn Bridge to Bristol
            That we CAN'T save Democracy
            And we don't much care.
            At the sound of a shot
            We'd just as soon as not

Take a hot-water bag and retire to bed
And while the press and the politicians nag nag nag
We'll wait until we drop down dead.

Refrain 4 There are bad times just around the corner
And the outlook's absolutely vile,
You can take this from us
That when they Atom bomb us
We are NOT going to tighten our belts and smile smile
     smile,
We are in such a mess
It couldn't matter less
If a world revolution is just ahead,
We'd better all learn the lyrics of the old 'Red Flag'
And wait until we drop down dead.
A likely story
Land of Hope and Glory,
Wait until we drop down dead.


## A RIBBON IN HER HAIR

Verse    In an album filled with daguerrotypes
A youthful face
Full of grace
Shines among the prim straight and narrow types
On every yellowing page,
Great Aunt Millicent Gertrude May
Photographed on a winter's day
Tripping home from a bygone school
In a very, very bygone age.

Refrain With her books and her satchel and a ribbon in her hair
And a neat winter coat discreetly braided,
You can see from the picture she was exquisitely fair,
Although the background's slightly faded,
She was like a day in spring,
Eyes rather wide apart,
Head held a little bit high,
Something worth remembering,
If you had seen her pass by,
Nobody could deny
She was gay and enchanting as a fairy tale retold
As she strolled every every evening through the square
With her books, pencil box and school satchel
And a bright blue ribbon in her hair.

## LOUISA

Verse    Louisa was a movie queen.
          Before she'd achieved the age of sweet sixteen,
          Long before Cagney threw those girls about,
          Little Louisa tossed her curls about.
          Later when the talkies came
          The whole world
          Resounded with her fame,
          Each time she married
          Every daily paper carried
          Headlines blazing her name.
          Not only headlines
          But photographs and interviews,
          Everything she did was news
          That held the world in thrall.

          Some said she read lines
          Better than Marlene could,
          No other entertainer could
          Compare with her at all.
          But regardless of the fact
          That she could sing and dance and act
          And owned furniture that wasn't 'Little Rockery',
          And regardless of her gems,
          Which were hers, not M.G.M.'s,
          Her life was one long mockery.

Refrain 1  Louisa was terribly lonely,
          Success brought her naught but despair.
          She derived little fun from the Oscars she'd won
          And none from her home in Bel Air.
          She declared she was weary of living
          On a bestial terrestrial plane.
          When friends came to visit their hands she would clutch
          Crying, 'Tell me, why is it I suffer so much?
          If only, if only, if only
          My life wasn't quite such a strain.'
          And soon after that she was terribly lonely,
          All over again.

Refrain 2  Louisa was terribly lonely,
          Louisa was terribly sad.
          It appears that the cheers that had rung in her ears
          For years had been driving her mad.
          She sobbed when men offered her sables

And moaned when they gave her champagne.
She remarked to her groom on their honeymoon night
As he tenderly kissed her and turned out the light,
'If only, if only, if only
I'd thrown myself out of the plane. . . . '
The very next day she was terribly lonely,
All over again.

Refrain 3   Louisa was terribly lonely
(Rhythm)   (The girl had no fun),
            Louisa was tired of it all
            (Not a call from anyone),
            She gazed like a dazed belated Sphinx
            At her hundred and eight mutated minks
            And she wrung her hands and she beat her breast
            Crying, 'My, my, my, I'm so depressed.'
            Nobody knew the trouble she'd seen,
            Nobody knew but you know who

            The tribulations of a movie queen.
            So farewell to lovely Louisa
            (Who just let life tease her),
            Let's leave her seeking in vain
            (To find someone to explain)
            Why destiny should single her out to be only lonely,
            Over and over again!


IRISH SONG
(Rosie O'Grady)

When first I was courtin' sweet Rosie O'Grady,
Sweet Rosie O'Grady she whispered to me,
'Sure you shouldn't be after seducin' a lady
Before she's had time to sit down to her tea.'

With a Heigho—Top-o-the-morning—Begorrah and Fiddle-
    dedee.

Her cheeks were so soft and her eyes were so trustin',
She tossed her bright curls at the dusk of the day,
She said to me, 'Darlin', your breath is disgustin','
Which wasn't at all what I hoped she would say.

With a Heigho, maybe Begorrah, and possibly Fiddlededee.

Our honeymoon started so blithely and gaily
But dreams I was dreaming were suddenly wrecked
For she broke my front tooth with her father's shillelagh
Which wasn't what I had been led to expect.

With a Heigho, maybe Begorrah, and certainly Fiddlededee.


## GIVE ME THE KINGSTON BY-PASS

*from* THE GLOBE REVUE

Verse   Pity the souls
           Cursed with a wanderlust,
           Each man builds his castle in the air,
           I've got a Rolls Daimler Lagonda lust,
           Pity me and say a short prayer.
           I'm well aware that my heart's desires
           Cost a bloody sight too much dough,
           Week-ends abroad I couldn't afford I know
           And so—

Refrain Give me the Kingston By-Pass
           On a Saturday afternoon
           In a bran' new Bugatti
           Made for Cincinnati
           Or a fairly flash Fraser Nash Town Saloon.
           Watching the country fly past
           In a carbon-monoxide swoon
           Is to me more romantic
           Than a South Atlantic
           Cruise,
           If I had to choose,
           I'd tearfully, cheerfully wipe out
           The sins that clutter my decks
           To take a Humber Snipe out,
           I'd even sacrifice Sex.
           But in our pre-war Seven
           That's the apple of Father's eye
           All I can do
           Is join the push-bike queue
           And let the By-Pass pass by.

           Give me the Kingston By-Pass
           And a thoroughly 'posh' machine
           Like a Healey three-litre

All complete with heater
Or a shiny grey Chevrolet Limousine.
Watching the summer sky pass
Through a blue haze of gasoline
Is to me more attractive
Than an over-active gland.
Try to understand
I take my pleasure gently,
My moral lapses are few,
But for a drop-head Bentley
I'd be convertible too.
But in our pre-war Seven
I'm immune from the evil eye,
Jekyll or Hyde,
I hug the left-hand side
And let the By-Pass pass by.


## FRENCH SONG

### CAFÉ DE PARIS

(*Paris est Toi*)


Paris ensorcelée, magique,
Dis que son nom et j'suis ému.
Quand j'me trouve loin d'son charme unique
Mon pauvre cœur est éperdu.
Je ne chercherai q'une autre maîtresse,
Elle ne me fera jamais cocu,
Elle tiendra toujours ma tendresse,
Tous mes vœux, toutes mes caresses
Dans mes bras vers elle tendus.
Ah les belles nuits que nous passions ensemble!
Ah les beaux jours quand j'étais si malheureux!
Ces souv'nirs brisent mon âme et je tremble
Chaque fois j'regarde tes yeux.


Tu es Paris et Paris est toi
Pour moi—pour moi—pour moi.
Ville bien aimée,
Chacun sa verité,
Pour moi la verité est claire,
Si extraordinaire
Que j'me dis, 'Que faire?'
Si tu m'ignore

Moi j't'aimerai encore,
Pourquoi—pourquoi—pourquoi?
Maîtresse troublante,
Plume de ma tante,
Toujours je crie—Paris.


Notre Dame, La Madeleine,
P'tits bistros au bord d'la Seine,
Opéra, Boul' Mich' et Bals Musettes.
Champs Élysées, Montparnasse,
Ceux qui restent et ceux qui passent,
Même Cecile Sorel et Mistinguette.
Tous les arbres dans les Bois,
Les marchands d'charcuteries,
Tous les pédicures Chinois
Si plein de nostalgie.
Toutes les filles d'la rue, narquoises,
Toutes les fraises et les framboises
Remplissent de joie mon âme fleuri,
De Montmartre a Père Lachaise
Paris est un doux malaise
Dont mon cœur ne sera jamais guéri,
Paris est un diable—Paris est un ange,
Tu es toujours tous les deux—quel affreux mélange.


Mystérieuse et vilaine blageuse,
Je bois—je bois—à toi
Bock, Fernet-Branca,
Hook, line et Sanka,
Toujours je crie—Paris!



DEVON

CAFÉ DE PARIS

Re-written from original in *London Calling* sung by Tubby Edlin.
Sung by N.C. Café de Paris.

Verse 1   Both near and far
I've followed my star
Wherever that star has led me,
From Zanzibar
To Leamington Spa
My vagabond feet have sped me,

But in my dreams
It always seems
I'm on some Devonshire hill
Where the earth is red
And the beer is red
And the girls are redder still,
Fill up—fill up—the girls are redder still.

Refrain 1　It's mighty fine to rattle home
　　　　　　To Tiverton or Torquay,
　　　　　　And Babbacombe Bay
　　　　　　The wise men say
　　　　　　Is just the only place to be,
　　　　　　Let others call the cattle home
　　　　　　Across the sands of Dee
　　　　　　For Francis Drake cried 'Toodle-oodle-oo'
　　　　　　In Devon by the sea.

Verse 2　　But when life's sky is overcast
　　　　　　And death is in the vale
　　　　　　Though we may go to rest at last
　　　　　　Thank God we've got our ale,
　　　　　　For Devon men are red throughout
　　　　　　In April, May and June,
　　　　　　So let your sturdy voices shout
　　　　　　For Drake and Lorna Doone,
　　　　　　Fie Doone—Fie Doone—Fie Doone, Fie Doone,
　　　　　　　　Fie Doone.

Refrain 2　For Wigan men are hearty
　　　　　　And Bolton men are bold,
　　　　　　There's something coy in a Blackpool boy
　　　　　　And the Bedford lads have hearts of gold,
　　　　　　But the chaps that live on Dartmoor
　　　　　　Are breezy, bright and gay,
　　　　　　Singing Hey ha ha with a fa la la and a hey nonny no
　　　　　　　and whack folly o,
　　　　　　Ha ha ha ha ha ha ha ha ha ha ha ha HA HA HA
　　　　　　　HA!

# DON'T MAKE FUN OF THE FAIR

*from* THE LYRIC REVUE

Verse 1   We're proud to say
    In every way
    We're ordinary folk,
    But please to observe
    We still preserve
    Our sturdy hearts of oak.
    Although as servants of the state
    We may have been coerced,
    As we've been told to celebrate
    We'll celebrate or burst.
    Though while we brag
    Our shoulders sag
    Beneath a heavy yoke
    We all get terribly heated
    If it's treated
    As a joke. So:

Refrain 1   Don't make fun of the festival,
    Don't make fun of the fair,
    We down-trodden British must learn to be skittish
    And give an impression of devil-may-care
    To the wide wide world,
    We'll sing 'God for Harry',
    And if it turns out all right
    Knight Gerald Barry,
    Clear the national decks, my lads,
    Everyone of us counts,
    Grab the traveller's cheques, my lads,
    And pray that none of them bounce.
    Boys and Girls come out to play,
    Every day in every way
    Help the tourist to defray
    All that's underwritten.
    Sell your rations and overcharge,
    And don't let anyone sabotage
    Our own dear Festival of Britain.

Verse 2   We've never been
    Exactly keen
    On showing off or swank
    But as they say
    That gay display
    Means money in the bank,

We'll make the dreadful welkin ring
From Penge to John O'Groats
And cheer and laugh and shout and sing
Before we cut our throats,
We know we're caught
And must support
This patriotic prank
And though we'd rather have shot ourselves
We've got ourselves
To thank. So:


Refrain 2    Don't make fun of the festival,
             Don't make fun of the fair,
             We must pull together in spite of the weather
             That dampens our spirits and straightens our hair.
             Let the people sing
             Even though they shiver
             Roses red and noses mauve
             Over the river.
             Though the area's fairly small,
             Climb Discovery's Dome,
             Take a snooze in the concert hall,
             At least it's warmer than home.
             March about in funny hats,
             Show the foreign diplomats
             That our proletariat's
             Milder than a kitten.
             We believe in the right to strike,
             But now we've bloody well got to like
             Our own dear Festival of Britain.


Refrain 3    Don't make fun of the festival,
             Don't make fun of the fair,
             We must have a look at a cookery book
             To prevent us from spreading alarm and despair.
             We can serve whale steaks
             When the weather's hotter
             And in place of entrecôtes,
             What's wrong with otter?
             Greet the gala with fervence, boys,
             Learn to dance in the dark,
             Build the Sunday observance boys
             A shrine in Battersea Park.
             Cross your fingers, hold your thumbs,
             Blow your trumpets, roll your drums,
             Even if nobody comes

Don't be conscience-smitten.
If no overseas trade appears
We'll have to work for a thousand years
To pay for the Festival of Britain.

Refrain 4    Don't make fun of the festival,
Don't make fun of the fair.
We mustn't look glum when the visitors come
And discover our cupboard is ever so bare.
We must cheer, boys, cheer,
Look as though we love it
And if it should be a bust
Just rise above it.
Take a nip from your brandy flask,
Scream and caper and shout,
Don't give anyone time to ask
What the Hell it's about.
Face the future undismayed,
Pray for further Marshall Aid,
Have the toast from Cavalcade
Drastically re-written.
Peace and dignity we may lack,
But wave a jolly Trades Union Jack,
Hurrah for the festival,
We'll pray for the festival,
Hurrah for the Festival of Britain!

Refrain 5    Don't make fun of the festival,
Don't make fun of the fair,
Our Government Bosses
Are counting their losses
And one of them's taken to brushing his hair.
We must all salute—those who double-crossed us,
Fire a round
For every pound
Ground-nuts have cost us,
Blow a kiss to the Board of Trade,
Learn to laugh like a drain
If a million has been mislaid,
Who are we to complain?
Join our civil servants' ball,
Cheer our near Decline and Fall,
Gibbon might have dreamed it all,
Also Bulwer-Lytton,
If our workers begin to slack
Let's get some enemy aliens back,
Hurrah for the Festival of Britain!

Refrain 6  Don't make fun of the festival,
Don't make fun of the fair,
We must have a look
At a cookery book
To prevent us from spreading alarm and despair.
You will find tinned Spam—much improved by mustard,
But when served Vanilla Shape
Scrape—off the custard.
Eat together or eat alone,
Order tea and a bun,
Break your teeth on a scone of stone
And enter into the fun.
Labour leaders lead us all
Though we know they bleed us all,
If the hands that feed us all
Should get badly bitten
Any surgeon without a fee
Would amputate them and shout with glee,
Hurray for the festival,
Make way for the festival,
Sing Hey for the Festival of Britain!

## A BAR ON THE PICCOLA MARINA

### (English Version)

Verse        In a 'bijou' abode
In St Barnabas Road
Not far from the Esher by-pass
Lived a mother and wife
Who, most of her life,
Let every adventure fly past.
She had two strapping daughters and a rather dull son
And a much duller husband who at sixty-one
Elected to retire
And, later on, expire,
Sing Hallelujah, Hey nonny-no, Hey nonny-no, Hey
        nonny-no!
He joined the feathered choir.
On a wet afternoon
In the middle of June
They all of them came home soaking
Having laid him to rest
By special request
In the family vault at Woking,
And then in the middle of the funeral wake

With her mouth full of excellent Madeira cake
His widow cried, 'That's done,
My life's at last begun,
Sing Hallelujah, Hey nonny-no, Hey nonny-no, Hey
nonny-no,
It's time I had some fun,
Today, though hardly a jolly day,
At least has set me free,
We'll all have a lovely holiday
On the island of Capri!'


Refrain 1  In a bar on the Piccola Marina
Life called to Mrs Wentworth-Brewster,
Fate beckoned her and introduced her
Into a rather queer
Unfamiliar atmosphere.
She'd just sit there, propping up the bar
Beside a fisherman who sang to a guitar.
When accused of having gone too far
She merely cried, 'Funiculi!
Just fancy me!
Funicula!'
When he bellowd 'Che Bella Signorina!'
Sheer ecstasy at once produced a
Wild shriek from Mrs Wentworth-Brewster,
Changing her whole demeanour.
When both her daughters and her son said,
'Please come home, Mama,'
She murmured rather bibulously, 'Who d'you think you
are?'
Nobody can afford to be so lahdy-bloody-da
In a bar on the Piccola Marina.


Interlude  Every fisherman cried.
'Viva Viva' and 'Che Ragazza',
When she sat in the Grand Piazza
Everybody would rise,
Every fisherman sighed,
'Viva Viva che bell' Inglesi',
Someone even said, 'Whoops-adaisy!'
Which was quite a surprise.
Each night she'd make some gay excuse
And beaming with good will
She'd just slip into something loose
And totter down the hill.

Refrain 2　To the bar on the Piccola Marina
　　　　　　Where love came to Mrs Wentworth-Brewster,
　　　　　　Hot flushes of delight suffused her,
　　　　　　Right round the bend she went,
　　　　　　Picture her astonishment,
　　　　　　Day in, day out she would gad about
　　　　　　Because she felt she was no longer on the shelf,
　　　　　　Night out, night in, knocking back the gin
　　　　　　She'd cry, 'Hurrah!
　　　　　　Funicula
　　　　　　Funiculi
　　　　　　Funic yourself!'
　　　　　　Just for fun three young sailors from Messina
　　　　　　Bowed low to Mrs Wentworth-Brewster,
　　　　　　Said 'Scusi' and politely goosed her.
　　　　　　Then there was quite a scena.
　　　　　　Her family, in floods of tears, cried,
　　　　　　'Leave these men, Mama.'
　　　　　　She said, 'They're just high-spirited, like all Italians are
　　　　　　And most of them have a great deal more to offer than
　　　　　　　　Papa
　　　　　　In a bar on the Piccola Marina.'


## A BAR ON THE PICCOLA MARINA

### (As sung at Las Vegas)

Verse　I'll sing you a song,
　　　　　It's not very long,
　　　　　Its moral may disconcert you,
　　　　　Of a mother and wife
　　　　　Who most of her life
　　　　　Was famed for domestic virtue.
　　　　　She had two strapping daughters and a rather dull son
　　　　　And a much duller husband, who at sixty-one
　　　　　Elected to retire
　　　　　And, later on, expire.
　　　　　Sing Hallelujah, Hey nonny-no, Hey nonny-no, Hey
　　　　　　nonny-no!
　　　　　He joined the feathered choir.
　　　　　Having laid him to rest
　　　　　By special request
　　　　　In the family mausoleum,
　　　　　As his widow repaired
　　　　　To the home they had shared,
　　　　　Her heart sang a gay Te Deum.
　　　　　And then in the middle of the funeral wake
　　　　　While adding some liquor to the Tipsy Cake

She briskly cried, 'That's done.
My life's at last begun.
Sing Hallelujah, Hey nonny-no, Hey nonny-no, Hey
     nonny-no!
It's time I had some fun.
Today, though hardly a jolly day,
At least has set me free,
We'll all have a lovely holiday
On the island of Capri!'


## ALICE IS AT IT AGAIN

Verse 1    In a dear little village remote and obscure
           A beautiful maiden resided,
           As to whether or not her intentions were pure
           Opinion was sharply divided.
           She loved to lie out 'neath the darkening sky
           And allow the soft breeze to entrance her,
           She whispered her dreams to the birds flying by
           But seldom received any answer.

Refrain 1  Over the field and along the lane
           Gentle Alice would love to stray,
           When it came to the end of the day,
           She would wander away unheeding,
           Dreaming her innocent dreams she strolled
           Quite unaffected by heat or cold,
           Frequently freckled or soaked with rain,
           Alice was out in the lane.
           Whom she met there
           Every day there
           Was a question answered by none,
           But she'd get there
           And she'd stay there
           Till whatever she did was undoubtedly done.
           Over the field and along the lane
           When her parents had called in vain,
           Sadly, sorrowfully, they'd complain,
           'Alice is at it again.'

Verse 2    Though that dear little village
           Surrounded by trees
           Had neither a school nor a college
           Gentle Alice acquired from the birds and the bees
           Some exceedingly practical knowledge.
           The curious secrets that nature revealed

She refused to allow to upset her
But she thought when observing the beasts of the
   field
That things might have been organized better.


Refrain 2  Over the field and along the lane
Gentle Alice one summer's day
Met a man who was driving a dray
And he whisked her away to London.
Then, after many a year had passed,
Alice returned to her home at last
Wearing some pearls and a velvet train,
Bearing a case of champagne.
They received her
Fairly coldly
But when wine had lifted the blight
They believed her
When she boldly
Said the Salvation Army had shown her the light.
When she had left by the evening train
Both her parents in grief and pain
Murmured brokenly, 'More champagne—
Alice is at it again!'


Rhythm  Over the field and along the lane
Refrain  Gentle Alice would make up
And take up—her stand.
The road was not exactly arterial
But it led to a town near by
Where quite a lot of masculine material
Caught her roving eye.
She was ready to hitchhike
Cadillac or motor-bike,
She wasn't proud or choosey,
All she
Was aiming to be
Was a prinked up,
Minked up
Fly-by-night Floosie.
When old Rajahs
Gave her pearls as large as
Nuts on a chestnut tree
All she said was, 'Fiddlededee,
The wages of sin will be the death of me!'
Over the field and along the lane
Gentle Alice's parents would wait hand in hand.

Her dear old white-headed mother wistfully sipping
    champagne
Said, 'We've spoiled our child—spared the rod,
Open up the caviar and say Thank God,
We've got no cause to complain,
Alice is at it,
Alice is at it,
Alice is at it again.'


# NINETY MINUTES IS A LONG, LONG TIME

*from* TOGETHER WITH MUSIC

with Mary Martin, New York 1955

| | |
|---|---|
| MARY:<br>(*speaking to<br>music*) | Noël dear,<br>Let's get things clear,<br>It's rather too late for bickering,<br>The warning lights are flickering,<br>We mustn't fool about. |
| NOËL:<br>(*speaking to<br>music*) | That's OK<br>But let me say<br>Before we go any farther, dear,<br>I'd really so much rather, dear,<br>You cut that number out. |
| (*singing*) | Apart from slowing up the pace<br>It truly isn't strong enough. |
| MARY:<br>(*singing*) | Without that number in that place<br>Our programme won't be long enough. |
| TOGETHER. | Ninety minutes is a long, long time,<br>A long, long time,<br>A long, long time,<br>To make people laugh<br>For an hour and a half<br>In this very exacting medium<br>Is a lot to expect<br>And the final effect<br>May be nothing but tears and tedium,<br>Don't imagine that we've not rehearsed,<br>We did that first |

But fear the worst
We hope to amuse the customers with music and with
    rhyme
But ninety minutes is a long, long time,
Ninety minutes is a long, long time.

*Second reprise*
Ninety minutes is a long, long time,
A long, long time,
A long, long time,
We need the Rockettes
And some marionettes
And a handful of stars supporting us
When we visualize
All those millions of eyes,
All those millions of screens distorting us,
Don't imagine it's a bagatelle
To cast a spell,
We know darned well
Whenever a song
Goes on too long
It isn't worth a dime
And ninety minutes is a long, long time,
Ninety minutes is a long, long time.


# TOGETHER WITH MUSIC

*from* TOGETHER WITH MUSIC

Refrain 1 Together with music,
        Together with music,
        We planned this moment long ago,
        Many a year we've sighed in vain
        For both of us knew
        Many a moon would wax and wane
        Before this dream came true.
        Together with music,
        Together with music,
        The thought of it enchants us so,
        When those first chords crash out
        We know beyond a doubt
        That everything's going to be divine
        Watch us rise and shine
        Riding as high as a kite
        Our hearts are fancy free
        Because at long long last we happen to be
        Together, with music tonight,

Verse  Bear with us, bear with us please,
     If we look a bit wild and overwrought,
     But we're dreaming a dream we never thought
     Would ever quite come true for us,
     Share with us, share with us please
     The excitement of standing hand-in-hand
     While this very select exclusive Band
     Plays a personal Tattoo for us.
     For many a year and many a day
     We've laid our plans away
     For many a day and many a year
     We've prayed that somewhere, sometime we'd
      appear . . .

Refrain 2 Together with music,
     Together with music,
     Now suddenly our hearts feel gay,
     Ever since that first day we met
     We both of us guessed
     Many a sun would rise and set
     Before we coalesced
     Together with music
     Together with music
     At last the Gods have said Okay,
     When those first notes we hear
     A million stars appear,
     Our personal world goes round and round
     Gaily wired for sound
     Everything's shining and bright
     This is our jubilee
     Because at long long last we happen to be
     Together with music tonight.


# WHAT'S GOING TO HAPPEN TO THE TOTS?
## (American Version)

Verse 1 Life today is hectic,
     Our world is running away,
     Only the wise
     Can recognize
     The process of decay,
     Unhappily all our dialectic
     Is quite unable to say
     Whether we're on the beam or not
     Whether we'll rise supreme or not

Whether this new régime or not
Is leading us astray.
We all have Frigidaires, radios,
Television and movie shows
To shield us from the ultimate abyss,
We have our daily bread neatly cut,
Every modern convenience, but
The question that confronts us all is this:

Refrain 1   What's going to happen to the children
When there aren't any more grown-ups?
Having been injected with some rather peculiar glands
Darling Mum's gone platinum and dances to all the
    rhumba bands,
The songs that she sings at twilight
Would certainly be the highlight
For some of those claques
That Elsa Maxwell takes around in yachts.
Rock-a-bye, rock-a-bye, rock-a-bye, my darlings,
Mother requires a few more shots,
Does it amuse the tiny mites
To see their parents high as kites?
What's, what's, what's going to happen to the tots?

Verse 2   Life today's neurotic,
A ceaseless battle we wage,
Millions are spent
To circumvent
The march of middle-age,
The fact that we grab each new narcotic
Can only prove in the end
Whether our hormones jell or not
Whether our cells rebel or not
Whether we're blown to hell or not
We'll all be round the bend
From taking Benzedrine, Dexamil,
Every possible sleeping pill
To knock us out or knock us into shape,
We all have shots for this, shots for that,
Shots for making us thin or fat,
But there's one problem that we can't escape:

Refrain 2   What's going to happen to the children
When there aren't any more grown-ups?
Thanks to plastic surgery and Uncle's abrupt demise
Dear Aunt Rose has changed her nose but doesn't
    appear to realize

The pleasures that once were heaven
Look silly at sixty-seven
And youthful allure you can't procure
In terms of perms and pots—so
Lullaby, lullaby, lullaby, my darlings,
Try not to scratch those large red spots.
Think of the shock when Mummy's face
Is lifted from its proper place,
What's, what's, what's going to happen to the tots?

Refrain 3   What's going to happen to the children
When there aren't any more grown-ups?
It's bizarre when Grandmamma, without getting out of
   breath,
Starts to jive at eighty-five
And frightens the little ones to death,
The police had to send a squad car
When Daddy got fried on Vodka
And tied a tweed coat round Mummy's throat
In several sailor's knots.
Hush-a-bye, hush-a-bye, hush-a-bye, my darlings,
Try not to fret and wet your cots,
One day you'll clench your tiny fists
And murder your psychiatrists,
What's, what's, what's going to happen to the tots?

# WHY MUST THE SHOW GO ON?

Verse 1   The world for some years
Has been sodden with tears
On behalf of the Acting profession,
Each star playing a part
Seems to expect the 'Purple Heart',
It's unorthodox
To be born in a box
But it needn't become an obsession,
Let's hope we have no worse to plague us
Than two shows a night at Las Vegas.
When I think of physicians
And mathematicians
Who don't earn a quarter the dough,
When I look at the faces
Of people in Macey's
There's one thing I'm burning to know:

Refrain 1  Why must the show go on?
It can't be all that indispensable,
To me it really isn't sensible
On the whole
To play a leading role
While fighting those tears you can't control,
Why kick up your legs
When draining the dregs
Of sorrow's bitter cup?
Because you have read
Some idiot has said,
'The Curtain must go up'!
I'd like to know why a star takes bows
Having just returned from burying her spouse.
Brave boop-a-doopers,
Go home and dry your tears,
Gallant old troupers,
You've bored us all for years
And when you're so blue,
Wet through
And thoroughly woe-begone,
Why must the show go on?
Oh Mammy!
Why must the show go on?

Verse 2  We're asked to condole
With each tremulous soul
Who steps out to be loudly applauded,
Stars on opening nights
Sob when they see their names in lights,
Though people who act
As a matter of fact
Are financially amply rewarded,
It seems, while pursuing their calling,
Their suffering's simply appalling!
But butchers and bakers
And candlestick makers
Get little applause for their pains
And when I think of miners
And waiters in 'Diners'
One query for ever remains:

Refrain 2  Why must the show go on?
The rule is surely not immutable,
It might be wiser and more suitable
Just to close
If you are in the throes

Of personal grief and private woes.
Why stifle a sob
While doing your job
When, if you use your head,
You'd go out and grab
A comfortable cab
And go right home to bed?
Because you're not giving us much fun,
This 'Laugh Clown Laugh' routine's been overdone,
Hats off to Show Folks
For smiling when they're blue
But more comme-il-faut folks
Are sick of smiling through,
And if you're out cold,
Too old
And most of your teeth have gone,
Why must the show go on?
I sometimes wonder
Why must the show go on?

Refrain 3  Why must the show go on?
Why not announce the closing night of it?
The public seem to hate the sight of it,
Dear, and so
Why you should undergo
This terrible strain we'll never know.
We know that you're sad,
We know that you've had
A lot of storm and strife
But is it quite fair
To ask us to share
Your dreary private life?
We know you're trapped in a gilded cage
But for Heaven's sake relax and be your age,
Stop being gallant
And don't be such a bore,
Pack up your talent,
There's always plenty more
And if you lose hope
Take dope
And lock yourself in the John,
Why must the show go on?
I'm merely asking
Why must the show go on?

## SPINNING SONG

Here at my spinning wheel I stay
While the robin sings 'Ho!' on the orchard bough,
Where is my love who rode away,
Where be he, be he now?
Where be he, be he, be he, be he, be he, be he, be he
   now?
Winter comes and then the Spring,
I weave and weave and weave and weave,
I've worked for a year
On a coat for my dear
And I've not yet finished the sleeve.
Here at my spinning wheel I stay,
My bobbin goes click-clack, click-clack,
I've got my warp right up my woof
And I can't get the bloody thing back.

# The Sixties

# NOTE ON 'THE SIXTIES'

This particular decade has not, as yet, progressed very far and what with the prevalent 'ill will to all men', nuclear fission, and the industrious piling up of weapons of annihilation, it may not even get beyond the half-way mark. However, regardless of evil portents, prophetic despair and a great deal too much writing on the wall, I have managed so far to write two fairly cheerful musical comedies. The first of these, *Sail Away*, contains some good lyrics, notably 'Why Do The Wrong People Travel', 'Useless Useful Phrases' and 'The Passenger's Always Right'. The second, *The Girl Who Came To Supper*, for which I was responsible for the music and lyrics only, has, at the time of writing, just opened on Broadway. Most of the lyrics in this were inspired, as they should be, by the book—Harry Kurnitz via Terence Rattigan. I would like to draw the reader's attention, if he is still with me, to the four 'London' songs and the intricate rhyming of the 'Coronation Chorale'. There are also some pleasant pastiche lines in the period musical comedy sequence, 'The Coconut Girl'.

I think I must take this opportunity of apologizing to the gentle reader for having written so very very much for such a very very long time, but as I stated in the preface to this book, the compulsion to make rhymes was born in me. For those sated readers of my works who wish ardently that I would stop, the future looks dark indeed.

# 'Sail Away'

## COME TO ME

*from* SAIL AWAY

STEWARDS: Thank the Lord,
Mimi Paragon's on board,
She can organize the horde
Of morons—we said morons—
That we take abroad,
She will see that they're occupied every moment of
   the day,
Keep the fatheads out of the way,
Hurray! Hurray! Hurray!
Give a cheer,
Mimi Paragon is here,
She will firmly commandeer
The dumb-clucks—we said dumb-clucks—
Till they're on their ear,
She will ride 'em till they qualify for the psychopathic
   ward,
Hallelujah—thank the Lord,
Mimi Paragon's on board.

MIMI: They christened me Mimi,
My tiny hand is frozen
But heaven forbid that I should shirk
The work that I have chosen,
To be a professional pepper-upper
Isn't everyone's cuppa tea
But I've wit and guile
And a big false smile
And the tourists rely on me.

BOYS: That's quite, quite true,
They always do,
They're crazy about Mimi.

MIMI: On the very first dreadful day
I stand them in line,

BOYS:     She stands them in line,

MIMI:     I keep them in line,

BOYS:     She keeps them in line,

MIMI:     I stand them in line and say:

If you're mad keen to be cultural
I'm the gal
With whom you should roam,
I can show you every ruin from Jerusalem to Greece,
Also quite a few between Antibes and Nice,
If you can't live without antique pots
I'll find lots for you to take home,
If you long to take bad photographs of classical
    débris
Come to me—come to me,
If you want to crouch in churches till you've water
    on the knee
Come to me, poor fools—come to me.

BOYS:     She's terribly energetic,
She's so full of vim and zip,
If we hit a gale
And the turbines fail
She can easily drive the ship.

MIMI:     And if to play games is what you call fun
I'm the one
To keep you in form,
I can organize a treasure hunt or even clockwork
    trains,
Anything to occupy four poor dim brains.
We've some fine backgammon boards on board
If the Lord should send us a storm,
If Canasta, Bridge or Bingo are your kind of Jamboree
Come to me—come to me.
But if you want to play strip poker with the girls in
    Cabin B
Come to me—dear boys—come to me—dear boys.
(*spoken*)
We will now have one fast chorus of 'Beyond the
    Blue Horizon'.
(*resume singing*)
Come to me!

And if you feel lonely and need a pal
I'm the gal
To take you in tow.
If you're pining for affection and a sympathetic friend
I've a large collection I can recommend.
If you want something discreetly planned
On this grand
And gracious bateau,
If you're basically frustrated and a martyr to ennui
Come to me—come to me.
Or if you need a marijuana or a quiet cup of tea
Come to me—lost lamb—
Come to me—lost lamb—come to me!

# SAIL AWAY

### *from* SAIL AWAY

JOHNNY: A different sky,
New worlds to gaze upon,
The strange excitement of an unfamiliar shore,
One more goodbye,
One more illusion gone,
Just cut your losses
And begin once more.

When the storm clouds are riding through a winter
        sky
Sail away—sail away.
When the love-light is fading in your sweetheart's eye
Sail away—sail away.
When you feel your song is orchestrated wrong
Why should you prolong
Your stay?
When the wind and the weather blow your dreams
        sky high
Sail away—sail away—sail away!

### *Reprise*

JOHNNY: When you can't bear the clamour of the noisy town

ALL:      Sail away—sail away!

JOHNNY: When the friends that you've counted on have let
you down

ALL: Sail away—sail away!

JOHNNY: But when soon or late
You recognize your fate
That will be your great,
Great day.
On the wings of the morning with your own true
love
Sail away—

ALL: Sail away—

JOHNNY: Sail away!

## WHERE SHALL I FIND HIM

*from* SAIL AWAY

NANCY: Oh, darling Mother, this
Was a mistake. I can never do the job.
I never should have come,
I'm far too dumb.
I know she's going to miss
That other girl, for at least she knew the job.
Can you imagine how she'd rage at me
Should she discover
I'm really searching for a lover?

*Refrain*

Where shall I find him?
Where will he be?
Where shall I find him,
The one for me?
Suddenly, suddenly maybe we'll meet
On an ordinary day on some ordinary street.
How shall I know him?
What will he wear?
How shall I show him
How tenderly I care?
How shall I prove to him,
Make him clearly see
That he's the only one for me?

*Reprise*

BARNABY: Maybe I've found her,
Can this be she?
Maybe I've found her,
The one for me.
Suddenly, suddenly I wonder why
Such a lot of extra stars
Seem to shimmer in the sky.
Can this be my girl
Do you suppose?
This rather shy girl
With freckles on her nose?
How can I prove to her,
Make her clearly see
That she's the only love for me?

## BEATNIK LOVE AFFAIR

*from* SAIL AWAY

Why suffer from moral convictions?
Social restrictions?
Let's thumb our noses at
Cold Wars and atomic predictions.
They're only a waste of time.
Let's make a romantic decision,
Follow a vision,
Now is the moment to see clearly
And realize that really
We are on the brink of it,
Come to think of it.

You and I could have an upright, downright,
Watertight, Dynamite
Love affair.
We could either play it up-beat, down-beat,
On-the-beat, off-the-beat,
Fair or square.
Hey for those flip Calypsos,
Ho for that rhythmic din,
Heigho for those dopes and dipsos,
Rum punch, coconuts, Gordon's gin
Think if we tried out
Some little hide-out

On some tropical isle.
Naked and warm
From dawn to moonrise,
Somerset Maugham-wise,
Blue Lagoon-wise.
We could lie upon the beach at nights, dear,
Watching all those Russian satellites, dear,
Whizzing through the air
While we carried on with our off-beat, on-beat, Beatnik
Love affair.

You and I could have an in-board, out-board,
Overboard, bed-and-board
Love affair,
All we need's a little off-key, on-key,
King-sized, organized
Time to spare,
There by the Caribbean
We'll cross the Rubicon.
We'll have, by the deep blue sea, an
All-out roustabout carry-on.
We'll get a 'Man-Tan',
Gargantuan tan
On those shimmering sands.
Nothing to do but read and rest, dear,
We could get through 'By Love Possessed', dear,
Every time we hear a seagull whistle
We'll forget our last misguided missile
Just destroyed Times Square,
As we carry on with our king-sized, organized,
    Beatnik Love Affair . . .

## LATER THAN SPRING

*from* SAIL AWAY

Have no fears for future years
For sweet compensation you may find,
Make your bow
To the moment that is now
And always bear in mind:

Refrain     Later than Spring
The warmth of Summer comes,
The charm of Autumn comes,
The leaves are gold.
Poets say
That the blossoms of May
Fade away
And die.
Yet, don't forget
That we met
When the sun was high.
Later than Spring
Words that were said before,
Tears that were shed before
Can be consoled.
Realize that its wise to remember
Though Time is on the wing,
Song birds still sing
Later than Spring.

Refrain 2   Later than Spring
Though careless rapture's past
No need to gaze aghast
At days gone by,
You can still if you will
Feel the thrill
Of a new desire,
Still
Feel that glow
When you know
That your world's on fire.
Later than Spring
Remembered April showers
May bring our present hours
A clearer sky.
We pretend and pretend it's the end
But the pendulum must swing,
Nightingales sing
Later than Spring.

Reprise     Later than Spring
Much disillusion comes,
Sometimes confusion comes,
You lose your way.
Need it be such unbearable sadness
To face the truth?

Love, with its passionate madness
Belongs to youth.
Later than Spring
Our values change, my dear,
It would be strange, my dear,
If they should stay.
Waste no tears
On the hurrying years,
For whatever they may bring
Song birds still sing
Later than Spring.


# THE PASSENGER'S ALWAYS RIGHT

### *from* SAIL AWAY

CARRINGTON: The woman in cabin forty-nine has lost her diamond
brooch.

JOE: Calm her, Carrington,
Charm her, Carrington,
That's the correct approach.

HOSKINS: A gentleman on the Promenade Deck just called me
a lazy slob.

JOE: Smile at him, Hoskins,
Smile at him, Hoskins,
That is part of your job.

STEWARD: The three fat children in B Deck 3
Have thrown their bathmat in the sea.

SHUTTLE-
WORTH: The silly old broad in Main Deck 2
Has dropped her dentures down the loo.

JOE: Passengers since the world began
Have been querulous, rude and snooty.
England expects that every man
This day should do his duty.

Weatherby?

| | |
|---|---|
| WEATHERBY: | Here. |
| JOE: | Hoskins? |
| HOSKINS: | Here. |
| JOE: | Green, Blake, Richardson? |
| GREEN, BLAKE, RICHARDSON: | Here. Here. Here. |
| JOE: | Crawford? |
| CRAWFORD: | Here. |
| JOE: | Shuttleworth? |
| SHUTTLE-WORTH: | Here. |
| JOE: | Smith, Brown, Parkinson? |
| SMITH, BROWN, PARKINSON: | Here. Here. Here. |
| JOE: | Where the devil are Bruce and Frome? |
| HOSKINS: | One's got shingles and the other's gone home. |
| JOE: | Where's O'Reilley and Jock McBride? |
| GREEN, BLAKE, RICHARDSON: | One got married, the other got fried. |
| JOE: | Carrington? |
| CARRINGTON: | Here. |
| JOE: | Brewster? |
| BREWSTER: | Here. |
| JOE: | Where's young Fawcett and Windermere? |
| WEATHERBY: | Fawcett stayed at home in bed. |
| STEWARDS: | Poor old Windermere dropped down dead. |
| JOE: | In the course of each cruise<br>I always choose<br>To lecture each subordinate. |

You're not damned fools
And you know the rules,
So see you all co-ordinate.

STEWARDS:        We've heard all this before.

HOSKINS:         I can't stand any more.

JOE:             Bow, smile, charm, tact,
                 Never forget one vital fact:

                 The passenger's always right, my boys,
                 The passenger's always right.
                 Although he's a drip
                 He's paid for his trip,
                 So greet him with delight.
                 Agree to his suggestions.
                 However coarse or crude,
                 Reply to all his questions,
                 Ply him with drink—stuff him with food.
                 The passenger may be sober, boys,
                 The passenger may be tight,
                 The passenger may be foe or friend
                 Or absolutely round the bend,
                 But calm him,
                 Charm him,
                 Even though he's higher than a kite
                 The passenger's always right.

                 The passenger's always right, my boys,
                 The passenger's always right.
                 Those dreary old wrecks
                 Who litter the decks
                 Demand that you're polite.
                 Don't count on any free time,
                 Be kind to all the jerks,
                 And every day at teatime
                 Stuff 'em with cake . . . give 'em the works.
                 The passenger may be dull, my boys,
                 The passenger may be bright,
                 The passenger may be quite serene
                 Or gibbering with Benzedrine,
                 But nurse him,
                 Curse him
                 Only when the bastard's out of sight.
                 Remember, boys,
                 The goddamned passenger's always right.

## USELESS USEFUL PHRASES

*from* SAIL AWAY

When the tower of Babel fell
It caused a lot of unnecessary Hell.
Personal 'rapport'
Became a complicated bore
And a lot more difficult than it had been before,
When the tower of Babel fell.

The Chinks and the Japs
And the Finns and Lapps
Were reduced to a helpless stammer,
And the ancient Greeks
Took at least six weeks
To learn their Latin grammar.
The guttural wheeze
Of the Portuguese
Filled the brains of the Danes
With horror,
And verbs, not lust,
Caused the final bust
In Sodom and Gomorrah.

If it hadn't been for that
Bloody building falling flat
I would not have had to learn Italiano
And keep muttering 'Si, si'
And 'Mi Chiamano Mimi'
Like an ageing Metropolitan soprano!

I should not have had to look
At that ghastly little book
Till my brain becomes as soft as mayonnaise is,
Messrs Hugo and Berlitz
Must have torn themselves to bits
Dreaming up so many useless useful phrases.

Refrain 1   Pray tell me the time,
It is six,
It is seven,
It's half past eleven,
It's twenty to two,
I want thirteen stamps,
Does your child have convulsions?

Please bring me some rhubarb,
I need a shampoo,
How much is that hat?
I desire some red stockings,
My mother is married,
These boots are too small,
My Aunt has a cold,
Shall we go to the opera?
This meat is disgusting,
Is this the town hall?

Refrain 2  My cousin is deaf,
Kindly bring me a hatchet,
Pray pass me the pepper,
What pretty cretonne,
What time is the train?
It is late,
It is early,
It's running on schedule,
It's here,
It has gone,
I've written six letters,
I've written no letters,
Pray fetch me a horse,
I have need of a groom,
This isn't my passport,
This isn't my hatbox,
Please show me the way
To Napoleon's tomb.

Refrain 3  The weather is cooler,
The weather is hotter,
Pray fasten my corsets,
Please bring me my cloak,
I've lost my umbrella,
I'm in a great hurry,
I'm going,
I'm staying,
D'you mind if I smoke?
This mutton is tough,
There's a mouse in my bedroom,
This egg is delicious,
This soup is too thick,
Please bring me a trout,
What an excellent pudding,
Pray hand me my gloves,
I'm going to be sick!

# THE LITTLE ONES' A.B.C.

### *from* SAIL AWAY

#### *Verse*

MIMI:  A. B. C. D. E. F. G.
H. I. J. K. L. M. N. O.
Oh what a jolly little jocular
Group we are.

ALVIN:  Bla—Bla—Bla!

MIMI:  Vocalize and harmonize
When mother cries
One, two, three—go.
Try, if it's possible to keep on key,
Sing the letters after me.

CHILDREN:  Just how corny can you be?

MIMI:  If you sing when you are blue
You find you
Never have to care a rap,
When the skies are dark and grey,
You just say—

CHILDREN:  What a lot of crap!

MIMI:  P. Q. R. S. T. U. V.
And W. X. Y. Z. or Zee.
This is my personal recipe
For the little ones' A.B.C.

#### *Refrain 1*

A. Stands for Absolutely Anything,
B. Stands for Big Brass Bands,
C. Stands for Chlorophyll,
D. Stands for Dexamil,
E. Stands for Endocrine Glands,
F. and G. Don't suggest a thing to me.
Nor do H. I. J. K. L.
But after L. comes M. for Mother
And Mother's going to give you Hell.

*Refrain 2*

MIMI:              A. Stands for Artichokes and Adenoids,
                   B. Stands for Bolts and Belts,
                   C. Stands for Cottage Cheese,
                   D. Stands for Dungarees,
                   E. Stands for Everything Else,
                   G. Of Course
                   Stands for Getting a Divorce
                   And F. Sometimes stands for Fridge,
                   But if I really were your mother
                   I'd throw myself from Brookyn Bridge.

                   A.  Stands for Romeo and Juliet,
                   B. Stands for Ku Klux Klan,
                   C. Stands for Bethlehem,
                   D. Stands for M.G.M.,
                   E. Stands for 'So's Your Old Man',
                   F. and G. Stand for Home in Tennessee
                   And we know H. Stands for Stoats,
                   But after L. comes M. for Mother
                   And Mother'd like to slit your throats!

# GO SLOW, JOHNNY

*from* SAIL AWAY

Go slow, Johnny,
Maybe she'll come to her senses
If you'll give her a chance.
People's feelings are sensitive plants,
Try not to trample the soil and spoil romance.
Go slow, Johnny,
No sense in rushing your fences,
Till you know that you know
Your stars are bright for you,
Right for you,
Mark their courses,
Hold your horses,
Speak low, Johnny,
Tip toe, Johnny,
Go slow, Johnny,
Go slow.

Go slow, Johnny,
Slow goes it,
Wait a bit, Johnny,
There's no need to stampede.
Don't forget if you wish to succeed
One truth had better be faced,
More Haste less Speed.
Watch those road signs,
They'll indicate a bit, Johnny,
Which direction to go,
Rely on time and tact,
Face the fact
You're no Brando,
Rallentando,
Speak low, Johnny,
Tip toe, Johnny,
Go slow, Johnny,
Go slow,
Go slow, Johnny,
Go slow!

# YOU'RE A LONG LONG WAY FROM AMERICA

*from* SAIL AWAY

### *Verse*

MIMI: Hail Pioneers! Hail Pioneers! Hail Pioneers!
You have survived
The mighty ocean's turbulence,
The sudden tempest's fearful roar,
The fury of the elements
Until at last the welcome shore
Rises against a star-filled sky
To crown your glorious Odyssey.

ALL: We have arrived! We have arrived! We have arrived!

MIMI: Give thanks to him, this blessed day,
To one above, who set the course,
I am referring, need I say,
To Captain Wilberforce.

ALL:  All praise to him,
      All praise to him,
      We heartily endorse
      Your most appropriate salute
      To Captain Wilberforce.


MIMI:  You are about to land
       Tomorrow morning,
       Upon an alien strand
       Your feet will tread,
       Accept from me I pray
       A final warning,
       Remember what I say,
       Remember what I say,
       Remember what I've said . . .


### Refrain 1

You're a long long way from America,
You're a long long way from home,
Let the standard guide books
Be your bedside books
And don't read snide books
Like *The Lays of Ancient Rome.*
If you're not put off
By the continental coffee
That arrives on your breakfast tray
You'll find you've learned a little from the bad old
    world
When you're back in the U.S.A.


### Refrain 2

You're a long long way from America,
Be prepared to face the worst,
While guitars are strumming
'The Yanks are coming',
You'll find the plumbing
Rather frightening at first.
Do not be surprised
If the milk's not pasteurized
And appears just a wee bit grey,
You'll have learned a little something from the bad
    old world
When you're back in the U.S.A.

*Counter-Melody*

ALL: Get out the greenbacks,
Get out the greenbacks,
They will extricate us
If we should go astray,
In ancient nations
The populations
Have learned to count upon
American donations,
Travellers' cheques can
Do more than sex can
To consolidate us,
Don't let the status quo go,
Hand out those dollar bills,
Be loyal, brave and true
To the traditions of the U.S.A.

*Refrain 3*

You're a long long way from America,
Be prepared for stress and strain,
Don't expect hot showers
Or search for hours
To find fresh flowers
That are wrapped in cellophane,
You need not suspect
If you've had enough injections
Every fish dish that comes your way,
You'll have learned some hints on cooking in the
    bad old world
When you're back in the U.S.A.


# THE CUSTOMER'S ALWAYS RIGHT

*from* SAIL AWAY

ALI: When a cruise ship comes
I expect you bums
To make your own deductions.
Inspired by greed
You will all proceed
According to instructions.

ARABS: The suckers land today,
Hurray, hurray, hurray!

ALI:    The customer's always right, my boys,
        The customer's always right.
        The son-of-a-bitch
        Is probably rich
        So smile with all your might.
        Be wiser than a monkey,
        Be on to all the tricks,
        If one of them's a junky
        Give him a break. Give him a fix.
        The customer may be black, my boys,
        Or yellow or brown or white,
        He may have a yen for raw recruits
        Or mountain goats or football boots,
        But smooth him,
        Soothe him,
        Pander to him morning, noon and night,
        The customer's always right.

        The customer's always right, my boys,
        The customer's always right.
        They may pay a price for curious vice
        Or merely want a fight.
        They may have inhibitions,
        And yearn for secret joys,
        Obey your intuitions,
        Offer them girls . . . offer them boys.
        The customer may be dumb, my boys,
        Or terribly erudite,
        Perhaps you can satisfy his needs
        With strings of rather nasty beads,
        Compel him,
        Sell him
        Anything from sex to dynamite.
        Remember, boys,
        The God-damned customer's always right.


## SOMETHING VERY STRANGE

### *from* SAIL AWAY

Verse   This is not a day like any other day,
        This is something special and apart.
        Something to remember
        When the coldness of December
        Chills my heart.

Refrain 1  Something very strange
Is happening to me,
Every face I see
Seems to be smiling.
All the sounds I hear,
The buses changing gear,
Suddenly appear
To be beguiling.
Nobody is melancholy,
Nobody is sad,
Not a single shadow on the sea.
Some Magician's spell
Has made this magic start
And I feel I want to hold each shining moment in
    my heart.
Something strange and gay
On this romantic day
Seems to be
Happening to me.

Refrain 2  Something very strange
Is happening to me,
Every cat I see
Seems to be purring.
I can clearly tell
In every clanging bell
Some forgotten melody
Recurring.
Tinker, tailor, soldier, sailor,
Beggar-man or thief,
Every single leaf
On every tree
Seems to be aware
Of something in the air.
And if only I were younger I'd put ribbons in my
    hair.
Something strange and gay
On this romantic day
Seems to be
Happening to me!

## DON'T TURN AWAY FROM LOVE

*from* SAIL AWAY

Don't turn away from love
Because you know there'll be an end to it.
No lyric lover's song
Has ever lasted long,
Why not be tender to it?
Let your heart surrender to it.
Don't turn away from love,
Don't play it false or condescend to it,
Here in the moonlight with the eager stars above
Don't turn away from love.

Don't turn away from love
No matter what it holds in store for you,
Don't fear the pain it brings
If once again it brings
That sweetness every lover
In his heart can re-discover.
Don't turn away from love,
Please let the music play once more for you,
Here in the moonlight with the eager stars above,
Don't turn away from love,
Don't run away from love!

## BRONXVILLE DARBY AND JOAN

*from* SAIL AWAY

Verse 1   We do not fear the verdict of posterity,
          Our lives have been too humdrum and mundane,
          In the twilight of our days
          Having reached the final phase
          In all sincerity
          We must explain:

Refrain 1 We're a dear old couple and we HATE one another
          And we've hated one another for a long, long time.
          Since the day that we were wed, up to the present,
          Our lives, we must confess,
          Have been progressively more unpleasant.

We're just sweet old darlings who despise one another
With a thoroughness approaching the sublime,
But through all our years
We've been affectionately known
As the Bronxville Darby and Joan.

Verse 2   Our Golden Wedding passed with all our family,
An orgy of remembrance and rue,
In acknowledgement of this
We exchanged a loving kiss
A trifle clammily
Because we knew:

Refrain 2  We're a dear old couple who DETEST one another,
We've detested one another since our bridal night,
Which was squalid, unattractive and convulsive
And proved, beyond dispute,
That we were mutually repulsive.
We're just sweet old darlings who torment one another
With the utmost maliciousness and spite,
And through all our years
We've been inaccurately known
As the Bronxville Darby and Joan.

Refrain 3  We're a dear old couple and we LOATHE one another
With a loathing that engulfs us like a tidal wave,
With our deep sub-conscious minds we seldom dabble
But something *must* impel
The words we spell
When we're playing 'Scrabble'.
We're just sweet old darlings who abhor one another
And we'll bore each other firmly to the grave,
But through all our years we've been referred to more or less
As the Bronxville Porgy and Bess.


## WHEN YOU WANT ME

*from* SAIL AWAY

*Verse*

BARNABY:   I'll have to get the bees and birds to tell you
That I've loved you from the start,
I simply haven't got the words to tell you
What is truly in my heart,
Joking apart.

*Refrain*

When you want me—if you want me
Call me—call me—if you care.
When you need me—if you need me
Say so—say so—I'll be there.
I've nothing but my heart to bring to you,
No money but a questing mind,
But if this little song I sing to you
Means a thing to you
Please be kind.
When you're lonely—if you're lonely
Call me—call me—anyhow.
If you want me—need me—love me
Tell me,
Tell me,
Tell me now!

NANCY:        I'll love you longer than *The Forsyte Saga*
              And I'll tremble at your frown.

BARNABY:      I'd like to cable to Balenciaga
              To prepare your wedding gown,
              Don't let me down.

NANCY:    When you          BARNABY:    When you
          Want me,                      Want me,
          If you                        If you
          Want me,                      Want me,
          Call me,                      Call me,
          Call me.                      Call me.

NANCY &
BARNABY:      If you care.

BARNABY:      I've got an answer service.

BARNABY:  When you          NANCY:      When you
          Need me,                      Need me,
          If you                        If you
          Need me,                      Need me,
          Say so,                       Say so,
          Say so.                       Say so.

NANCY &
BARNABY:      I'll be there.

| | |
|---|---|
| NANCY: | I want to make my feelings clear to you,<br>I've never felt like this before. |
| BARNABY: | I'd sacrifice my whole career to you<br>To be near to you<br>Evermore. |
| NANCY &<br>BARNABY: | When you're lonely—if you're lonely<br>Call me—call me—anyhow. |
| NANCY: | You can reverse the charges. |
| NANCY &<br>BARNABY: | If you want me—need me—love me<br>Tell me—tell me—here and now! |
| BARNABY: | I really haven't any goods and chattels<br>But a beat-up Chevrolet. |
| NANCY: | I only know I've got a heart that rattles<br>Every time you look my way. |
| NANCY &<br>BARNABY: | There's really nothing more to say<br>Except that I should like to stay<br>With you for ever and a day,<br>*Olé!* |

*Reprise*

| | |
|---|---|
| NANCY, PAT &<br>ANN: | When you want me<br>Phone me, phone me. |
| ANN: | MU Six Two<br>Nine Four Three. |
| RAWLINGS: | We'll have a drink or something. |
| CANDIJACKS: | If I'm not in<br>Try Algonquin<br>Four three thousand<br>When you're free. |
| MRS LUSH: | All Saturdays are quite all right with us. |
| ELINOR: | Drop by and see my bulldog pup. |

ALL:          Maybe you'll stop and have a bite with us,
              Spend the night with us,
              Just call up.

NANCY:        Dial TE two
              Four one three two,
              That will get us
              Up to ten.

BARNABY:      You must come to the wedding.

ALVIN:        Try Filmore two
              Six five four two.

ALL:          That will find me
              Up to noon.

ALVIN:        If not just leave a message.

ALL:          It's been swell, pal,
              Give a yell, pal!
              What the hell, pal,
              See you soon!


# WHY DO THE WRONG PEOPLE TRAVEL?

### *from* SAIL AWAY

Verse 1   Travel they say improves the mind,
          An irritating platitude
          Which frankly, entre nous,
          Is very far from true.
          Personally I've yet to find
          That longitude and latitude
          Can educate those scores
          Of monumental bores
          Who travel in groups and herds and troupes
          Of various breeds and sexes,
          Till the whole world reels
          To shouts and squeals
          And the clicking of Rolliflexes.

Refrain 1 Why do the wrong people travel, travel, travel,
     When the right people stay back home?
     What compulsion compels them
     And who the hell tells them
     To drag their cans to Zanzibar
     Instead of staying quietly in Omaha?
     The Taj Mahal
     And the Grand Canal
     And the sunny French Riviera
     Would be less oppressed
     If the Middle West
     Would settle for somewhere rather nearer.
     Please do not think that I criticize or cavil
     At a genuine urge to roam,
     But why oh why do the wrong people travel
     When the right people stay back home
     And mind their business,
     When the right people stay back home
     With Cinerama,
     When the right people stay back home,
     I'm merely asking
     Why the right people stay back home?

Verse 2  Just when you think romance is ripe
     It rather sharply dawns on you
     That each sweet serenade
     Is for the Tourist Trade.
     Any attractive native type
     Who resolutely fawns on you
     Will give as his address
     American Express.
     There isn't a rock
     Between Bangkok
     And the beaches of Hispaniola,
     That does not recoil
     From suntan oil
     And the gurgle of Coca Cola.

Refrain 2 Why do the wrong people travel, travel, travel,
     When the right people stay back home?
     What explains this mass mania
     To leave Pennsylvania
     And clack around like flocks of geese,
     Demanding dry martinis on the Isles of Greece?
     In the smallest street
     Where the gourmets meet
     They invariably fetch up

And it's hard to make
Them accept a steak
That isn't served rare and smeared with ketchup.
Millions of tourists are churning up the gravel
While they gaze at St Peter's dome,
But why oh why do the wrong people travel
When the right people stay back home
And eat hot doughnuts,
When the right people stay back home
With all those benefits,
When the right people stay back home?
I sometimes wonder
Why the right people stay back home!

Refrain 3  Why do the wrong people travel, travel, travel,
When the right people stay back home?
What peculiar obsessions
Inspire those processions
Of families from Houston, Tex,
With all those cameras around their necks?
They will take a train
Or an aeroplane
For an hour on the Costa Brava,
And they'll see Pompeii
On the only day
That it's up to its ass in molten lava.
It would take years to unravel—ravel—ravel
Every impulse that makes them roam
But why oh why do the wrong people travel
When the right people stay back home
With all that Kleenex,
When the right people stay back home
With all that lettuce,
When the right people stay back home
With all those Kennedys?
Won't someone tell me
Why the right,
I say the right people stay back home?

# The Girl Who Came to Supper

## LONG LIVE THE KING

*from* THE GIRL WHO CAME TO SUPPER

### Verse 1

PRINCE: As regent of a Balkan state
I have to be realistic,
My loving people cultivate
An impulse to assassinate
That is positively sadistic.

POLICE: But nevertheless artistic.

PRINCE: My uncle, the Grand Duke Stanislas,
Slept tight—in a bullet-proof nightshirt
Until one fatal Michaelmas
His valet, like a stupid ass,
Forgot to lay out the right shirt.

POLICE: Believe it or not,
The naïve little clot
Forgot—to lay out the right shirt!

PRINCE: Everything went according to plan
And that, my friend,
Was the end
Of Uncle Stan.

### Refrain 1

Long live the King—if he can,
And if he can, it takes a most remarkable man
To remain undismayed
When a hand-made grenade
Makes a loud explosion every time the national
    anthem's played.
When launching a ship
With a stiff upper lip

Or opening a Church bazaar
He longs for the calm
And the gracious charm
Of a heavily armoured car.
Every procession of state
May, or may not, be lightly shot at as it leaves the
    palace gate,
If the Monarch's bodyguard is twenty seconds late,
He'll be as dead as Queen Anne,
Long live the King—if he can.

### Verse 2

PRINCE:  The ruler of a Balkan state
Must always be closely guarded,
No oil magnate, or potentate,
No nun, or undergraduate
Though he's mentally retarded

POLICE:  Must ever be disregarded.

PRINCE:  My uncle, the Grand Duke Vladimir,
Was brave, but they never forgave him
For every morning of the year
Throughout his brief, but gay career
No one but his wife could shave him.

POLICE:  Believe it or nay,
It grieves us to say
That even this didn't save him!

PRINCE:  They finally mined his hot-water pad
And that, my friend,
Was the end
Of Uncle Vlad.

### Refrain 2

Long live the King—if he can,
And if he can he'll be a very fortunate man.
From the womb to the tomb
He must always assume
That he might be strangled every time he enters the
    drawing-room,
He's wise, on the whole,
To refrain from a stroll
Down any little country lane,
It's a hundred to five
That he'll never arrive

Alive, on his private train.
Each Monarch learns when a boy
That Christmas parties, by and large, are not
    unmitigated joy,
On the tree there's apt to be
A dynamited toy
(Probably made in Japan),
Long live the King—if he can.


## I'VE BEEN INVITED TO A PARTY

*from* THE GIRL WHO CAME TO SUPPER

I've been invited
To a party.
Everyone will say,
'Who's that pretty girl?'
As they see me swirl
Round the floor
And before
The night is through
I'll be drinking champagne out of everyone's shoe.
People will murmur,
'But she's charming!
What a lovely smile!
What a sense of style!'
Nobody will guess
That my dress
Is the one that I wear in Scene Three
And the whole Royal Court will agree
That the Belle of the Ball—is me.

The most entrancing waltz will be
The waltz the Prince
Will dance with me
And as we're floating
Cheek to cheek
The pressure of his hand
Will make me understand
There's really no necessity to speak.
Guests will cheer
And cry 'Bravo!'
As round and round and round we go
And when the music comes to an end
He'll say—'Hey,
You've found a friend!'

I've been invited
To a party
And when they've at last
Played the final dance
Someone will advance
And I'll wait
Till a stately
Limousine
Drives me back through the sunrise to Camberwell
    Green
And when I write home
To Milwaukee
Mom will have a fit
When she reads the bit
Saying that I danced with a Prince
And that since
I've been asked round to tea.
Then she'll tell all the neighbours with glee
That the Belle of the Ball—was me!

Reprise          I was invited
To a party,
Though it wasn't quite
What I had in mind
I must be resigned
To the fact
That it lacked
That magic touch,
That I over-romantically
Wanted so much
And when I get back
To the Theatre
It will be a strain
Having to explain
How my pretty song
Went all wrong
And insisted on changing its key. . . .

# WHEN FOREIGN PRINCES COME TO VISIT US

(Footmen's Sextette)

*from* THE GIRL WHO CAME TO SUPPER

When foreign Princes come to visit us
Usually from the Balkans
We spend our time looking helpful and solicitous
And hovering about like falcons.
If one of them wants a—tra la la la la
We have to set the stage for a seduction
And what with the lighting, champagne and caviar
It's certainly the hell of a production.
For Emperors and Czars
Fresh flowers in every vase
And we introduce some spruce loose-covers,
We also burn some scent,
In a spoon that's rather bent,
Essential for potential royal lovers,
Arch-Dukes—Grand Dukes
And rather out-of-hand Dukes
Whose countries can't be found on any map,
To inflame their tepid blood
We release a gurgling flood
Of Cordon Rouge and Château Neuf Du Pape.
When foreign Princes come to visit us
Life is an exhausting strain,
We long and pray
For that happy happy day
When they bugger off home again.

# SIR OR MA'AM

*from* THE GIRL WHO CAME TO SUPPER

NORTHBROOK: The privilege of supping with a Royal Prince
Is granted to very few,
Allow me to give you one or two hints
As to what you may say or do,
Maintain a dignified demeanour,
Be relaxed but not too expectant
And always remember protocol . . .

MARY: It sounds like a disinfectant.

NORTHBROOK: Protocol, my dear,
Is just a set of simple rules
Designed to lubricate Pro-Consular machinery,
For example it is wiser
When you talk with King or Kaiser
To confine your conversation to the scenery.
But I digress,
The very first thing you must master is the method
of address . . .

*Refrain 1*

Sir or Ma'am,
Ma'am or Sir,
One's addressed to him of course,
The other's addressed to her,
Majesty or Highness
Can once a while be used
But you'll notice a certain dryness
If you get the terms confused.
Ma'am or Sir,
Sir or Ma'am,
Accompanied by a simple bob,
Not a profound salaam.
Don't have a stroke
If a casual joke
Is received with funereal gloom,
Smother a curse
And in quick reverse
Back right out of the room.

*Refrain 2*

Sir or Ma'am,
Ma'am or Sir,
The mumbling of this simple phrase
Betrays the amateur.
Royal condescension
May murmur a Christian Name
But you'll notice a certain tension
If you try to do the same.
Ma'am or Sir,
Sir or Ma'am
Makes every royal personage as happy as a clam.
If some remark
Should go wide of the mark
And you're suddenly conscious of doom
Sink to the ground
And in one swift bound
Back right out of the room.

## SOLILOQUIES

*from* THE GIRL WHO CAME TO SUPPER

REGENT: She looks quite sweet,
Perhaps a little young for me,
But still that youthful charm will be
A change.
I must arrange
For Northbrook to receive
Some sort of minor decoration,
He's really done exceedingly well
And shows—in fact
Much tact
Combined with shrewd discrimination.

MARY: He looks quite nice,
I'm not a bit afraid of him,
The image that I made of him
Was wrong,
His face is strong
But I can see
Some tired little lines of dissipation,
His eyes are kind and just a bit sad
I think—I'm glad
That I'm the girl who had the invitation.

*Reprise*

REGENT: It's too absurd,
I can't protest—my hands are tied,
I'm trapped in this undignified
Charade,
I find it hard,
On top of having
Passed a night of amorous frustration
To give this girl—for passing out cold
An old
Pure gold
And really quite expensive decoration.

MARY: He looks so cross,
His mouth is set—his eyes are grim
But still I'm not afraid of him
At all.
I knew I'd fall

In love with him
Which obviously wasn't very smart of me,
But even though I see him this way
I know
He'll stay
For ever in my heart a special part of me.

## LONELY

*from* THE GIRL WHO CAME TO SUPPER

REGENT: Imagine if you can
A solitary man
Eternally surrounded—yet alone,
A royal prince
Who ever since
He first began to dream
Has lived within the shadow of a throne,
Pity him and think of him
Weighed down by cares of state,
Hearing happy lovers laughing by
Weary and oppressed
But maybe you have guessed
The sad unhappy prince I am referring to
Is I.

Lonely—lonely,
A pawn of destiny,
A sawdust puppet on a string,
No one near to me to know or even care
That the heart behind this royal mask I wear
Beats out its melancholy days
Proving the falseness of the phrase
'To be as happy as a king'.

Only—only
Swift moments here and there,
A brief illusion that I'm free,
I know too well true happiness
Can never ever be
For a solitary soul like me.

Only—only
I hold deep in my heart
The foolish dream that there may be
Just one last blossom flowering
On true love's eternal tree
For a solitary soul like me.


# LONDON

*from* THE GIRL WHO CAME TO SUPPER

Verse    I was born and bred in London,
It's the only city I know,
Though it's foggy and cold and wet
I'd be willing to take a bet
That there ain't no other place I'd want to go

### *London Is A Little Bit of All Right*

Refrain 1  London—is a little bit of all right,
Nobody can deny that's true,
Bow Bells—Big Ben,
Up to the heath and down again
And if you should visit the monkeys in the zoo
Bring a banana,
Feed the ducks in Battersea Park
Or take a trip to Kew,
It only costs a tanner there and back,
Watch our lads in the Palace Yard
Troop the Colour and Change the Guard
And don't forget your brolly and your mack:
And I'd like to mention
London—is a place where you can call right
Round and have a cosy cup of tea,
If you're fed right up and got your tail right down
London town
Is a wonderful place to be.

### *What Ho, Mrs Brisket*

What ho, Mrs Brisket,
Why not take a plunge and risk it?
The water's warm,
There ain't no crabs
And you'll have a lot of fun among the shrimps and
    dabs,

If for a lark
Some saucy old shark
Takes a nibble at your chocolate biscuit
Swim for the shore
And the crowd will roar,
What ho, Mrs Brisket!

### Don't Take Our Charlie For The Army

Don't take our Charlie for the Army,
He's a sensitive lad
And like his dad
His heart is far from strong,
He couldn't do route marches
On account of his fallen arches
And his asthma's something terrible
When the winter comes along,
He's a nice boy—one of the best
But when he gets a cold on his chest
He coughs until he nearly drives us barmy,
So nightie-night—close the door,
Go back to the barracks and think some more
Before you take our Charlie for the Army.

### Saturday Night At the Rose and Crown

Saturday night at the Rose and Crown,
That's just the place to be,
Tinkers and Tailors
And Soldiers and Sailors
All out for a bit of a spree,
If you find that you're
Weary of life
With your trouble and strife
And the kids have got you down
It will all come right
On Saturday night
At the Rose and Crown.

### London Is A Little Bit of All Right

Refrain 2 London—is a little bit of all right,
Nobody can deny that's so,
Big Ben—Bow Bells,
Have a good laugh and watch the swells
Treating themselves to a trot in Rotten Row
Sitting on horses,
Grosvenor Square or Petticoat Lane,
Belgravia, Peckham Rye,

You can stray through any neighbourhood,
If you haven't a swanky club
Just pop into the nearest pub,
A little of what you fancy does you good,
And I'd like to mention
London—is a place where you can call right
Round and have a cosy cup of tea,
If you use your loaf a bit and know what's what
This old spot
Is a bloody good place to be.


## HERE AND NOW

*from* THE GIRL WHO CAME TO SUPPER

Verse   Here on this gay,
Glorious day
How can I keep my feet from dancing?
Some entrancing tune
Makes me want to fly
Higher than the moon
In the sky.
Who can I tell?
What can I say?
How can I breathe and not betray
To every soul I see
What today
Means to me?

Refrain Here and now
I've a wonderful secret that nobody knows,
Here and now
I've got rings on my fingers and bells on my toes,
When I woke as today was dawning
All the world seemed to glow
On this marvellous, magic morning,
Suddenly I know
I'm in love,
I adore every moment that's hurrying by,
Up above
There's a lovely new light in the sky,
When my prince appears
I'll burst into tears
And curtsy three times and bow,

Who could foresee
That such happiness could happen to me
Here and now?

Reprise Here and now
I've a wonderful secret that nobody knows,
Here and now
I've got rings on my fingers and bells on my toes,
Though it ought to be quite alarming
I'm not nervous at all,
Arm in arm with my young Prince charming
Going to the ball.


# CORONATION CHORALE

*from* THE GIRL WHO CAME TO SUPPER

ALL:    A Coronation is spectacular
And though, as pageantry, not easy to improve on,
To coin a phrase in the vernacular,
We wish to God they'd get a move on.
We hate the weight
Of our robes of state
And our jewellery weighs a ton
And we'd sell our souls
For some nice hot rolls
Or the smell of a Chelsea bun.
We rise at dawn and put our ermine on
And then we squeeze into a freezing open landau,
To lift our trains with all this vermin on
Requires the muscles of a Sandow,
With stays too tight
We sit bolt upright
In a rigidly unyielding pew,
Even British oak
Gets beyond a joke
When you've sat on it from nine till two.
Part of a royal education is
To be resigned
To your behind
Becoming numb.
The worst of every coronation is
We always wish we hadn't come.

Here we sit—exquisitely bored,
Hear our stomachs rumble
As we watch late-comers stumble
Up the nave.
Good Lord!
Look at Cousin Maud,
Someone should have given her a shave.

Here we all elegantly squat
Praying that Aunt Xenia
Won't give way to Schizophrenia
Again.
Great Scott!
Look at what she's got
Dragging from the bottom of her train.

MARY: It's all so wonderful—wonderful—wonderful,
It's like the most entrancing fairy tale I ever knew,
Diamonds, rubies and pearls,
As I can't quite believe it's true
How can I explain it to the girls,
They'll think that having got into some awful scrape
I'm trying—just by lying—to forget
And when I start to tell about this sable cape
They'll gape,
You bet.

ALL: Here we sit—dummies in a row,
Heaven knows how many
Of us long to spend a penny
But we're stuck
And so
Though it's touch and go
We shall simply have to trust to luck.

MARY: It's all so wonderful—wonderful—wonderful,
It's the most lovely lovely lovely sight I'll ever see,
All this glitter and gold,
In my heart this will always be
Something to remember when I'm old,
I'll think of it each time I see a summer sky
However sad and weary I may grow,
And every year another lovely June goes by
I'll sigh
Heigh-ho,
It was so wonderful—wonderful—wonderful
But it was long—long ago.

## MIDDLE AGE

*from* THE GIRL WHO CAME TO SUPPER

What's wrong?—What's wrong?
I'm behaving like an utter fool,
I've always hitherto
Seen clearly what to do
And remained—restrained
And cool,
But since this idiotic girl appeared
With her sentimental ignorance and youth,
Though I merely asked her to sup with me,
She's made me feel the years are catching up with me
And that now I must compromise slightly
And politely
Face the truth.

How do you do, middle age?
How do you do, middle age?
If you're planning to upset
And fret
And ultimately diminish me
Let—this wet
Soubrette—set to and finish me,
Knowing that I'm
In my prime
And mellow season
Must I permit her
To twitter
Pure high treason?
Give me one reason.
Can I still love now and then?
Shall I be sweet or gentle,
Sane or mental?
Must I spend my days in a blazing rage?
Give me a clue,
Over to you,
Middle age.

Comment ça va, middle age?
Qu'est ce que tu as, middle age?
Autumn winds begin to blow
And so
I'd better unbend my mind to you
Though—you know
I'm not quite yet resigned to you,
More relaxation,

More ease,
More time for snoozing,
What consolation
Are these
For those amusing
Pleasures I'm losing?
Shall I survive this decade
Or shall I merely fade out,
Done for—played out?
What are your designs for the final page?

It's too absurd
To let myself become morose,
Disconsolate and lachrymose
And dull
Because a nattering, chattering ingénue
Is making me feel I'm ninety-two
Instead of a muscular forty-five.
I've still got teeth—I'm still alive,
My legs still take me where I want to go
And so
I'm damned if I'll let this little whipper-snapper
      lay me low.

A feather-brained, garrulous small-part minx
Who never draws breath and seldom thinks,
Who teases my amorous appetites
And then recites the Bill of Rights
And lectures me about my son and heir,
I swear
I'll not let this dizzy little busybody see I care.

Why should I so upset myself?
Let myself
Get myself
In a state of acute dismay
Because some years have passed away?
Why should I crucify myself?
Sigh myself
By myself?
When I still feel bright of eye,
Clear of brain
And ready to start from scratch all over again.

Don't jump the gun,
Middle age,
Life is still fun,

Middle-age,
I'm not ready to kow-tow
Just now
And impotently unbend for you,
Stay
Away
And wait until I send for you,
Must taxes paid on the past be retroactive?
Waves of self-pity
Are pretty
Unattractive
When you're still active,
Don't be so dumb,
Middle-age,
Spare me that glum recital.
I'm still vital.
I've enough bombast
For one last
Rampage.
Just wait and see,
Leave it to me,
Fiddle-de-dee,
Middle-age.


## 'CURT, CLEAR AND CONCISE'

*from* THE GIRL WHO CAME TO SUPPER

REGENT:       Curt, Clear and Concise
REFRAIN 1     Is the way that a lady should be.
I am not a perfectionist who seeks the sublime,
All I ask is a woman who won't waste my time.
I'm frankly sick to death of females who procrastinate,
Who guard their virtue like a sort of holy grail,
I much prefer the type who's willing to co-operate,
Concentrate,
Smack on the nose,
Bang on the nail.
Coy maidens who shed
Bitter tears at the thought that they might be misled
And who faint dead away at the sight of a bed
Soon find out that my parting advice
Can be curt, clear and concise.

You must forgive me, Northbrook, if I should
  philosophize,
At moments such as these
I find myself at ease,
In matters of the heart I'm sure our points of view
  indubitably harmonize,
You're quite a connoisseur.

NORTHBROOK: You're flattering me, Sir.

REGENT:     I feel that really
            You look on sex clearly
            And factually
            Which saves you quite a lot of time and tears,
            You have an air,
            Libertine—debonair.

NORTHBROOK: Well, Sir—actually
            I've been engaged for nearly seven years.

REGENT:     You must excuse me, Northbrook, if I seem to minimize
            The prevalent idea
            That sex should be austere,
            I've always had a notion
            Sensual emotion
            Was a cracking bore
            And as I mentioned before,

REFRAIN 2   Curt, Clear and Concise
            Is the way that a lady should be,
            She should not sentimentalize the physical act
            And believe she can dodge biological fact,
            I think it is behaving really indefensibly
            To take exception to an amorous advance,
            Give me the kind of girl who mutters comprehensibly,
            Sensibly,
            Off with the lights.
            On with the dance.
            Though moralists say
            That it's better to honour and love and obey
            I have found that a casual roll in the hay
            Without bridesmaids, confetti or rice
            Is more curt, clear and concise.

# THE COCONUT GIRL

*from* THE GIRL WHO CAME TO SUPPER

*Opening Chorus: 'Welcome to Pootzie Van Doyle'*
Welcome to Pootzie Van Doyle
Who's made millions and millions from coconut oil,
He's travelled by train
And he's travelled by ship
And the dear little coconuts paid for his trip,
A man of the people,
A man of the soil,
All welcome to Pootzie Van Doyle.

*'The Coconut Girl'*
I am known as the Coconut Girl
Though my intimate friends call me Tina,
I'd be more contented
If dad hadn't rented
Quite such a grand place as the Villa Marina,
The style is ornate,
There's lots of gold plate
And my bathroom is mother of pearl,
But beneath all this show
I should like you to know
That I'm simply—just simply—The Coconut Girl.

*'Paddy MacNeil and His Automobile'*
Paddy MacNeil
Bought an automobile
And invited his girlie for a spin.
Everything was fine and dandy for the first few miles
Until he let the clutch right out
And couldn't let it in.
As they drove at full speed
Paddy tried to proceed
With a little original sin
But he found he couldn't cuddle her with both hands
    on the wheel (crash!),
That's why Paddy had to buy another automobile!

## DUET: 'SWING SONG'

*from* THE GIRL WHO CAME TO SUPPER (THE COCONUT GIRL)

### *Verse*

ALEXIS: Forgive me please for thus intruding
Upon a lady who is fairer than the day.

TINA: Kind sir, if it should be
To me you are alluding
I must beseech you pray
To go away.

ALEXIS: Be not unkind,
Be not unfair,
Moments so sweet
Are all too rare.

### *Refrain*

TINA: As I swing to and fro,
High and low—high and low,
All my cares melt away
Like the cold winter snow.

ALEXIS: Would you permit a stranger
For a while to stay with you?

TINA: Maybe.

ALEXIS: To share this beautiful day with you?

TINA: We'll see.
Not a cloud in the sky
And a lark singing high
And the sound of the sea far below.

ALEXIS: Would you permit a stranger
Who has nothing but a lonely heart to bring,
Just to kiss you as you swing
To and fro?

## SEXTETTE: 'LILIES OF THE VALLEY'

*from* THE GIRL WHO CAME TO SUPPER (THE COCONUT GIRL)

We're six lilies of the valley,
Rose, Maud, Kate, Jane, Marybelle and Sally,
We toil not neither do we spin much,
But we find, in the Casino, that we win much
More
By being gentle with the gentlemen
Playing at the tables,
Often sentimental men
Give emeralds and sables
To Rose, Maud, Kate, Jane, Marybelle and Sally,
Six pretty fillies,
Far from being silly billies,
Six little lilies of the valley.

## 'THE WALLA WALLA BOOLA'

*from* THE GIRL WHO CAME TO SUPPER (THE COCONUT GIRL)

When you dance the Walla Walla Boola,
Walla Walla Boola,
You will find it more exciting
Than the Honolulu Hula.
First you swing to the left,
Swing to the right,
It's got a kick that makes you want to dance all night,
Your hips start to wiggle,
You give a little giggle
And begin to wish the temperature was cooler,
So stand up and holler,
Throw away your collar,
Come on and dance the Walla Walla Boola,
Walla Walla Boola,
Walla Walla Walla Walla Boola!

# THIS TIME IT'S TRUE LOVE

*from* THE GIRL WHO CAME TO SUPPER

MARY:    There's nothing more to say
Because at last your heart has beckoned,
In this brief fleeting second,
I know
You really are a lonely man,
The one and only man
I dreamed of all my life ago.

This time it's true love,
This time it's real,
Last night I knew love,
Now I can feel
A lovely certainty at last has come true,
I know you care for me as I care for you.
This is no light love,
No passing phase,
This is the right love
For all my days,
I need no violins

MARY &    No moon, nor stars above . . .
REGENT:  You are my own true love.

MARY:    This time it's true love,
All else apart,
Out of the blue love
Has touched my heart.

REGENT:  Dare I believe that from one brief rendezvous
You've grown to care for me as I care for you?
This is no light love,
Too well I know
No fly-by-night love
Could move me so.

MARY &    We need no violins,
REGENT:  No moon nor stars above.

REGENT:  You are my own true love.

## I'LL REMEMBER HER

*from* THE GIRL WHO CAME TO SUPPER

I'll remember her,
How incredibly naïve she was,
I couldn't quite believe she was
Sincere,
So alert,
So impertinent
And yet so sweet.
My defeat
Was clear.
I'll remember her,
Her absurd exaggerating
And her utterly deflating
Repartee
And the only thing that worries me at all
Is whether she'll remember me.

I'll remember her
In the evenings when I'm lonely
And imagining if only
She were there.
I'll relive,
Oh, so vividly,
Our sad and sweet,
Incomplete
Affair.
I'll remember her
Heavy-hearted when we parted,
With her eyes so full of tears she couldn't see
And I'll feel inside a foolish sort of pride
To think that she remembers me.

# *Miscellaneous*

## COME THE WILD, WILD WEATHER

*from* WAITING IN THE WINGS

Time may hold in store for us
Glory or defeat,
Maybe never more for us
Life will seem so sweet
Time will change so many things,
Tides will ebb and flow,
But wherever fate may lead us
Always we shall know—

Come the wild, wild weather,
Come the wind and the rain,
Come the little white flakes of show,
Come the joy, come the pain,
We shall still be together
When our life's journey ends,
For wherever we chance to go
We shall always be friends.
We may find while we're travelling through the years
Moments of joy and love and happiness,
Reason for grief, reason for tears.
Come the wild, wild weather,
If we've lost or we've won,
We'll remember these words we say
Till our story is done.

# INDEX

# Index